THE SEARCH FOR THE ORIGINS
OF CHRISTIAN WORSHIP

THE SEARCH FOR THE ORIGINS OF CHRISTIAN WORSHIP

Sources and Methods for the Study of Early Liturgy

PAUL F. BRADSHAW

New York   *Oxford*
OXFORD UNIVERSITY PRESS
1992

Oxford University Press

Oxford   New York   Toronto
Delhi   Bombay   Calcutta   Madras   Karachi
Kuala Lumpur   Singapore   Hong Kong   Tokyo
Nairobi   Dar es Salaam   Cape Town
Melbourne   Auckland

and associated companies in
Berlin   Ibadan

Copyright © 1992 by Paul F. Bradshaw

Published by Oxford University Press, Inc.
198 Madison Avenue, New York, New York 10016-4314

First published in Great Britain 1992
by SPCK, Holy Trinity Church
Marylebone Road, London NW1 4DU

Oxford is a registered trademark of Oxford University Press, Inc.

Library of Congress Cataloging-in-Publication Data
Bradshaw, Paul F.
The search for the origins of Christian worship : sources
and methods for the study of early liturgy / Paul F. Bradshaw.
p. cm.   Includes bibliographical references and indexes.
ISBN 0-19-508050-5
ISBN 0-19-508051-3 (pbk.)
1. Liturgies, Early Christian. I. Title.
BV185.B734   1992   264'.009'015—dc20
92-19531

3 5 7 9 8 6 4

Printed in the United States of America
on acid free paper

To my students

past and present

Contents

Preface

In an article entitled 'Quest for the Mother Tongue' in *The Atlantic Monthly*, April 1991, the author, Robert Wright, maintained that 'there are two kinds of people. In different fields they go by different names. In comparative linguistics they are known as the lumpers and the splitters. The lumpers like to put many languages into few families. The splitters like to inspect the resulting lumps and find fault lines' (p. 68). In the field of early Christian liturgical study, I am a self-confessed splitter in an arena traditionally dominated by lumpers, who have tried to arrange the evidence so as to suggest that a single coherent line of liturgical evolution can be traced from the apostolic age to the fourth century. This book, therefore, is an attempt to present the case for the splitters' view of primitive Christian worship.

The volume has been long in gestation. Its conception can be dated from the late 1970s when I was engaged in exploring the subjects of daily prayer and ordination in early Christianity, which eventually resulted in several articles and two books — *Daily Prayer in the Early Church* (ACC 63, London 1981/New York 1982) and *Ordination Rites of the Ancient Churches of East and West* (New York 1990). In the course of my research it became clear to me that those engaged in the study of Christian liturgical origins were in general unaware of recent developments in Jewish liturgical study which had profound consequences for the reconstruction of early Christian practices, and were often also unacquainted with recent advances in biblical scholarship, just as New Testament scholars were similarly frequently unfamiliar with the way in which early Christian liturgy evolved from the first-century world on which their attention was focused. It was also apparent that the interpretation of that enigmatic genre of ancient Christian literature, the pseudo-apostolic church orders, was an important key to understanding many aspects of early liturgical practice.

These two concerns in turn led me to publish the first English edition of the *Canons of Hippolytus* (A/GLS 2, 1987), and to develop an interest in the whole question of the appropriate methods which should be used in the study of the early history of Christian liturgy, a preliminary essay on which I also published in 1987: 'The Search for the Origins of Christian Liturgy: Some Methodological Reflections' (*SL* 17, pp. 26 –34). The following year I was involved in convening what I believe was the first ever joint Jewish-Christian liturgical conference, held at the University of Notre Dame, and was able to present there an attempt to list some methodological principles which I believe should guide the student in the field of early Christian liturgical study. This paper was subsequently published in a symposium which Lawrence Hoffman and I edited, *The Making of Jewish and Christian Worship* (University of Notre Dame Press, 1991), and I am grateful to the publishers for allowing me to include an expanded version of it as chapter 3 of this current book. The invitation to contribute to a memorial volume for my former colleague Niels Rasmussen, *Fountain of Life*, ed. Gerard Austin (Washington DC, Pastoral Press, 1991), also afforded me the opportunity to put together a systematic overview of the ancient church orders, and once again I am grateful to the publishers for permitting me to include an expanded version of that essay as chapter 4.

It had originally been my aspiration that I might produce a volume to replace that classic work by Joseph Jungmann, *The Early Liturgy to the Time of Gregory the Great* (Notre Dame 1959/London 1960), now more than thirty years old and largely out of date in the light of more recent research. But that same research is making it clear that a single, simple picture of early liturgical practice can no longer be painted. We are in many ways less sure now than we once were as to what the worship of the early Church was like. What this book sets out to do, therefore, is to offer a guide or handbook for the journey through the field of Christian liturgical origins. It seeks to explain what are perceived as the problems inherent in interpreting the source-documents on which our knowledge of early Christian worship is based, and also the reasons why we can no longer always share the methodological presuppositions adopted by earlier generations of scholars — nor consequently the conclusions that they reached. My hope is that readers will thereby be in a better position to examine the available primary sources for themselves and to see what may—and may not—be said about the ways in which early Christians worshipped.

While I have tried to keep in mind the needs of those who may be venturing into this field for the first time, extensive annotation has also been provided so that the more advanced may be able to proceed easily to further research and my fellow scholars may be able readily to check the veracity of my claims. Indeed, the whole book may in a sense be seen as an annotated bibliography of primary and secondary literature pertaining to Christian worship in the first four centuries. Hence no separate bibliography is provided at the end, but readers should easily be able to locate the sources relevant to their interests by use of the indices, as full bibliographical details are given in the notes at the first mention of a text or study.

I wish to express my gratitude to all those who have assisted me in enabling this work to come to birth. My special thanks are due to Roger Brooks, Professor of Judaism at Connecticut College, and Lawrence Hoffman, Professor of Liturgy at the Hebrew Union College—Jewish Institute of Religion, New York, for their helpful comments and insights on material in chapter 1; to my colleagues at Notre Dame in the field of New Testament Studies, Harold Attridge and Gregory Sterling, for their willingness to examine critically what I have written in chapter 2; to the Association of Theological Schools for a grant towards the costs of research; to my graduate assistant, John Klentos, for his painstaking labour in checking references; and above all to my students both past and present, to whom the book is dedicated and whose needs, questions, and own contributions to scholarship have challenged and stimulated me in my writing.

Paul F. Bradshaw
December 1991

Abbreviations

ACC	Alcuin Club Collection
A/GLS	Alcuin/GROW Liturgical Study, Nottingham
ALW	*Archiv für Liturgiewissenschaft*
B.C.E.	Before the Common Era
C.E.	Common Era
EL	*Ephemerides Liturgicae*
GLS	Grove Liturgical Study, Nottingham
JBL	*Journal of Biblical Literature*
JEH	*Journal of Ecclesiastical History*
JJS	*Journal of Jewish Studies*
JQR	*Jewish Quarterly Review*
JTS	*Journal of Theological Studies*
NTS	*New Testament Studies*
OCA	Orientalia Christiana Analecta, Rome
OCP	*Orientalia Christiana Periodica*
PO	Patrologia Orientalis, Paris
QLP	*Questions liturgiques et paroissiales*
RevSR	*Revue des sciences religieuses*
SC	Sources chrétiennes, Paris
SJT	*Scottish Journal of Theology*
SL	*Studia Liturgica*
SP	*Studia Patristica*
ZKTh	*Zeitschrift für katholische Theologie*
ZNW	*Zeitschrift für die neutestamentliche Wissenschaft*

THE SEARCH FOR THE ORIGINS
OF CHRISTIAN WORSHIP

1. 'The rock whence ye were hewn':
The Jewish Background of Christian Worship

When C. F. D. Moule used the above quotation from Isaiah 51.1
as the title of the first chapter of his now classic work, *Worship in
the New Testament*,[1] it seemed perfectly possible to state with a
considerable degree of assurance what Jewish worship was like
in the first century of the Common Era. Thirty years later,
however, things are by no means so clear. In the intervening
period what can only be described as a revolution in Jewish
liturgical studies has taken place, a revolution which has almost
completely changed our perception of how sources should be
used to reconstruct the forms of worship of early Judaism. This
has resulted in the need to be much more cautious about affirming what would have been the liturgical practices with which
Jesus and his followers were familiar.

The basic problem for the reconstruction of the early history
of Jewish worship is that extant liturgical texts as such are of a
late date. The earliest comprehensive prayer book known to us
is that compiled by Amram Gaon in the ninth century,[2] although
there are in addition some liturgical fragments from the Cairo
Genizah[3] which may antedate Amram by a century or so.
Knowledge of the growth and development of Jewish liturgy
prior to this time has to rely to a large extent on attempts to
divine the pre-history of these later texts with the assistance of
the comments on and discussion of liturgical matters found in
the Mishnah, Tosefta, and Talmud; and recent scholarship has
shown that the interpretation of this material presents not
inconsiderable difficulties.[4] To complicate matters further,

---

[1] London/Richmond VA 1961 = GLS 12/13, 1983.

[2] *Seder R. Amram Gaon*, Part I ed. David Hedegard, Lund 1951, Part II ed.
Tryggve Kronholm, Lund 1974.

[3] For this, see below, p. 3.

[4] The Mishnah is the first systematic collection of rabbinic judgements
made at the end of the second century C.E.; the Tosefta is a later supplement
to this; and the Talmud is an extensive compilation of rabbinic discussion span-
ning several centuries after the Mishnah's promulgation and organized as a
running commentary on that work. There are two Talmuds, the Palestinian,

Amram's text is Babylonian in origin, whereas it is the less easily discernible Palestinian tradition which is of most immediate relevance to the search for the roots of Christian worship.

Earlier Jewish liturgical scholarship[5]

The scientific study of the history of Jewish liturgy is usually regarded as having begun with Leopold Zunz (1794–1886), although its roots can be traced back even before his time. In his monumental work, *Die gottesdienstlichen Vorträge der Juden*, published in 1832, Zunz became the first scholar to stress the gradual evolution of the liturgy in the course of history. His methods were those of classical philology, which he had learned at the University of Berlin from August Boeckh and Friedrich August Wolf. Zunz regarded differences in the wording of prayers in the various manuscripts to which he had access as being variations on, or additions to, a single archetype, an *Urtext*, which lay behind them all. Thus, he believed that words and phrases which were common to all the manuscripts must be of greater antiquity than those which differed from one to another, and hence by comparing the variant forms of the material and peeling off the layers of what appeared to be subsequent accretions, it was possible to recover the original, briefer core of the text.

Not only does his approach—and all those which are derived from it —presuppose that liturgical texts necessarily evolved from simplicity to greater complexity, but it also contains several other assumptions:

---

which in its final form is traditionally dated *c.* 400 C.E., and the Babylonian, which is said to have been completed *c.* 500–600, though in actuality it was not finally edited until some time thereafter, perhaps as late as the seventh century or even the eighth. For further details, see Roger Brooks, *The Spirit of the Ten Commandments* (San Francisco 1990), pp. 36–45; and his articles, 'Mishnah' and 'Gemara', in the (forthcoming) *Anchor Bible Dictionary*.

[5] In whats follow I am heavily indebted to the detailed survey and critique by Richard S. Sarason, 'On the Use of Method in the Modern Study of Jewish Liturgy', in W. S. Green, ed., *Approaches to Ancient Judaism: Theory and Practice* (Brown Judaic Studies 1, Missoula MT 1978), pp. 97–172; reprinted in Jacob Neusner, ed., *The Study of Ancient Judaism* I (New York 1982), pp. 107–79.

(a) that throughout the process of historical evolution there was in existence, as the Talmudic literature itself implies, a centralized rabbinic authority which established and regulated a single, normative pattern of worship, which instituted all legitimate changes 'from above' in an orderly manner, and which effectively disseminated them throughout the Judaism of the period;

(b) that textual variations were generally best understood sequentially (that is, as reflecting subsequent chronological stages along this single line of development, with the different changes following one after the other in the course of history in a cumulative fashion) rather than, for example, occurring simultaneously in parallel versions of similar material;

(c) that variations which could not be explained within this linear progression must either be deliberate heretical deviations from the norm or unimportant modifications which were not part of the mainstream of liturgical life, or be examples of a later liturgical diversity which was brought about primarily by the geographical dispersion of the Jews, an assumption that once again the Talmudic literature encourages;

(d) that it was possible to postulate the date when each of the changes had taken place by looking for some appropriate historical context which would have caused that change to occur, or at least have been congruent with its development.

The methodological criteria established by Zunz were followed by the scholars who came after him, and not even Solomon Schechter's discovery in 1896 in the Genizah of the Ben Ezra synagogue in Cairo of a vast quantity of fragmentary liturgical texts of a distinctly Palestinian character which frequently differed in wording from the European manuscripts was sufficient to shake these foundations. Subsequent scholars may have made minor modifications to their conclusions, but the basic principles survived in the work of such major figures as Ismar Elbogen (1874–1943) and Louis Finkelstein (1895–1991). While Elbogen (whose comprehensive study, *Der jüdische Gottesdienst in seiner geschichtlichen Entwicklung,*[6] continues to

---

[6] Leipzig 1913, 2nd edn, Frankfurt 1924, 3rd edn 1931 = Hildesheim 1962. There is also a revised Hebrew edition, ed. J. Heinemann, *Ha-tefillah Be-Yisrael*, Tel-Aviv 1972.

be used as a basic source today) acknowledged that the precise wording of prayers had not originally been fixed, but that there were several alternative versions in existence for some time, he still used philological methods to analyse the history of texts, viewing the original 'seed' of the liturgy as having been gradually encapsulated in layers of 'rind'.[7]

Finkelstein, on the other hand, whose reconstructions of the supposed *Urtext* of the *Tefillah* (the prescribed form of Jewish daily prayer) and of the *Birkat ha-mazon* (the grace after meals)[8] still tend to be cited as authoritative by Christian scholars, had no such reservations. On the contrary, he carried Zunz's method to an extreme, articulating his operational rules as follows:

> In attempting to establish on the basis of these later forms the earliest text of the benedictions, we must bear in mind that for many centuries the prayers were not written down but transmitted orally. Under these circumstances new material could be added, but changes and omissions were difficult. It is comparatively easy to issue an edict changing the wording of written prayers, and in an age of printing it is a slight matter to prepare a new edition of a prayer book. But when people recited their prayers from memory, they were willing to learn new verses or phrases, but found it difficult to unlearn what they already knew.
>
> It follows that in dealing with various formulae of prayer we must remember that *in general* these rules hold. 1. The old text is retained as a nucleus of the later formula. 2. Where various versions differ, the part that is common to all of them is the more likely to contain the original form. 3. The briefest form is very often the most akin to the original.[9]

The influence of Joseph Heinemann (1915–1977)

Although form-critical methods had begun to be applied to biblical studies at the beginning of the twentieth century, they had virtually no impact upon the study of Jewish liturgy until very recently. It is true that in the 1930s Arthur Spanier (1884–1944) began to question the appropriateness of the pure philological method and to suggest a generic classification of prayer-material

[7] (3rd edn), pp. 41f., 254. See Sarason, 'On the Use of Method', p. 109 = 120.

[8] 'The Development of the Amidah', *JQR* 16 (1925/6), pp. 1–43, 127–70; 'The Birkat Ha-Mazon', *JQR* 19 (1929), pp. 211–62.

[9] ibid., p. 224 (emphasis in original).

according to characteristics of form and style, but this initiative came to an end when he perished in the Holocaust.[10]

It was not until the 1960s that this approach was taken up again. In his doctoral dissertation, published in Hebrew in 1964,[11] Joseph Heinemann posited the origin of individual Jewish liturgical texts on the basis of the particular stylistic features which they displayed, arguing that some forms appeared more congruent with the Temple, others with the nascent synagogue, the law court, the house of study, and so on. So, to take a simple example, he held that texts which addressed the congregation in the second-person plural ('you') were unlikely to have originated in the synagogue, where the prayer-leader was expected to use the first-person plural ('we, us') and include himself along with those on whose behalf he was praying. On the other hand, the second-person address was common in Temple services, where the priests were accustomed to bless the people.[12]

But Heinemann's work did much more than add a new analytical tool to the study of the history of Jewish worship: it challenged the fundamental principles of interpretation hitherto adopted, and set forth a completely different model of liturgical development. He did not deny the value of the philological method, when applied to genuine literary texts, but insisted that 'it cannot be transferred as a matter of course to the field of liturgy without first determining whether or not the methodological tools are appropriate to the subject matter which is to be analyzed by them'.[13] He argued that there never had been a single *Urtext* of Jewish liturgical forms, but that a variety of oral versions had existed from the first, and only later were these subjected to standardization:

> The Jewish prayers were originally the creations of the common people. The characteristic idioms and forms of prayer, and indeed the statutory

[10] See the analysis of his work in Sarason, 'On the Use of Method', pp. 140−5 = 155−60.

[11] *Prayer in the Period of the Tanna'im and the Amora'im: Its Nature and its Patterns*, Jerusalem 1964, 2nd edn 1966; English translation: *Prayer in the Talmud: Forms and Patterns*, Berlin/New York 1977.

[12] *Prayer in the Talmud*, pp. 104ff.

[13] ibid., p. 6.

prayers of the synagogue themselves, were not in the first place products of
the deliberation of the Rabbis in their academies, but were rather the
spontaneous, on-the-spot improvisations of the people who gathered on
various occasions to pray in the synagogue. Since the occasions and places
of worship were numerous, it was only natural that they should give rise to
an abundance of prayers, displaying a wide variety of forms, styles, and patterns. Thus, the first stage in the development of the liturgy was characterized by diversity and variety —— and the task of the Rabbis was to
systematize and to impose order on this multiplicity of forms, patterns, and
structures. This task they undertook after the fact; only after the numerous
prayers had come into being and were familiar to the masses did the Sages
decide that the time had come to establish some measure of uniformity and
standardization. Only then did they proceed carefully to inspect the existing
forms and patterns, to disqualify some while accepting others, to decide
which prayers were to be statutory on which occasions, and by which
prayers a man 'fulfilled his obligation'.[14]

Heinemann thus called into question the underlying presuppositions of earlier scholarship. Since he denied that — at least
in the earliest period of liturgical evolution — there had been a
centralized rabbinic authority which regulated worship practices,
textual differences were not necessarily always reflective of
sequential stages of development, nor alternatively to be dismissed as deviations from some putative norm. On the contrary,
they might often be indicative of simultaneous, parallel strands,
some of which ultimately converged, while others in time disappeared from use. Hence, neither the simplest version nor that
which has most features in common with others is necessarily
the earliest. Similarly, parallel occurrences of the same phraseology in widely different contexts could well be the natural use of
certain stock phrases rather than actual literary dependency.[15]
Heinemann argued that the process of standardization took
place only gradually. By the second century C.E. 'only the number of the benedictions, their order of recitation, and their general content had been fixed, as well as the occasions of their
recitation and the rules which governed them, but not their exact
wording'.[16] At this time 'each worshipper was still basically
allowed to formulate his own benedictions as long as he "mentioned in them" those items and idioms which, in the meantime,

14 ibid., p. 37.
15 ibid., pp. 37—69.
16 ibid., p. 26.

had become customary'. The next step came in the late Amoraic period (fifth century C.E.), 'when it was no longer deemed sufficient merely to set down the particular items which had to be mentioned in specific benedictions, but it was also felt necessary to fix exact wordings of the opening formula, the concluding eulogy, and ultimately certain important phrases in the body of the benediction itself'. However, even this did not prove that non-normative formulations did not go on being used.[17] The process, he believed, did not end until the Geonic period (600–1100 C.E.), and even when the exact wording of the prayers was finally determined, different versions became authoritative in Babylonia and in Palestine.[18]

Contemporary Jewish scholarship

Heinemann's methodology has since been adopted by other Jewish scholars, and most notably by Lawrence Hoffman, who has traced in greater detail the slow movement towards the standardization of the synagogue liturgy in later centuries.[19] However, not all have accepted Heinemann's conclusions unreservedly. E. Daniel Goldschmidt (1895–1973), for example, continued to defend the philological approach.[20] Even Heinemann's translator, Richard Sarason, while accepting the arguments for an original multiplicity of forms, has expressed caution about the detail of his theory of origins, since so little is known of the period in question:

> While Heinemann's general characterization of the synagogue as a popular folk institution over which the rabbis gradually came to exercise control seems valid, it is not at all clear that the prayer texts and formulae, as well as most of the structures, which the rabbis set down in the Mishnah, Tosefta, and the two Talmuds as 'normative' necessarily originated with the masses and not within rabbinic circles themselves.[21]

[17] ibid., pp. 51–3.
[18] ibid., p. 29.
[19] *The Canonization of the Synagogue Service*, Notre Dame 1979. On this process, see also the study by Stefan C. Reif, 'The Early History of Jewish Liturgy', in Bradshaw & Hoffman, *The Making of Jewish and Christian Worship*, pp. 109–36.
[20] See Sarason, 'On the Use of Method', pp. 124–7 = 137–40.
[21] ibid., p. 146 = 161.

In other words, while Heinemann's theory of the origins of Jewish prayer may indeed be accurate, what survives in the later liturgy may in fact derive from an elitist group rather than from these more populist prayer-patterns —which increases the difficulty of discovering just what the latter were. This suspicion is further encouraged by the existence of occasional incidental references in the rabbinic literature to ongoing ritual practices of the common folk which meet with disapproval. Such glimpses of alternative patterns of worship may well represent only the tip of the iceberg with regard to the customs of the masses.

Similarly, Tzvee Zahavy would maintain that more credence needs to be given to social and political influences in the shaping of Jewish prayers, and both Zahavy and Stefan Reif have argued that Heinemann went too far in his emphasis on the superiority of the form-critical over the philological method. They have advocated as the direction for the future a more comprehensive, integrated interdisciplinary approach, incorporating the use of such things as literary criticism, archaeology, art history, history of religions, and the history of law.[22] Hoffman, too, in his more recent work has criticized all schools of liturgical scholarship for being too narrowly focused on the textual dimension of worship to the exclusion of other perspectives.[23]

On the other hand, it can also be argued that in some respects Heinemann did not go far enough, in that he tended to accept the genuine historicity of statements in the Mishnah, Tosefta, and Talmud which were attributed to rabbinic figures of earlier centuries. In the period since he wrote, such an assumption has been seriously questioned by a new school of rabbinic studies

[22] Tzvee Zahavy, 'A New Approach to Early Jewish Prayer', in Baruch M. Bokser, ed., *History of Judaism: The Next Ten Years* (Brown Judaic Studies 21, Chico CA 1980), pp. 45—60; idem, 'The Politics of Piety: Social Conflict and the Emergence of Rabbinic Liturgy', in Bradshaw & Hoffman, *The Making of Jewish and Christian Worship*, pp. 46—69; idem, *Studies in Jewish Prayer* (Lanham MD 1990), pp. 1ff.; Stefan C. Reif, 'Jewish Liturgical Research: Past, Present and Future', *JJS* 34 (1983), pp. 161—70. See also Richard S. Sarason, 'Recent Developments in the Study of Jewish Liturgy', in Neusner, *The Study of Ancient Judaism* I, pp. 180—7.

[23] *Beyond the Text: A Holistic Approach to Liturgy*, Indianapolis 1987; 'Reconstructing Ritual as Identity and Culture', in Bradshaw & Hoffman, *The Making of Jewish and Christian Worship*, pp. 28—45.

which is particularly associated with Jacob Neusner. If Heinemann's contribution to Jewish liturgical study parallels the form-critical phase of biblical scholarship, then this new movement may be compared to the redaction-criticism which developed in scriptural studies in the second half of the twentieth century. Previously the compilers of biblical books, and especially those responsible for the final redaction of the canonical Gospels, had tended to be seen as little more than mere scribes, mechanically recording historical material more or less exactly in the form they received it. Redaction-criticism took the compilers' role rather more seriously and viewed them as playing a much more creative part in the process of composition —recognizing that they selected and shaped the written and/or oral traditions which they inherited according to their own particular theological outlook, literary purposes, and personal prejudices. They had thus impressed their individual viewpoint on the material, and in the process had sometimes obliterated our access to the earlier sources themselves.

In the same way, scholars had held until recently that the rabbinic literature contained a highly accurate record of the oral judgements of individual rabbis which had been carefully handed down, in some cases over many centuries. Hence it was believed that this material could be used as a reliable historical chronicle for the periods which it purported to represent. More than that, there was a tendency to treat texts which had been edited over a four-century span—from 200 to 600 C.E.—as a seamless whole, regardless of geographical or chronological provenance, and to see a harmonious picture of a developing 'normative Judaism', in which a single sage's opinion could be thought to represent the universal practice; and even the cataloguing of a multitude of differing claims as to the origin of some institution was not thought to cast any serious doubts on its antiquity.

The newer school of rabbinic scholarship, however, approaches the sources with an awareness that one cannot automatically assume a simple historical reading to be reliable. Rabbinic literature, like the biblical books, was created not simply to chronicle the past but to promote and justify the world-view of those responsible for its redaction. For that reason, they were inevitably selective in their approach, restricting themselves to those rabbinic opinions that came within their own view of acceptable limits and omitting whatever did not, and arranging and shaping the material that they did include so that it reflected their own intellectual and theological system.

In other words, the literature is seen as more revealing about the redactors and the age in which they lived than about the earlier periods of history from which it draws. Thus, a saying may be attributed to an ancient authority, but that does not necessarily mean that he must have said it or, if he did say it, that it had the same meaning in its original context as it is given by the redactor of the material or by a later commentator on it. A story may be told about a particular rabbi, but that does not necessarily mean that the events described actually took place in the historical period to which they are ascribed, or even at all. Transmitters and redactors of oral tradition regularly attribute anonymous stories and sayings to ancient authorities so as to increase their prestige, as well as supplementing and reinterpreting their content.[24]

Yet here, too, as in the case of philology versus form-criticism, one must beware of rushing to one extreme or another. As Stefan Reif has said,

> to accept uncritically the historicity of all talmudic reports, particularly as they relate to events in the pre-Christian period, and the attribution of all statements to particular personalities is as misguided as the approach that claims all previous studies antiquated and distinguished talmudists obsolete and refuses to credit the rabbis with any reliable information about the origin of their own religious traditions.[25]

[24] See Jacob Neusner, 'The Teaching of the Rabbis: Approaches Old and New', *JJS* 27 (1976), pp. 23—35; 'The Use of the Later Rabbinic Evidence for the Study of First-Century Pharisaism', in Green, *Approaches to Ancient Judaism*, pp. 215—28; 'The Formation of Rabbinic Judaism: Methodological Issues and Substantive Theses', *Formative Judaism: Religious, Historical and Literary Studies* III (Brown Judaic Studies 46, Chico CA 1983), pp. 99—146.

[25] Stefan C. Reif, 'Some Liturgical Issues in the Talmudic Sources', *SL* 15 (1982/3), p. 190. On the essential continuities within Judaism, see also Roger Brooks, 'Judaism in Crisis? Institutions and Systematic Theology in Rabbinism', in Jacob Neusner et al., *From Ancient Israel to Modern Judaism* II (Brown Judaic Studies 173, Atlanta 1989), pp. 3—18.

On the other hand, we must not underestimate the radical transformation which Judaism underwent after the destruction of the Temple in 70 C.E. The religion which emerged in the period afterwards was by no means identical with the religion which had been current in the decades preceding it. That catastrophic event spelled the demise of many varieties of thought and practice which had previously flourished within Judaism, as groups like the Sadducees and Essenes failed to adapt to the new situation and left the traditions of the Pharisaic party in a position of pre-eminence. And yet even those traditions did not simply continue unchanged: the loss of the Temple and of its sacrificial cult deprived Jews of the way of serving God which was prescribed in the Torah, and so for the faith to survive required a massive reinterpretation of much that they had previously believed. Indeed, the whole of post-70 C.E. Judaism may be viewed as a kind of cultic surrogate, in which the former sacrificial activities were metaphorically transferred to the daily life of the Jewish people — to the act of Torah study, to the obedient observance of the commandments, and to prayer in the synagogue.[26]

Consequently, many things which had earlier been a part of Temple liturgy alone gradually came to have a place within the daily life of ordinary Jews and within the worship of the synagogue. For example, the rules of ritual purity which had formerly pertained only to those engaged in the service of the cult were now reinterpreted as applying to everyone, and such ceremonies as the procession seven times around the altar at the festival of Sukkot were eventually transferred to the synagogue. While among the Pharisees some of these developments — and especially the application of the rules about ritual purity — certainly ante-dated the destruction of the Temple and thus prepared the way for further moves in that direction, it seems

[26] This idea is extensively developed in Richard S. Sarason, 'Religion and Worship: The Case of Judaism', in Jacob Neusner, ed., *Take Judaism, For Example: Studies toward the Comparison of Religions* (Chicago 1983), pp. 49–65. See also Arnold Goldberg, 'Service of the Heart: Liturgical Aspects of Synagogue Worship', in Asher Finkel & Lawrence Frizzell, eds., *Standing before God* (New York 1981), pp. 195–211; B. T. Viviano, *Study as Worship: Aboth and the New Testament*, Leiden 1978.

likely that others underwent transformation only after that event made it impossible to observe them in their original setting.

All this should lead to great caution in assuming that many of the features of later Jewish life and synagogue worship would necessarily have been familiar to Jesus and his followers. The issue can perhaps best be illustrated by considering briefly the question of the statutory synagogue services themselves, which take place three times each day, in the morning, the afternoon, and the evening. Rabbinic literature records a variety of explanations as to their origin, among them that the prayers were instituted by the patriarchs (*B. Ber.* 26b), by Moses (*J. Ber.* 7.11c), or by one hundred and twenty elders, including several prophets (*B. Meg.* 17d). Heinemann, having listed these and other rabbinic claims, confidently concluded that

> since almost every one of these dicta attributes the institution of fixed prayer to a different generation, public body, or personage, nothing can be deduced from their joint testimony with any degree of surety, save for the great antiquity of that institution itself. . . . The evolution of the fixed prayers began hundreds of years before the destruction of the Second Temple.[27]

His conclusion, however, does not necessarily follow. The testimony reveals only that rabbis of the fourth and fifth centuries C.E. are said to have *thought* that the practice was an ancient one, not that it really was. An important dimension of post-70 C.E. Judaism was the obvious need to stress its continuity with the past, and to give authority to the practices it then prescribed by affirming their antiquity. It is, moreover, a natural tendency of all religions to regard whatever is current as having always been observed. So, while it is possible that prayer three times a day was an ancient Jewish custom which was later organized and regulated by Simeon of Paqoli at Yavneh (*c.* 90 C.E.), as the Babylonian Talmud also claims (*B. Meg.* 18b), it is also possible that in reality it had only just emerged at that time as a substitute for the former daily sacrifices of the Temple. Which of these explanations is the more likely requires the consideration of evidence other than the rabbinic traditions alone,

[27] *Prayer in the Talmud,* p. 13.

and to this we shall return when we discuss the question of early synagogue liturgy.

Reconstructing the Jewish background to Christian worship

In our efforts to assess the influence of Jewish practices upon Christian worship we ought to focus primarily upon the first century. It is true that contact between Jews and Christians did not end after 70 C.E., and there is evidence for some continuing links down to at least the fourth century: some of the early Fathers were clearly influenced by Jewish sources, and John Chrysostom tells us that some ordinary Christians were attending both synagogue and church, though it is not clear how widespread, geographically or chronologically, this practice was.[28] On the other hand, after the close of the first century, liturgical influence from Judaism to a now predominantly Gentile Church is likely to have been only marginal, and any really significant effects must be sought in the earlier formative period.

Furthermore, in the task of reconstructing first-century Jewish worship, we should treat as primary sources only material that is contemporary with, or older than, the period. The historicity of evidence from later sources that is not largely substantiated by these earlier witnesses must be regarded with a degree of suspicion. It is possible that such sources may contain genuine records of earlier times, but that cannot automatically be assumed. Even descriptions of Temple rituals may sometimes be projecting back what later Jews thought should have happened rather than what actually was the case.[29] The probable veracity of statements like this must be carefully tested by considering

[28] See James H. Charlesworth, 'A Prolegomenon to a New Study of the Jewish Background of the Hymns and Prayers in the New Testament', *JJS* 33 (1982), pp. 269–70; William Horbury, 'The Benediction of the Minim and Early Jewish-Christian Controversy', *JTS* 33 (1982), pp. 19–61; Robert Wilken, *John Chrysostom and the Jews*, Berkeley 1983.

[29] So, for example, the material in the Mishnah tractate *Middot* seems at times to be more closely related to biblical projections of the Temple than to what is now known through archaeological research to have been true of the actual Temple site. Similarly, the liturgical descriptions in the tractate *Tamid* do not yield a single consistent picture such as one might expect if its purpose had really been to record accurately the daily ritual.

such matters as the chronological proximity of the written testimony to the event or person mentioned in it and the possible motives which might lie behind the propagation of the narrative.

What is equally important for the background of Christian worship is that we should not single out any one Jewish tradition as normative and treat others as deviations, nor restrict our focus to asking which elements of later Jewish liturgy go back to the first century. While Pharisaism may have been the prevailing school of thought in the first century, it was not necessarily the chief influence on the early Christians. Hence, if we wish to see the whole picture without bias, our sources must encompass the total evidence for early Jewish worship — both those expressions that survived in the rabbinic corpus and those that found no place there but were just as much a part of earlier Jewish piety — and we should be as open to the possibility of a diversity as to a uniformity of practice, and not try to force the various pieces of evidence that we have into a false harmony with one another. Testimony that a custom was practised is not *ipso facto* proof that it was universally observed, to the exclusion of all alternatives.

Although not as much contemporary material pertaining to worship may have survived from this period as we might wish, there is in fact much more than is often assumed. James Charlesworth has recently catalogued what he describes as 'an abundance of unexamined data' relating to forms of Jewish hymns and prayers that predate 70 C.E.[30] As he indicates, much work remains to be done on this material before it can yield useful results for our picture of first-century Jewish worship:

> Here, these hymns and prayers are brought together for the first time, and I confess that the best I can do at present is to attempt a prolegomenous outline for a synthesis. We need a synthesis of this data. We need to explore

[30] 'A Prolegomenon', pp. 274–6. For an introduction to some of these sources, see Charlesworth, 'Jewish Hymns, Odes, and Prayers (ca. 167 B.C.E.–135 C.E.)', in Robert A. Kraft & George W. E. Nickelsburg, eds., *Early Judaism and its Modern Interpreters* (Atlanta 1986), pp. 411–36; David Flusser, 'Psalms, Hymns and Prayers', in Michael E. Stone, ed., *Jewish Writings of the Second Temple Period* (Assen, Netherlands/Philadelphia 1984), pp. 551–77.

the relationships of shared themes, perspectives, symbols, and metaphors. We need to explore the possibility of a development of the ancient forms of Semitic poetry, rhythm and rhyme. We need to clarify the social setting of the compositions, and to explore whether there is a significant relation between the prayers composed by the apocalypticists and the statutory prayers of the Synagogue, *Bet Midrash*, and other liturgically formalized Jewish settings. Especially, we need to probe the possible kinship among those that phenomenologically had a life within some liturgical setting. In terms of these concerns, the above outlined data is a promised land without maps.[31]

In the light of all this, what can be said about Jewish worship in the first century? For the purposes of this study, we shall omit consideration of the Temple. While it is beyond doubt that regular sacrifices were being offered there, there is very little literary evidence which provides reliable details of the cult at this period. In any case, although the sacrifical imagery of the Temple certainly did continue to figure in early Christian thought, and more strongly from the fourth century onwards in actual liturgical practice,[32] the source for this was the literary description of the Temple liturgy in the Hebrew Scriptures rather than the first-century institution itself. Thus, we shall examine briefly three areas: forms of prayer themselves; possible elements of synagogue liturgy; and grace at meals. Reference to the Passover and its influence upon early Christian worship will be reserved to the next chapter.

First-century Jewish prayer-patterns

While it is true —as Christian scholars have constantly asserted —that the *berakah* was a first-century Jewish prayer-form, it was not the only form that prayer could then take in the Jewish tradition, nor was there only one standard form of *berakah* in current use.[33] The *berakah* (plural *berakot*) derives its name

[31] 'A Prolegomenon', p. 277.

[32] See Robert Daly, *The Origins of the Christian Doctrine of Sacrifice*, London/Philadelphia 1978; R. P. C. Hanson, *Eucharistic Offering in the Early Church*, GLS 19, 1979; Kenneth Stevenson, *Eucharist and Offering* (New York 1986), pp. 10—37; Rowan Williams, *Eucharistic Sacrifice: The Roots of a Metaphor*, GLS 31, 1982; Frances Young, *The Use of Sacrificial Ideas in Greek Christian Writers from the New Testament to John Chrysostom*, Cambridge MA 1979.

[33] See further Bradshaw, *Daily Prayer in the Early Church*, pp. 11—16.

from the Hebrew verb *barak*, 'to bless', and several variant types of liturgical formulae utilizing its passive participle *baruk* (or in Greek, *eulogetos*) in reference to God can be detected in the Hebrew Bible and in intertestamental literature. As well as very short doxological formulae, such as 'Blessed is the Lord for ever' (Ps. 89.52), there are also longer acclamations containing either a relative clause or a participial phrase. The use of a relative clause to express the particular actions of God which were the reason for the blessing (as in Exod. 18.10: 'Blessed is the Lord, who has delivered you out of the hands of the Egyptians and out of the hand of Pharaoh') appears to be older than the use of the participial phrase, which tends to speak in more general terms of the qualities of God, as in Tobit 13.1: 'Blessed is God, the one living for ever, and [blessed is] his kingdom.'

In either case, however, this simple *anamnesis* of God might be expanded into a more complex structure by the addition of other elements. A more detailed narrative description of God's works (as, for example, in 1 Kings 8.15−21 or in Tobit 13.2) is very common, as are supplication and intercession —the remembrance of God's past goodness constituting the ground on which he might be asked to continue his gracious activity among his people (as in 1 Kings 8.56−61) —but confession of sin or protestations of unworthiness and faithfulness are also found. The petitionary element often ends with a statement that its purpose is not just the benefit of the suppliants but the advancement of God's glory (as in 1 Kings 8.60: 'that all the peoples of the earth may know that the Lord is God'), and both the narrative description and such petition may lead back to praise in a concluding doxology. Although in the Hebrew Bible these *berakot* are nearly all cast in the third person, there developed in the intertestamental period an increasing preference for the second person instead, as, for example, in 1 Macc. 4.30ff.: 'Blessed are you, O Saviour of Israel, who. . . .'

On the other hand, the praise of God might be expressed in ways other than the *berakah*. An alternative construction (sometimes called the *hodayah*) instead used the Hebrew verb *hodeh*, or sometimes some other verb, but in an active and not a passive form, with God addressed directly in the second person. Although *hodeh* is usually translated into English as 'give thanks', its primary meaning is not the expression of gratitude but rather confession or acknowledgement that something is the case, the same verb also being used for the confession of sin. It was at first rendered into Greek by compound forms of the verb *homologeo*, although later *eucharisteo* became established as an alternative. Like *barak*, it could be used in brief doxologies, as in Ps. 30.12, 'O Lord my God, I will give thanks to you for ever', or with a subordinate clause to articulate the reason for the praise, usually introduced with the conjunction *ki*, 'that' (in Greek *hoti*), as in Isa. 12.1: 'I will give thanks to you, O Lord my God, that though you were angry with me, your anger turned away and you comforted me'; and the formula could be expanded with further narrative description or by the addition of supplication before returning to a doxological conclusion. This liturgical form is common among the material from Qumran.

Similarly, Jewish prayers of praise in this period might dispense entirely with any introductory formula, and begin directly to recount the mighty works of God, either speaking of God in the third person or addressing God directly in the second person, and could then pass on to supplication and to a concluding doxology, as in the Prayer of Manasses. More complex liturgical forms might combine elements of different types. So, for example, Dan. 2.20−3 begins with a *berakah* and continues (v. 23) with the *hodayah* form; 2 Macc. 1.11−17 is in *hodayah* form but with a *berakah* conclusion; and 1 Esd. 4.59−60 has all three forms: 'From you comes victory, from you comes wisdom, and yours is the glory, and I am your servant. Blessed are you, who has given me wisdom; for to you I give thanks, O Lord of our fathers.' Furthermore, the difference between the constructions could be blurred to some extent by the fact that the *hodayah* might occasionally use a relative clause, like the *berakah*, and the *berakah* a subordinate clause like the *hodayah*.

The liturgy of the synagogue in the first century

The Mishnah lists five actions which it says cannot be performed communally without the presence of a quorum of ten adult males: the recitation of the *Shema*, the recitation of the *Tefillah*, the priestly blessing, the reading from the Torah, and the reading from the Prophets (*Meg.* 4.3). Scholars have usually assumed that these constituted the main elements of the Sabbath synagogue service of the time, and took place in the order in which they are listed, especially as they correspond with the order of the later synagogue liturgy. But this assumption is open to doubt. Since they form merely the first part of a longer list of nine liturgical activities requiring ten males in which the others clearly refer to different situations (weddings, funerals, and the grace after meals), it is by no means certain that all five must belong to a single occasion; and even if they do, it still remains an open question whether the Mishnah is here describing what was the accepted practice of the period or attempting to prescribe some innovation. Hence, the further assumption that this form of service, even if not the rabbinic rule about the need for a mimimum of ten men, was already in existence in the first century C.E. is even more questionable.

The Shema

In its fully developed form the *Shema* consists of three Pentateuchal passages (Deut. 6:4–9; 11:13–21; Num. 15:37–41) and takes its name from the opening Hebrew word of the first passage ('Hear'). The Mishnah presupposes that it is recited twice each day, in the morning and in the evening, accompanied by *berakot* —in the morning two before it and one after, in the evening two before it and two after (*Ber.* 1.1–4). It also claims that the *Shema* had been recited by the priests in the Jerusalem Temple, where it had been preceded by the recitation of a single *berakah* and the Decalogue, and followed by three *berakot* (*Tamid* 5.1). It appears, therefore, that the general obligation to recite the *Shema* developed out of an earlier Temple ritual. Zahavy, however, has disputed this and proposed instead that it originated as a popular scribal rite, the alleged link with the Temple being an attempt by the scribal group to give added authority to the practice.[34] If this is so, it seems a little surprising that this group did not make their description of the Temple ritual correspond more exactly in its details (and especially the number of *berakot*) with the form which later became normative.

[34] 'The Politics of Piety', pp. 53–6; *Studies in Jewish Prayer*, pp. 87–94.

Whatever its origins, there are signs that the twice-daily recitation of the *Shema* was already widely practised prior to the destruction of the Temple. There are apparent allusions to it in the *Letter of Aristeas* (which was probably composed in the middle of the second century B.C.E.), in Philo, in Josephus, and in the Dead Sea Scrolls.[35] The Decalogue and the beginning of the *Shema* occur in the Nash papyrus (*c.* 150 B.C.E.),[36] and the scriptural verses of the *Shema* appear in the earliest phylacteries found at Qumran. While the Mishnah makes no reference to the use of the Decalogue with the *Shema* outside the Temple, both the Nash papyrus and the evidence of the Cairo Genizah suggest that at least in some places the two were combined.

The Tefillah

The *Tefillah*, 'prayer' (later also known as the *Amidah*, 'standing', indicating the posture to be adopted for it), was also called the *Shemoneh Esreh* (the 'Eighteen [*berakot*]'), from the fact that its contents came to be fixed at eighteen[37] separate sections, each of which eventually had a short *berakah* appended to its conclusion in order to conform to the later rabbinic requirement that all prayers must have the *berakah* form. According to the Mishnah, the *Tefillah* was to be said three times each day—in the morning, the afternoon, and the evening (*Ber.* 4.1)—and there are indications that the custom of threefold daily prayer was well established in earlier Judaism. It is mentioned in Dan. 6.10; the afternoon time of prayer is referred to in the New Testament (Acts 3.1; 10.3, 30); and prayer three times a day may even have been the practice at Qumran.[38] What is less certain, however, is the content of the prayer which was said at those times. Only at the end of the first century C.E. was the number of *berakot* fixed at eighteen, together with the general theme of

---

[35] *Letter of Aristeas* 158—60; Philo, *De Spec. Leg.* 4.141; Josephus, *Ant.* 4.8.13; 1 QS 10.10. For an English translation of the *Letter of Aristeas*, see James H. Charlesworth, ed., *The Old Testament Pseudepigrapha* II (Garden City NY 1985/London 1986), pp. 7—34.

[36] See W. F. Albright, 'A Biblical Fragment of the Maccabean Age: The Nash Papyrus', *JBL* 56 (1937), pp. 145—76.

[37] Later nineteen.

[38] See Bradshaw, *Daily Prayer in the Early Church*, pp. 4ff.

each and the order in which they were to be said. Even then some variation still remained: the precise wording was not yet established, and on Sabbaths and festivals a different order of only seven *berakot* was substituted. Prior to this date it appears that a number of different forms of prayer were in use, of varying lengths and with a diversity of themes, according to local custom.[39]

Zahavy has argued that the *Shemoneh Esreh* originated as the main liturgical practice of the deposed priestly aristocracy after the destruction of the Temple, and hence both *Shema* and *Tefillah* represent the prototypical liturgies of competing social factions. Only later, during the second century, he believes, was a compromise reached and the two were amalgamated to form the core of rabbinic liturgy.[40] His identification of the priestly aristocracy as the *originating* group — rather than as those who adopted a pre-existent practice — is questionable, since we have seen that the custom of threefold daily prayer appears to be much older than the destruction of the Temple. In any case, the connection of *thrice*-daily prayer with the times of the *twice*-daily sacrifices looks more like a secondary adaptation than its primary motivation, since there is no equally significant correspondence in the Temple cult for the evening hour of prayer, and even the Mishnah's suggestion that it was linked to the closing of the Temple gates (*Taan.* 4.1) has the appearance of a later rationalization.[41]

Nevertheless, the notion that the two customs — reciting the *Shema* with its accompanying prayers twice each day and praying three times a day — first emerged as the distinctive practices of quite different religious groups and were only harmonized in the second century does seem to be well founded, especially as even within later Judaism the rules pertaining both to the time-limits for the fulfilment of the duty and to the persons who were obligated to perform it were quite different in each case.

[39] See Jacob Petuchowski, 'The Liturgy of the Synagogue: History, Structure, and Contents', in W. S. Green, ed., *Approaches to Ancient Judaism* IV (Brown Judaic Studies 27, Chico CA 1983), pp. 6ff.

[40] 'The Politics of Piety', pp. 58−63; *Studies in Jewish Prayer*, pp. 94−101.

[41] See Bradshaw, *Daily Prayer in the Early Church*, pp. 2−11.

The priestly blessing

According to the Mishnah, the pronouncing of the Aaronic blessing, Num. 6.24–6, over the people originated in the Temple ritual in connection with the daily sacrifices (*Tamid* 7.2). It is possible, therefore, that it was not transplanted to the synagogue until after 70 C.E. Its position in the later synagogue service — after the *Shema* and *Tefillah* but before the scriptural reading(s) — is interesting, since one might have expected it to have been placed at the end of the whole liturgy. A possible explanation may be that the *Tefillah* and the blessing were viewed as a single liturgical unit, perhaps because the *Tefillah* came to be thought of as a substitute for the Temple sacrifices and hence the blessing followed it, as it had done in the cult.

The readings from the Torah and the Prophets

The reading of a portion of the Torah on every Sabbath and festival seems to have been a regular feature of the synagogue from the outset, and may have constituted *the* fundamental reason for the emergence of that institution. Indeed, James McKinnon would go further still and argue, largely on the basis of a total silence in early sources with regard to the practice of prayer in relation to the synagogue, that while the reading of Scripture and discourse upon it took place there prior to the destruction of the Temple, it was not a place for formal, communal worship until after that event necessitated the creation of a substitute centre for liturgical activity.[42]

Be that as it may, portions of the Torah also came to be read at the Sabbath afternoon service and on Monday and Thursday mornings. This, however, is almost certainly a later development than the reading on Sabbath mornings, and the choice of Mondays and Thursdays for this purpose seems to be governed by the fact that these were market days in Palestine when people might be expected to gather in villages and towns in some numbers. The morning service on Sabbaths and festivals also included a second reading from the Prophets (which in the Jewish division of the Scriptures includes the historical books of

---

[42] 'On the Question of Psalmody in the Ancient Synagogue', *Early Music History* 6 (1986), pp. 170–80.

Joshua, Judges, Samuel, and Kings). This too was probably a later development, though Luke 4.16–30 and Acts 13.15 indicate that it was established in the first century C.E. The readings were followed by a translation into the vernacular and could be concluded with a discourse or homily.

The Babylonian Talmud prescribed that the entire Pentateuch should be read through in a year, on a consecutive basis interrupted only by special lections on festal days. The Palestinian practice, however, was different, and the traditional scholarly theory has been that in this case there was a standard lectionary cycle lasting exactly three years, both for the Torah and for the Prophets.[43] Heinemann has demonstrated, however, that any idea of a uniform cycle of readings in early times runs contrary to the evidence and 'belongs clearly to the realm of fiction'.[44] While, for example, the Mishnah prescribes twenty-one verses of the Torah as the minimum to be read each Sabbath morning (there are to be at least seven readers, who must each read no fewer than three verses: *Meg.* 4.4), it does not set any maximum, and consequently different synagogues could have reached different places in the Torah on any given occasion. Moreover, while some read passages consecutively on Sabbath mornings, Sabbath afternoons, Mondays, and Thursdays, others did not, but repeated the Sabbath morning reading on the other occasions in the week. Even less is known about how the Prophetic readings were originally arranged, whether, for instance, they were simply read consecutively or were chosen to complement the Pentateuchal lection or were determined by the season of the liturgical year.

The question of psalmody
Liturgical and musical historians have tended to assert confidently that psalmody was a standard part of the early synagogue

---

[43] This theory was first advanced by Adolph Büchler, 'The Reading of the Law and Prophets in a Triennial Cycle', *JQR* 5 (1893), pp. 420–68; 6 (1894), pp. 1–73.
[44] 'The Triennial Lectionary Cycle', *JJS* 19 (1968), pp. 41–8. See also Charles Perrot, *La lecture de la Bible dans la synagogue*, Hildesheim 1973; 'The Reading of the Bible in the Ancient Synagogue', in M. J. Mulder, ed., *Mikra* (Philadelphia 1988), pp. 137–59.

liturgy, and some have even gone so far as to suggest that there was once a triennial cycle for the Psalter at the Sabbath afternoon service, corresponding to that for the Torah, in which the psalms were read through in order.[45] There is, however, an almost total lack of documentary evidence for the inclusion of psalms in synagogue worship. The Mishnah lists a psalm for each of the seven days of the week (24, 48, 82, 94, 81, 93, 92) which was sung by the Levites at the Temple sacrifices (*Tamid* 7.4), and at the important festivals the *Hallel* (Pss. 113–118) accompanied the sacrifices. But, while the *Hallel* seems to have been taken over into the domestic Passover meal at an early date, and apparently also into the festal synagogue liturgy, the first mention of the adoption of the daily psalms in the synagogue is not until the eighth century.[46]

Nor are there earlier references to the use of other psalms in the synagogue, except for an enigmatic statement in the Mishnah concerning 'those who complete a *hallel* every day' (*Meg.* 17b). The Babylonian Talmud identifies this *hallel* as *pesukei de-zimrah*, 'verses of song' (*B. Shab.* 118b), a phrase which was later used to denote Pss. 145–150, but there is no way of knowing whether the Talmudic expression was originally understood in this sense or not, still less whether the Mishnaic *hallel* referred to the same psalms. Hoffman has suggested that both were probably intended simply as generic terms for any group of psalms of praise.[47] In any case, it would appear that what is envisaged is private recitation by pious individuals rather than a formal part of the synagogue liturgy, just as also seems to be true of the Baylonian Talmud's reference to some who recite Ps. 145 three times a day (*b. Ber.* 4b).

On the other hand, although there may be no evidence for the use of the canonical psalms in early Judaism, there are at

[45] See the scholars cited in J. A. Lamb, *The Psalms in Christian Worship* (London 1962), pp. 14–15.

[46] See McKinnon, 'On the Question of Psalmody in the Ancient Synagogue', pp. 180ff.; Zahavy, *Studies in Jewish Prayer*, pp. 103–9.

[47] *The Canonization of the Synagogue Service*, pp. 127–8. See also Sarason, 'On the Use of Method', p. 130 = 145; and cf. a spirited defence of the notion that the *hallel* did comprise Pss. 145–150 in W. Jardine Grisbrooke, 'The Laudate Psalms: A Footnote', *SL* 20 (1990), pp. 175–9.

least some indications that hymns and songs were being composed and used in some way.[48] These, however, may have belonged rather to more informal and domestic situations than to formal synagogue assemblies.

Daily synagogue services?

Although, as we have seen, the Mishnah presupposes that both the *Shema* and the *Tefillah* will be said every day, the impression given is that private recitation by individuals is understood to be the normal practice, rather than a corporate liturgical action in the synagogue, which belongs rather to those days of the week when people might gather together to read the Scriptures —the Sabbath, Mondays, and Thursdays.[49] Moreover, while the community life of the Essenes apparently did lead to daily prayer in common,[50] Matt. 6.5 regards public prayer by some Pharisees at street-corners *and in synagogues* as a particular act of ostentation rather than as a regular religious custom. Thus there appears to be no sure foundation for the confident assertion by C. W. Dugmore (1910−1990) that in first-century Judaism, at least in the larger towns, 'daily attendance at the public worship of the community would be the practice of every devout Jew'.[51]

Grace at meals

According to the Mishnah, nothing was to be eaten without God having first been blessed for it, and the short *berakot* to be used for each kind of food are quoted (*Ber.* 6.1−3). Zahavy has suggested, however, that this fully-fledged system of food-blessings, recited before eating, was not formalized until at least the middle of the second century, and was built upon an older tradition

[48] See, for example, the collection of Qumran *Hodayoth*; Philo, *In Flaccum* 121−4 and *De Vita Contemplativa* 29, 80, 83, 84.

[49] See McKinnon, 'On the Question of Psalmody in the Ancient Synagogue', pp. 176−8; Roger T. Beckwith, *Daily and Weekly Worship — From Jewish to Christian* (A/GLS 1, 1987), pp. 11−12; Zahavy, *Studies in Jewish Prayer*, pp. 45−52.

[50] See Josephus, *Jewish War* 2.128−9; 1 QS 6.3. The Therapeutae described by Philo, however, lived in recluse and only assembled for worship on the Sabbath (*De Vita Contemplativa* 30).

[51] *The Influence of the Synagogue upon the Divine Office* (London 1944, 2nd edn, ACC 45, London 1964), p. 43.

of saying blessings over wine and at the end of a meal.[52] Although the Mishnah does not give the text of the grace at the end of a meal, its general outline must by then have been well established, for it is referred to as comprising three *berakot* (*Ber.* 6.8). It is usually assumed that at least the substance of the later *Birkat ha-mazon* was already in regular use, as this too has a tripartite structure: a *berakah* for the gift of food; a *hodayah* for the gift of the land, the covenant, and the law; and a supplication for mercy on the people, the city of Jerusalem, and the Temple.[53] Some confirmation of the antiquity of this form is provided by the *Book of Jubilees*, usually dated somewhere in the middle of the second century B.C.E. There a grace which is put into the mouth of Abraham displays a very similar tripartite structure: a blessing of God for creation and the gift of food; thanksgiving for the long life granted to Abraham; and a supplication for God's mercy and peace.[54]

We should beware, however, of too readily drawing the conclusion that this grace after meals had a standardized form in the first century. Since we have already observed a considerable degree of variation and fluidity in other prayer-patterns from this time, it would be natural to expect some similar diversity in domestic food rituals prior to the attempts to set limits to orthodoxy after the destruction of the Temple. There is obviously an element of continuity between the general structure and themes of the grace known to the author of *Jubilees* and the later *Birkat ha-mazon*, but it is likely that the precise contents varied considerably between different groups of people in the intervening centuries. A fragmentary text of what may be a somewhat different meal-prayer has survived from the synagogue at Dura-Europos,[55] and it is possible that some tradi-

---

[52] *Studies in Jewish Prayer*, pp. 14—16. See also Baruch M. Bokser, 'Ma'al and Blessings over Food: Rabbinic Transformation of Cultic Terminology and Alternative Modes of Piety', *JBL* 100 (1981), pp. 557—74.

[53] For an English translation of the later text, see R. C. D. Jasper & G. J. Cuming, eds., *Prayers of the Eucharist: Early and Reformed* (3rd edn, New York 1987), pp. 7—12.

[54] *Jubilees* 22.6—9. For an English translation, see Charlesworth, *Old Testament Pseudepigrapha* II, p. 97.

[55] See Jacob Neusner, *A History of the Jews in Babylonia* I (Leiden 1969 = Chico CA 1984), p. 161, n. 3.

tions within early Judaism had forms of grace which diverged more widely still from this pattern.

Unfortunately, no more detailed information about meal-prayers in this period has been preserved. While, for example, both Josephus and the Qumran literature witness to the fact that the Essenes prayed before and after eating, they do not give any clear indication of the content of the prayers.[56] On the other hand, the *Letter of Aristeas* refers to prayer before eating as a regular Jewish custom, and the only words which it cites are petitionary rather than an act of blessing or thanksgiving.[57] It should also be noted that Philo consistently uses *eucharisteo* rather than *eulogeo* to refer to prayer at meals, which may possibly be an indication that there were forms of grace in Hellenistic Judaism which began with that verb.[58]

The Mishnah directed that when three or more people ate together, one of them was to say the grace on behalf of all, and it prescribed before the prayer a formula of invitation and a communal response, which varied according to the number of people present (*Ber.* 7.1–3). Thus, for example, the form for use with one hundred people was:

> Let us bless the Lord our God.
> Blessed be the Lord our God.

Heinemann argued that this bidding must be of great antiquity and that its wording would have become fixed at an early date.[59] However, that some variation in wording could apparently still be countenanced when the Mishnah was compiled seems a strong indication that its text had not been definitively established at an earlier time. This in turn suggests the possibility that there may once have existed even more diverse forms both of the bidding and of the grace itself which lay beyond the limits that the rabbinic tradition was prepared to recognize.

---

[56] Josephus, *Jewish War* 2.8.5; 1 QS 6.3–8; 1 QSa 2.17f.

[57] *Letter of Aristeas* 185.

[58] See Jean Laporte, *La doctrine eucharistique chez Philon d'Alexandre* (Paris 1972), pp. 82–4; English translation, *Eucharistia in Philo* (New York 1983), pp. 53–5.

[59] 'Birkath ha-Zimmun and Havurah Meals', *JJS* 13 (1962), pp. 23–9.

Christian views of first-century Jewish worship

The recognition that Christianity probably inherited many of its liturgical practices from Judaism can be traced back at least to the late seventeenth century. The Dutch Protestant theologian, Campegius Vitringa (1659–1722), appears to have been the first to suggest the connection,[60] and similar views apppeared in the works of eighteenth- and nineteenth-century scholars.[61] F. E. Warren (1842–1930) argued that a priori 'the law of evolution would lead us to expect a natural continuity between Jewish and Christian worship', though he recognized that there were difficulties when it came to deciding whether specific resemblances between the two were the result of a direct connection or not, especially as 'there are not extant sufficient authentic Jewish liturgical remains of the first century A.D., for us to base an independent conclusion upon them with certainty'. In contrast to other scholars, however, Warren thought it unlikely that the synagogue, 'with such painful and degrading associations and recollections' for the first Christians, would have been the quarter to which they would have turned for a model, but that 'their thoughts would more naturally centre round the temple'.[62]

The early twentieth century saw an increasing number of attempts to postulate a link between Jewish and Christian liturgical forms,[63] and especially after the publication in 1945 of Gregory Dix's magisterial work, *The Shape of the Liturgy*,[64] it became axiomatic for those searching for the origins of every aspect of primitive Christian liturgical practice to look primarily for Jewish antecedents. However, because they have generally continued to accept uncritically the conclusions reached by older

[60] *De synagoga vetere*, Francquerae 1696; English translation by J. L. Bernard, *The Synagogue and the Church*, London 1842.

[61] See, for example, Joseph Bingham, *Origines Ecclesiasticae: The Antiquities of the Christian Church* (London 1710), Bk. XIII, ch. V, sect. 4; William Smith, *Dictionary of the Bible* (London 1863), 'Synagogue, V.1'.

[62] *The Liturgy and Ritual of the Ante-Nicene Church* (London 1897), pp. 201–7.

[63] See, for example, W. O. E. Oesterley, *The Jewish Background of the Christian Liturgy*, Oxford 1925 = Gloucester MA 1965; Frank Gavin, *The Jewish Antecedents of the Christian Sacraments*, London 1928 = New York 1969.

[64] For this, see below, pp. 137ff.

Jewish liturgical scholarship, it is hardly surprising that they have tended to be convinced of the fixity and uniformity of Jewish liturgical practices in the first century C.E. Thus, for example, Walter Frere (1863–1938) said of the *Kiddush*[65] that 'there has been a reliable and uniform tradition which has kept the observance unchanged in Jewish usage; so the Jewish Prayer-book of to-day may be taken as evidence of what was customary in a Jewish home of our Lord's time, or in a group such as He had gathered round Him'.[66] Similarly, Dix could write that 'the various formulae of blessing for the different kinds of food were fixed and well-known, and might not be altered'.[67] Finkelstein's methodology was lauded by Frederick Grant (1891–1974),[68] and his reconstruction of the supposed *Urtext* of the Jewish daily prayers was accepted unhesitatingly in C. W. Dugmore's work on the origins of Christian daily prayer.[69]

Since few Christian liturgical scholars have competence in Hebrew, the language in which Heinemann's dissertation was first published in 1964, his work remained almost totally unknown until its appearance in an English translation in 1977 (though an English abstract did accompany the original edition). And even since then, it has all too rarely been cited in studies of the origins of Christian worship;[70] still less has its full significance been appreciated, or the changing face of rabbinic scholarship taken into account. Yet recent Jewish studies challenge the very foundations upon which reconstructions of early Christian liturgy have been built. As Stefan Reif has said, 'suddenly it becomes clear that the basic work in Jewish liturgy has, after all, not been definitively completed. *Au contraire*, even

[65] Literally 'Sanctification': a domestic ceremony which marked the beginning of the Sabbath.

[66] *The Anaphora* (London 1938), p. 7.

[67] *The Shape of the Liturgy*, p. 51.

[68] 'Modern Study of the Jewish Liturgy', *Zeitschrift für die Alttestamentliche Wissenschaft* 65 (1953), pp. 59–77.

[69] *The Influence of the Synagogue upon the Divine Office*, pp. 24–5.

[70] Louis Ligier made passing reference to the Hebrew edition (see below, p. 148, n. 76), but my citation of it in my essay, 'Authority and Freedom in the Early Liturgy', in Kenneth Stevenson, ed., *Authority and Freedom in Liturgy* (GLS 17, 1979), p. 4, appears to be the first reference to the English translation in a Christian liturgical study.

the most basic facts about the early liturgical relationship between Jews and Christians must be rethought.'[71]

[71] 'Jewish Liturgical Research', p. 168.

2. Worship in the New Testament

The number of studies in the last few decades relating to various aspects of worship in the New Testament has been so great that a detailed account is quite impossible within the limits of this chapter. We shall content ourselves, therefore, with indicating a number of major trends or tendencies which can be observed within this literature, and noting some methodological criticisms which may be raised in connection with them. Some of these trends are more pronounced in the work of New Testament scholars; some are more evident in the work of liturgical scholars; while others are common to both groups.

The tendency towards 'panliturgism'

While some scholars have been inclined to deny that the New Testament supplies much evidence at all for what the early Christians were doing in their regular worship, others have sometimes displayed what has been called a certain 'panliturgism' — a tendency to see signs of liturgy everywhere,[1] which, as C. F. D. Moule observed, brings with it 'the temptation to detect the reverberations of liturgy in the New Testament even where no liturgical note was originally struck'.[2] This tendency can be clearly illustrated in the multifarious attempts to discern a liturgical context behind the New Testament writings themselves. Many scholars have claimed to see here reflections of certain Jewish liturgical practices which more recent research into the origins of Jewish worship would consider post-date the composition of the New Testament books.

For example, it has often been stated that the Gospels were intended for public reading within regular Christian worship, and hence their composition would have been shaped to some extent by the Jewish lectionary which they would then have accompanied and on which they would have constituted a com-

---

[1] W. C. van Unnik, '*Dominus vobiscum*: The Background of a Liturgical Formula', in A. J. B. Higgins, ed., *New Testament Essays: Studies in Memory of T. W. Manson* (Manchester 1959), p. 272 = *Sparsa Collecta* 3 (Supplements to Novum Testamentum 31, Leiden 1983), p. 363.

[2] *Worship in the New Testament*, p. 7.

mentary. Thus attempts have been made to discern the lectionary material lying behind them. R. G. Finch in 1939 seems to
have been the first to do this, maintaining that Jesus' teaching
was not only given in the synagogue but affected by what was
read there.[3] Subsequently G. D. Kilpatrick suggested that Matthew was intended for public reading at worship, but did not
attempt to propound a detailed lectionary arrangement.[4] Philip
Carrington developed the idea in relation to Mark, seeing it as
laid out in accordance with an annual cycle of Sabbaths and
feasts.[5] Michael Goulder went further, and regarded all three
Gospels as lectionary books —Mark for half a year, Matthew
for a full year following the festal cycle, and Luke for a full year
following the Sabbath cycle[6] —while Aileen Guilding tried to
show that the Fourth Gospel was intended as a commentary on
the Jewish triennial lectionary and was attempting to preserve
the traditions about Jesus in a form suitable for liturgical use in
the churches.[7]

---

[3] *The Synagogue Lectionary and the New Testament*, London 1939.

[4] *The Origins of the Gospel according to St Matthew* (Oxford 1946), ch. V.

[5] *The Primitive Christian Calendar: A Study in the Making of the Markan
Gospel*, Cambridge 1952. He was severely criticized by W. D. Davies, 'Reflections on Archbishop Carrington's "Primitive Christian Calendar" ', in W. D.
Davies & D. Daube, *The Background of the New Testament and its Eschatology*
(Cambridge 1954), pp. 124—52, reprinted in W. D. Davies, *Christian Origins
and Judaism* (London/Philadelphia 1962), pp. 67—95. Carrington, however,
defended his position in a long appendix to his *According to Mark* (Cambridge
1960), pp. 346—71.

[6] *Midrash and Lection in Matthew*, London 1974; *The Evangelists' Calendar*,
London 1978. Goulder has subsequently admitted that 'in the present state of
knowledge the Sabbath readings in the synagogue are speculative', and so the
hypothesis of a correspondence between the Gospels and a Sabbath lectionary
'needs to be shelved, though it does not need to be abandoned'; but he still
insists that correspondence with the main feasts of the year is much stronger:
Luke: A New Paradigm (Journal for the Study of the New Testament Supplement Series 20, Sheffield 1989) I, pp. 147—77.

[7] *The Fourth Gospel and Jewish Worship* (Oxford 1960), pp. 54—7. But cf.
the criticisms in Leon Morris, *The New Testament and the Jewish Lectionaries*,
London 1964; idem, 'The Gospels and the Jewish Lectionaries', in R. T. France
& David Wenham, eds., *Gospel Perspectives* 3 (Sheffield 1983), pp. 129—56.
While not going as far as Guilding, Oscar Cullmann, *Early Christian Worship*
(London/Philadelphia 1953), pp. 37—59, considered that one of the chief con-
cerns of the Fourth Gospel was to set forth the connection between the con-
temporary Christian worship and the historical life of Jesus.

Most of these theories do not have the slightest evidence to support them. Not only has recent Jewish scholarship revealed that there was no fixed Sabbath lectionary in existence in the first century,[8] but we have no reason to suppose that Gentile churches would necessarily have wanted to preserve a Jewish system of Scripture reading in their worship, nor is there any sign that Christians assigned particular passages of Scripture to specific occasions. On the contrary, Justin Martyr, writing in the middle of the second century, stated that the readings lasted 'for as long as time allows'.[9]

Efforts to find a liturgical background in Judaism have not been restricted to the Gospels alone. T. W. Manson thought that the early part of Romans took its form from the liturgy of the Day of Atonement, and that the Corinthian letters contained reminiscences of the feasts of Passover, New Year, and Tabernacles.[10] Carrington believed that some of the themes of the Corinthian correspondence were derived from a synagogue lectionary used during the period from Passover to Pentecost, and that Hebrews may have been intended for reading at a Jewish-Christian celebration of the Day of Atonement.[11] Ernst Lohmeyer also saw a reflection of the Day of Atonement in Col. 1.13−20,[12] while James Charlesworth has suggested that the influence of that feast lies behind Phil. 2.6−11.[13] Here, too, the connection is tenuous. While it is possible at least in some cases that the author's experience of Jewish festivals and the concepts associated with them have coloured the expression of the theological ideas of some of the New Testament material, it is a quite unjustified leap from there to posit the text's original *Sitz im Leben* within that worship.

[8] See above, pp. 21−2.
[9] Justin Martyr, *I Apol.* 67.3. See below, pp. 111−12, 139.
[10] '*Hilasterion*', *JTS* 46 (1945), pp. 1−10.
[11] *The Primitive Christian Calendar*, pp. 42−4. See also T. W. Manson, *The Epistle to the Hebrews* (London 1951), p. 131.
[12] *Die Briefe an die Philipper, an die Kolosser und an Philemon* (Göttingen 1930), pp. 41−7. See also Stanislas Lyonnet, 'L'hymne christologique de l'Épître aux Colossiens et la fête juive du Nouvel An', *Recherches de science religieuse* 48 (1960), pp. 92−100.
[13] 'A Prolegomenon', p. 279, n. 46.

Closely related to these claims is the question of the extent to which Christianity separated itself from Judaism from the outset, and therefore the degree to which Jewish liturgy would have continued to exercise a formative influence on Christian worship, especially in the predominantly Gentile churches founded by Paul. Scholars have adopted different positions on this issue. Some have stressed the element of continuity with Judaism in almost every aspect of Christian liturgy; others have minimized the connection between Church and synagogue, often seemingly more on the basis of a dogmatic conviction that the Christian faith necessarily involved a radical transformation or even rejection of the former religion than on the basis of a dispassionate examination of the evidence. Gerhard Delling, for example, in what has often been viewed as a standard study of worship in the New Testament, asserted that 'the Worship which belongs to the kingdom which has come in Jesus is fundamentally and completely detached from that of Israel'.[14]

Other attempts have been made to discover a specifically Christian liturgical context behind New Testament material. Carrington concluded that the similar moral exhortations in Colossians, Ephesians, 1 Peter, and James implied that the writers were drawing upon a common pattern of teaching designed for pre-baptismal catechesis.[15] E. G. Selwyn added material from Romans and 1 Thessalonians and believed that he had discovered a baptismal catechism with five different sections which circulated *c.* 50−55 C.E.[16] While many scholars have subscribed to the view that 1 Peter contains a baptismal homily of some sort,[17] Herbert Preisker and F. L. Cross went further and

---

[14] D. G. Delling, *Worship in the New Testament* (London 1962), p. 6. See also Ferdinand Hahn, *The Worship of the Early Church* (Philadelphia 1973), pp. 32ff., 50−2, who believes that the early Christians were originally free from Jewish ritual practices, but gradually returned to such customs as fasting and Sabbath observance.

[15] *The Primitive Christian Catechism*, Cambridge 1940.

[16] *The First Epistle of St Peter*, London 1947. Cf. the careful evalution of a possible liturgical background for 1 Thessalonians by Raymond F. Collins, 'I Thes. and the Liturgy of the Early Church', *Biblical Theology Bulletin* 10 (1980), pp. 51−64.

[17] See, for example, F. W. Beare, *The First Epistle of Peter* (2nd edn, London 1958), pp. 196−202, (3rd edn, Oxford 1970), pp. 220−6.

argued that the epistle incorporates a complete baptismal liturgy.[18] J. C. Kirby extended this idea to Ephesians and claimed to find there an act of worship which 'may have had a close connection with baptism, though not necessarily with the administration of the sacrament itself', but was more likely 'a Christianized form of the renewal of the covenant'.[19] John Coutts argued that similar forms of prayer, which were baptismal in context, could be seen in 1 Peter and Ephesians;[20] A. T. Hanson discerned elements of a baptismal liturgy in Titus 2–3;[21] Ernst Käsemann saw Col. 1.12–20 as a primitive Christian baptismal liturgy;[22] and Massey Shepherd put forward the notion that the outline of the Book of Revelation was probably suggested by the order of the paschal liturgy.[23]

Other scholars have rightly questioned many of these claims. James Dunn, for example, doubts whether it is valid to argue from similarities in teaching to established catechetical forms, and his 'unease grows when these catechetical forms become explicitly *baptismal* catechisms', since not only is testimony lacking for a formal catechumenate lacking in the first century, but the New Testament itself implies that one did not exist; and the evidence for elaborate baptismal liturgies at this period is 'even more flimsy'.[24]

---

[18] H. Preisker, revision of H. Windisch, *Die katholischen Briefe* (3rd edn, Tübingen 1951), pp. 49–82, 156–62; F. L. Cross, *1 Peter — A Paschal Liturgy*, London 1954. See also M.-E. Boismard, 'Une liturgie baptismale dans la Prima Petri', *Revue biblique* 63 (1956), pp. 182–208; 64 (1957), pp. 161–83; idem, *Quatre hymnes baptismales dans la Première Épître de Pierre*, Paris 1961; A. R. C. Leaney, 'I Peter and the Passover: An Interpretation', *NTS* 10 (1963/4), pp. 238–51.

[19] *Ephesians: Baptism and Pentecost* (London 1968), pp. 150, 170.

[20] 'Ephesians 1.3–14 and 1 Peter 1.3–12', *NTS* 3 (1956/7), pp. 115–27.

[21] *Studies in the Pastoral Epistles* (London 1968), ch. 7.

[22] *Essays on New Testament Themes* (London/Naperville IL 1964 = Philadelphia 1982), pp. 149–68.

[23] *The Paschal Liturgy and the Apocalypse*, London/Richmond VA 1960.

[24] *Unity and Diversity in the New Testament* (London/Philadelphia 1977), pp. 143–7, (2nd edn 1990), pp. 141–8. See also C. F. D. Moule, 'The Nature and Purpose of 1 Peter', *NTS* 3 (1956/7), pp. 1–11; T. C. G. Thornton, '1 Peter a Paschal Liturgy', *JTS* 12 (1961), pp. 14–26.

The tendency to read back later liturgical practices

Many conclusions about worship in the New Testament —
including some of those listed above — are arrived at only by
assuming that liturgical customs found in later centuries must
have been in continuous existence from the first century. But
that is precisely to beg the question. If there is no unambiguous
witness in the New Testament documents themselves to a particular liturgical practice but it can only be detected by interpreting
obscure allusions there in the light of evidence from several
centuries later (and often from a quite different geographical
region), are we justified in making such a connection? While it is
certainly possible that in some cases a line of historical continuity *may* run from New Testament times to the liturgical practices of later ages, there are enough instances where recent
scholarship is able to demonstrate the improbability of such a
trajectory (and to propose instead a much more likely genesis
for a particular liturgical custom in the circumstances of a later
period) as to make all similar speculation highly risky.

Abundant illustrations could be offered of the pitfalls of such
an approach, but Massey Shepherd's theory about the link
between the Book of Revelation and the paschal liturgy will
serve as a good example. Although he admitted the danger of
reading the liturgical developments of a later period back into
early sources, and agreed that 'it would be very difficult, if not
impossible, to construct from the Apocalypse an order of Paschal celebration, if we did not have the outline of such an order
in the *Apostolic Tradition* of Hippolytus', yet he was so convinced
of the reliability of the claim of this third-century document to
embody genuine first-century traditions that he believed that,
'apart from certain details of ceremonial, there is nothing in the
general *ordo* of the Paschal rite described by Hippolytus that
could not have been in use in the first century'.[25] He therefore
proceeded to see behind the structure of the Book of Revelation
a full-blown baptismal liturgy, comprising: scrutinies, vigil with
readings, the initiation itself, prayers, readings from the Law,
Prophets, and Gospel, psalmody, and eucharist. Many of these

---

[25] *The Paschal Liturgy and the Apocalypse*, pp. 78—9. For the *Apostolic Tradition*, see below, pp. 89—92.

elements, however, are not in fact found in the *Apostolic Tradition*, but are also being read back from even later sources; and more recent scholarship (as we shall see later in chapter 7) casts serious doubt on the notion that such a standardized paschal initiation liturgy existed anywhere before at least the fourth century.

A further illustration of the dangerous temptation posed by this tendency is provided by Michael Goulder's claim that the precise chronology of the death of Jesus given in the Gospels is an indication that the first Christians turned the Passover into a memorial of their Lord's Passion lasting twenty-four hours. He justifies this conclusion by reference to the evidence of the fourth-century Jerusalem pilgrim, Egeria, and what he calls 'hints' in second- and third-century sources.[26] While there may perhaps be a liturgical dimension to the Passion chronology, possibly in relation to the hours of daily prayer observed throughout the year by some early Christians,[27] there is no evidence to support a connection with a Christian Passover. Not only does the Jerusalem commemoration of the Passion of Jesus seem to be a fourth-century creation derived from the gospel chronology and the earlier 'hints' turn out to be allusions merely to an all-night paschal vigil and not to a more extended observance, but what positive testimony there is to the earliest Christian Pascha suggests that it was celebrated at cockcrow and not prolonged throughout the following day.[28]

The tendency towards harmonization

Not least because of the paucity of evidence in the New Testament for first-century Christian worship, there has been a tendency among some scholars to amalgamate the various scraps of information that do exist in order to form a single composite picture. Thus, for example, references to liturgical activities from the Acts of the Apostles or from the Pauline letters may be combined with apparent allusions to worship from the Johannine literature or from one of the synoptic Gospels to constitute

---

[26] *Luke: A New Paradigm* I, pp. 151−2. For Egeria, see below, pp. 128−9.
[27] See Bradshaw, *Daily Prayer in the Early Church*, pp. 60−2.
[28] See below, p. 196.

a supposed description of how the first Christians worshipped. Behind this approach lies the assumption of a basic unity of liturgical practice within the apostolic period.[29]

Contemporary currents in New Testament scholarship, however, present a strong challenge to this presupposition, since they stress the essentially pluriform nature of primitive Christianity,[30] and so render improbable the traditional idea that a single, uniform archetype ultimately underlies the later diversity in Christian worship practices. Each of the New Testament books, therefore, needs to be examined for what it may have to reveal about the worship of the particular Christian community from which it emerges, as well as for remnants of even earlier liturgical traditions which it may have preserved, before any attempt is made to look for common features shared by these different churches.[31]

There is a further danger inherent in the process of harmonization, and that is of treating as standard liturgical customs those practices which are described or advocated by the authors whose works happen to have come down to us. Since these represent only a limited number of the many diverse forms which early Christianity appears to have taken, we simply do not know whether all Christian communities worshipped in this way or not. It is even difficult to be sure, when a series of liturgical references are given in a New Testament source, whether they reflect an actual sequence within a rite or are mentioned in that order for some quite different reason.[32]

Liturgy in the Acts of the Apostles

One of the major problems with regard to the New Testament is that nearly all the explicit references to and descriptions of

[29] Cullmann, *Early Christian Worship*, pp. 7–36, is guilty of this fault.

[30] See, for example, Raymond E. Brown, *The Churches the Apostles Left Behind* (New York 1984), pp. 19–30; Dunn, *Unity and Diversity in the New Testament*, passim; Käsemann, *Essays on New Testament Themes*, pp. 95–107.

[31] Despite some weaknesses, Hahn's *Worship of the Early Church* (to which reference has already been made) is a notable attempt to trace patterns of worship in the New Testament in this way.

[32] See, for example, G. J. Cuming, 'Service-endings in the Epistles', *NTS* 22 (1975/6), pp. 110–13: and cf. J. M. Gibbs, 'Canon Cuming's "Service-endings in the Epistles": A Rejoinder', *NTS* 24 (1977/8), pp. 545–7.

Christian worship occur in one book—the Acts of the Apostles. Because of the shortage of other evidence, there has been a not unnatural tendency for scholars to generalize about forms of worship in the New Testament period on the basis of this source alone. In the light of the recognition of the extent of the diversity of thought and practice within first-century Christianity, however, such a tendency is called into serious question. This work may possibly be able to tell us about what went on in one tradition within the early Church, but we have no grounds for assuming that it was necessarily typical of all the rest.

But which tradition of worship, if any, does it reflect? When, for example, the author describes the procedure adopted to appoint a replacement for Judas (Acts 1.23−6) and the initiation of Cornelius and his household (Acts 10.44−8), just what is it that is being described? Are these accounts reasonably reliable historical records of what actually went on in the earliest Palestinian Christian communities, carefully preserved and communicated to the author? Or do they, on the contrary, derive from the author's own experience of Christian liturgy, so that, while they may not tell us anything about the first generation of Christians, they do instead offer valuable evidence about what ordination and baptismal practices were like in a predominantly Gentile church in the second half of the first century?[33] Or are they neither of these, but rather the products of the author's own imagination, intended perhaps by their form to make specific theological points —for instance, the casting of lots in the appointment of Matthias symbolizing that the choice was not human but divine,[34] and the gift of the Spirit preceding the act of immersion in the case of the household of Cornelius symbolizing a Gentile equivalent of the Pentecost experience[35]—

[33] Ernst Haenchen, *The Acts of the Apostles* (Oxford/Philadelphia 1971), p. 354, suggests that because Peter himself does not perform the actual baptism of Cornelius and his household, 'Luke is no doubt reproducing here the position obtaining in his own day.'

[34] See William A. Beardslee, 'The Casting of Lots at Qumran and in the Book of Acts', *Novum Testamentum* 4 (1960), pp. 245−52.

[35] See, for example, Geoffrey Lampe, *The Seal of the Spirit* (London 1951, 2nd edn 1967), p. 75. Gerd Lüdemann, *Early Christianity according to the Traditions in Acts* (Minneapolis 1989), p. 129, claims that 'the bestowal of the Spirit comes before the baptism only for reasons of narrative technique'.

and consequently say nothing about what ordinary Christians actually did at any time in the first century?

Similar questions can be posed about other descriptions of acts of worship elsewhere in the Book of Acts. When, for example, the Jerusalem church gather at night to pray for the imprisoned Paul (Acts 12.5, 12), and Paul and Silas pray and sing hymns to God at midnight while in prison (Acts 16.25), are these reflections of a regular custom of night-prayer known to the author, or an unusual activity occasioned by the special circumstances?[36] Again, does the occurrence of the 'breaking of the bread' at Troas after midnight on the first day of the week, preceded by a lengthy sermon (Acts 20.7−11), reflect the regular time and manner of the eucharistic celebration with which the author was familiar or is it an exceptional form and occasion brought about by Paul's impending departure?[37] In any case, which evening is meant — Saturday (which in Jewish reckoning would be the beginning of the first day of the week) or Sunday?[38] The account of the resurrection appearance on the Emmaus road (Luke 24.13−32) has caused similar speculation: is the sequence of events — the explanation of Moses and the prophets followed by the meal — indicative of the regular order of the eucharist known to the compiler or not?

Such questions have perhaps been raised most acutely in connection with the various references to baptism which occur in Acts. In 8.14−17, for example, the apostles at Jerusalem send Peter and John to the Samaritans who have been baptized by

[36] Hans Conzelmann, *A Commentary on the Acts of the Apostles* (Philadelphia 1987), p. 132, suggests that in Acts 16.25 the midnight hour is simply part of the 'numinous mood' and the singing of hymns of praise is a common motif of the 'prison release'.

[37] Haenchen (*The Acts of the Apostles*, p. 586) suggests the former: a eucharist, without a meal, preceded by a sermon. Conzelmann, however (*A Commentary on the Acts of the Apostles*, p. 169), would see verses 7 and 11 as a liturgical embellishment to an older form of the story, and maintains that 'no conclusions about the course and the components of the liturgy can be drawn from the redactional additions, since they do not intend to provide ritual exactitude'.

[38] See the discussion in Willy Rordorf, *Der Sonntag* (Zurich 1962) = *Sunday* (London/Philadelphia 1968), pp. 196−202; Samuele Bacchiocchi, *From Sabbath to Sunday* (Rome 1977), pp. 101−11.

Philip. They pray that the Samaritans may receive the gift of the Holy Spirit 'for it had not yet fallen on any of them. . . . Then they laid their hands on them and they received the Holy Spirit.' Some would see this merely as a more detailed description of what would have happened at all baptisms. Ernst Haenchen, for example, affirms that 'in Luke's community baptism and the laying on of hands must still have been associated';[39] Hans Conzelmann concludes that 'the laying on of hands must have been customary at baptism, even if Tertullian is the first to state it explicitly';[40] and Wolfgang Dietrich thinks that in the early Jerusalem community there was a rule that the bestowal of the Spirit was reserved to the apostles.[41] Others argue that what is described is an exceptional practice occasioned by the particular situation: the story provides a means whereby the mission of the Hellenists in Samaria can be seen to be endorsed by the Jerusalem apostles, and tells us nothing about normal initiatory practice in the author's community.[42]

A similar difference of opinion exists over the parallel instance in Acts 19.1–7, where the baptism is followed by the imposition of Paul's hands and the reception of the Holy Spirit. Was the post-baptismal imposition of hands conveying the gift of the Spirit a standard initiation procedure in the author's experience, or alternatively is the account constructed in an unusual way to make the point that only after baptism in the name of Jesus can the Holy Spirit be received?[43]

Although various scholars have expressed a strong preference for one position or another in both these and other instances in the Book of Acts, the inevitable uncertainty which is raised by the alternative explanations means that it is difficult to use the evidence of this source with any degree of confidence to reconstruct first-century Christian liturgy.

[39] *The Acts of the Apostles*, p. 304. See also ibid., p. 308.

[40] *A Commentary on the Acts of the Apostles*, p. 65.

[41] *Das Petrusbild der lukanischen Schriften* (Stuttgart 1972), pp. 249f.

[42] See Lampe, *The Seal of the Spirit*, pp. 66–75; Lüdemann, *Early Christianity according to the Traditions in Acts*, pp. 96–7.

[43] See Lampe, *The Seal of the Spirit*, pp. 75ff.; Lüdemann, *Early Christianity according to the Traditions in Acts*, pp. 210–11.

Literary metaphor or liturgical practice?

The other New Testament books, and especially the Epistles, tend to offer possible allusions to what Christians were doing liturgically more often than explicit descriptions of practices. But once again there is a serious difficulty about how these should be interpreted. When, for instance, Gal. 3.27 speaks of the baptized as having 'put on Christ', and Col. 3.9–10 and Eph. 4.22–4 speak of putting off the old nature and putting on the new, are these images occasioned by an already existing baptismal custom of stripping off one's clothing before being immersed and of being clothed with a white garment after emerging from the water, such as we find in fourth-century evidence?[44] Or are they simply vivid metaphors coined by the writer, which only much later encouraged or gave rise to the liturgical usage? The latter might seem the more probable explanation, but to these examples may be added the accounts in Mark's Gospel of the young man at the arrest of Jesus who left the linen cloth he was wearing and ran away naked (14.51–2) and of the young man sitting on the right side of the empty tomb, dressed in a white robe (16.5). Robin Scroggs and Kent Goff have put forward the suggestion that this pair of stories are intended as a baptismal image,[45] and this is certainly an attractive interpretation of passages which have often puzzled commentators.

The same questions have been asked of other baptismal images in the New Testament. For example, Christians are spoken of as having been sealed with the Holy Spirit (see 2 Cor. 1.22; Eph. 1.13; 4.30), and Rev. 7.3f. describes the sealing of the servants of God as being 'upon their foreheads'. Is this merely a metaphor, or an allusion to a liturgical ceremony of making the sign of the cross on the foreheads of the newly baptized, such as we find in later practice? Do references to anointing (see 1 John 2.20, 27) reflect a literal use of oil or are they meant metaphorically?

Obviously, in all such cases there is a real danger of the unwarranted reading back of later practices into New Testament

---

[44] Cf. also the similar eschatological images of 2 Cor. 5.1–5.

[45] Robin Scroggs & Kent I. Goff, 'Baptism in Mark: Dying and Rising with Christ', *JBL* 92 (1973), pp. 531–48.

times that we have spoken of earlier. Yet, at least in some instances, we cannot entirely rule out the possibility that the development may not always have been from metaphor to later literal fulfilment, but rather from early practice to literary image. The difficulty consists in knowing which direction the development took in any given case.

The Book of Revelation presents a particular problem in this area. Some have regarded much of its imagery of heavenly worship as a clear reflection of liturgical practices familar to the author. So, for example, Oscar Cullmann could say: 'the whole Book of Revelation from the greeting of grace and peace in chapter 1.4 to the closing prayer: Come Lord Jesus, in chapter 22.20, and the benediction in the last verse, is full of allusions to the liturgical usages of the early community'.[46] Other scholars, on the other hand, question the too ready assumption of the existence of parallels between heavenly and earthly worship in many of the details described.[47] After all, it is generally taken for granted that the early Christians did not use incense in their worship, in spite of the references to it in Rev. 5.8 and 8.3f. How then can we be sure that other elements do correspond to regular Christian liturgical customs?

Possible early Christian hymns and prayers

One aspect of research into early Christian worship which has received considerable attention in recent years is the detection of actual liturgical texts, and especially hymns, within the New Testament books themselves.[48] Among the more obvious examples of hymnic material are the Lukan canticles (1.46−55, 68−

---

[46] *Early Christian Worship*, p. 7.

[47] See, for example, Delling, *Worship in the New Testament*, pp. 44−8; Hahn, *Worship of the Early Church*, pp. 80−1.

[48] Important studies of hymnic material include: R. Deichgräber, *Gotteshymnus und Christushymnus in der frühen Christenheit*, Göttingen 1967; J. M. Robinson, 'Die Hodajot-Formel in Gebet und Hymnus des Frühchristentums', in W. Eltester, ed., *Apophoreta. Festschrift für Ernst Haenchen* (Berlin 1964), pp. 194−235; J. T. Sanders, *The New Testament Christological Hymns*, Cambridge 1971; J. Schattenmann, *Studien zum neutestamentlichen Prosahymnus*, Munich 1965; G. Schille, *Frühchristliche Hymnen*, Berlin 1965; K. Wengst, *Christologische Formeln und Lieder des Urchristentums*, Gütersloh 1972.

79; 2.29−32);[49] John 1.1−16;[50] Phil. 2.6−11;[51] Col. 1.15−20;[52] and the various acclamations and songs in the Book of Revelation.[53] Some scholars would add to this list such passages as Heb. 1.3; 1 Tim. 3.16; 1 Pet. 3.18−22, and others still more, but these suggestions immediately reveal how extremely difficult it is to establish objective criteria to distinguish actual hymns from mere poetic passages,[54] or to know whether the composition simply originated with the author or some other anonymous person, or was in real liturgical use in a Christian community. It is often equally difficult to determine when the New Testament authors are citing typical prayer-forms with which they are familiar and when they are not,[55] or even to separate hymns from prayers, since both may employ a similar construction.

Some scholars have attempted not only to identify passages as hymnic material but also to classify them as being either (a) Jewish compositions with little or no Christian editing, (b) Christian redactions of Jewish originals, (c) pre-Christian Hellenistic compositions, or (d) purely Christian compositions, though perhaps influenced by Jewish or other traditions. Some would further subdivide the material as being of either Palestinian or Hellenistic Jewish-Christian origin, or even envisage different types of Hellenistic Jewish-Christianity.[56]

[49] For full discussion and bibliography, see Raymond E. Brown, *The Birth of the Messiah* (New York 1977), pp. 346−66.

[50] See Rudolf Schnackenburg, *The Gospel according to St John* I (London 1968/New York 1980), pp. 229−30.

[51] See especially the study by R. P. Martin, *Carmen Christi*, Cambridge 1967, 2nd edn, Grand Rapids 1983.

[52] See the bibliography in W. G. Kümmel, *Introduction to the New Testament* (London 1966/Nashville 1975), p. 343.

[53] For these, see E. Cothenet, 'Earthly Liturgy and Heavenly Liturgy according to the Book of Revelation', in *Roles in the Liturgical Assembly* (New York 1981), pp. 115−35; K.-P. Jörns, *Das hymnische Evangelium*, Gütersloh 1971; Pierre Prigent, *Apocalypse et liturgie*, Neuchâtel 1964. See also Ugo Vanni, 'Liturgical Dialogue as a Literary Form in the Book of Revelation', *NTS* 37 (1991), pp. 348−72.

[54] See the comments by Charlesworth, 'A Prolegomenon', p. 280.

[55] See, for example, P. T. O'Brien, *Introductory Thanksgivings in the Letters of Paul*, Leiden 1977; and G. P. Wiles, *Paul's Intercessory Prayers*, Cambridge 1974, who tends to see rather more such passages than are actually there.

[56] See, for example, Dunn, *Unity and Diversity in the New Testament*, pp. 132−41.

While, however, there might be some measure of agreement as to the categories, there is a conspicuous lack of consensus about where the various hymns ought to be located. So, for example, while Käsemann regards Col. 1.15–20 as in origin a Gnostic hymn,[57] Reinhard Deichgräber[58] and Eduard Lohse[59] trace it back to Hellenistic Judaism, and others would attribute its composition entirely to the author of the epistle.[60]

Nevertheless, in spite of all this uncertainty, those passages which have been identified by general consensus as hymns and prayers can legitimately be seen as reflecting the sort of liturgical material which early Christians would have used. Even if these particular examples are not taken directly from common worship but are the product of the authors' creativity, they would inevitably have been influenced to a considerable extent by the liturgical forms with which they were familiar. This conclusion is confirmed by a comparative analysis of the passages in question, which reveals a large number of common stylistic and linguistic features persisting across differences of author, theology, and background, and so suggests that this commonality derives from the similarities within their various liturgical traditions. For example, early Christian forms of prayer reveal an apparently growing preference for *eucharisteo* over *eulogeo*. Although it is frequently said that these verbs are simply synonyms, our study of Jewish prayer patterns has indicated that this is not the case, but that each word was used in a quite different liturgical construction. Thus, the preference points to the dominance of the *hodayah/eucharistia* form over the *berakah/eulogia* in primitive Christianity.[61]

---

[57] *Essays on New Testament Themes*, pp. 154–9.

[58] *Gotteshymnus und Christushymnus in der frühen Christenheit*, p. 154.

[59] *Colossians and Philemon* (Philadelphia 1971), p. 45.

[60] See, for example, A. Hamman, *La Prière, I: Le Nouveau Testament* (Tournai 1959), pp. 255–6. Some would not consider it a hymn at all but an example of a eucharistic prayer: see Klaus Gamber, 'Anklänge an das Eucharistiegebet bei Paulus und das jüdische Kiddusch', *Ostkirchliche Studien* 9 (1960), pp. 254–64; E. J. Kilmartin, 'Sacrificium Laudis: Content and Function of Early Eucharistic Prayers', *Theological Studies* 35 (1974), p. 273.

[61] See above, pp. 15–17, and also Bradshaw, *Daily Prayer in the Early Church*, pp. 30–7.

In addition to the general methodological questions outlined so far in this chapter, there are some further, specific problems with regard to the interpretation of the baptismal and eucharistic references in the New Testament, and to these we now turn.

The origins of Christian baptism

The custom of baptizing new converts to Christianity appears to have been derived from John the Baptist, but the source of his practice is uncertain. Some scholars have argued that it was based on the ablutions of the Essene community at Qumran, but these were repeated washings related to the need for ritual purity and do not seem to have included an initiatory baptism. Others have suggested that John was influenced by the practice of baptizing new converts to Judaism, but there is some doubt whether this was being done in his time or whether it was only adopted at a later date. A third possibility is that it arose out of the Israelite traditions of ritual purification (see, for example, Lev. 15.5 – 13) and/or of prophetic symbolism, which had spoken of God's people being cleansed with pure water in preparation for the advent of the messianic age (see, for example, Ezek. 36.25 – 8).[62]

Whether the Christian adoption of baptism began with Jesus himself or only in the Church after his resurrection cannot easily be resolved. All three synoptic Gospels record Jesus' own baptism by John but say nothing of him baptizing his followers. The Gospel of John, on the other hand, does not mention Jesus being baptized but does speak of him baptizing others (John 3.22, 26; 4.1; but cf. 4.2). Matt. 28.16 – 20 contains the command

---

[62] For further details, see Adela Yarbro Collins, 'The Origin of Christian Baptism', *SL* 19 (1989), pp. 28ff. See also Edward R. Hardy, 'Jewish and Christian Baptism: Some Notes and Queries', in Robert H. Fischer, ed., *A Tribute to Arthur Vööbus* (Chicago 1977), pp. 309 – 18; S. Legasse, 'Baptême juif des proselytes et baptême chrétien', *Bulletin de littérature ecclésiastique* 77 (1976), pp. 3 – 46; Derwood C. Smith, 'Jewish Proselyte Baptism and the Baptism of John', *Restoration Quarterly* 25 (1982), pp. 13 – 32; Barbara E. Thiering, 'Inner and Outer Cleansing at Qumran as a Background to New Testament Baptism', *NTS* 26 (1980), pp. 266 – 77; idem, 'Qumran Initiation and New Testament Baptism', *NTS* 27 (1981), pp. 615 – 31.

to baptize all nations, but there are difficulties in accepting this as an authentic saying of the risen Lord.[63]

Whatever its origins, however, it appears that from early times it became the usual custom to initiate new converts into the Church through a process which included baptism, performed perhaps in a river, a pool, or a domestic bath-house. What else besides the immersion might have been involved is not made explicit in the New Testament. We have already noted the difficulties in deciding whether allusions to anointing and clothing are to actual baptismal practices and whether the references to a post-baptismal imposition of hands in Acts are to a regular part of the initiation rite (cf. also Heb. 6.2). There may possibly have been a preliminary period of instruction, though this is not certain, and it is likely that the ritual included a confession of faith in Jesus in one form or another. It is equally uncertain whether infants and young children were baptized as well as adults.[64]

On the other hand, what is clear from the New Testament is that the process of becoming a Christian was interpreted and expressed in a variety of different ways.[65] So, for example, in some traditions the emphasis was placed on the forgiveness of sins and the gift of the Holy Spirit (see Acts 2.38); in others the metaphor of birth to new life was used (John 3.5f.; Titus 3.5—7); in others baptism was understood as enlightenment (Heb. 6.4; 10.32; 1 Pet. 2.9); and in Paul's theology the primary image was

[63] See Collins, 'The Origin of Christian Baptism', pp. 37ff.; Benjamin J. Hubbard, *The Matthean Redaction of a Primitive Apostolic Commissioning: An Exegesis of Matthew 28:16—20*, Missoula MT 1974.

[64] The classic discussion of this question is between Joachim Jeremias, *Infant Baptism in the First Four Centuries*, London 1960, and Kurt Aland, *Did the Early Church Baptize Infants?*, London 1963. See also Jeremias' reponse to Aland, *The Origins of Infant Baptism*, London 1963, and the contribution to the debate by Everett Ferguson, 'Inscriptions and the Origin of Infant Baptism', *JTS* 30 (1979), pp. 37—46.

[65] Among the standard works on baptism in the New Testament are G. R. Beasley-Murray, *Baptism in the New Testament*, London 1962 = 1972; Oscar Cullmann, *Baptism in the New Testament*, London 1950/Philadelphia 1978; W. F. Flemington, *The New Testament Doctrine of Baptism*, London 1964; Rudolf Schnackenburg, *Baptism in the Thought of St Paul*, Oxford/New York 1964; Günter Wagner, *Pauline Baptism and the Pagan Mysteries*, Edinburgh 1967; R. E. O. White, *The Biblical Doctrine of Initiation*, London/Grand Rapids 1960.

union with Christ through participation in his death and resurrection (Rom. 6.2ff.). This variation in baptismal theology encourages the supposition that the ritual itself may also have varied considerably from place to place.

Last Supper and Lord's Supper

One of the major difficulties faced by scholars with regard to the origins of the eucharist is the question of how far the accounts of the Last Supper (Matt. 26.17–30; Mark 14.12–26; Luke 22.7–38; 1 Cor. 11.23–6) may be treated as reliable descriptions of an actual historical event and how far they have been affected by the later liturgical practices of the first generation of Christians. Some scholars, among them Rudolf Bultmann, have argued that, while Jesus may indeed have held a final meal with his disciples, the narratives as we have them are creations of the early Church and so can tell us nothing about the actual historical roots of the eucharist but can only witness to its later development.[66] The majority of scholars, however, would accept that the accounts have certainly been influenced by the liturgical practices of the first Christians, but maintain that still discernible within them is a firm historical core.

Since there are significant differences between the various narratives, scholars have been divided over which of them, if any, has best preserved the historical details. Joachim Jeremias, for example, opted for the Markan version of the interpretative words of Jesus over the bread and the wine as coming closest to the original,[67] Heinz Schürmann expressed a strong preference for the Lukan narrative, with its eschatological emphasis,[68] and

[66] See, for example, R. Bultmann, *Theology of the New Testament* (London/New York 1952) I, pp. 144–51; W. Marxsen, *The Lord's Supper as a Christological Problem*, Philadelphia 1970; Eduard Schweizer, *The Lord's Supper according to the New Testament*, Philadelphia 1967.

[67] *Die Abendmahlsworte Jesu*, Göttingen 1935, 3rd edn 1960 = *The Eucharistic Words of Jesus*, London/New York 1966. Many other scholars have followed him, including most recently Rudolf Pesch, *Das Abendmahl und Jesu Todesverständnis*, Freiburg 1978.

[68] *Eine quellenkritischen Untersuchung des lukanischen Abendmahlberichtes Lk 22, 7–38*, published in 3 parts, Münster 1953, 1955, 1957. A similar position was adopted by H. Merklein, 'Erwägungen zur Überlieferungsgeschichte der neutestamentlichen Abendmahlstraditionen', *Biblische Zeitschrift* 21 (1977), pp. 88–101, 235–44.

Eduard Schweizer considered the Pauline account the most primitive in form, in spite of its more obvious liturgical character.[69] More recently, Xavier Léon-Dufour has taken up a mediating position and argued that older and newer elements are combined in all the traditions.[70]

To speak of the narratives as being 'influenced by the liturgical practices of the first Christians' requires some clarification. This does not necessarily mean that they were regularly recited as part of the eucharistic liturgy itself from early times, whether within the eucharistic prayer or as an independent formula, as many scholars have concluded. We simply have no way of knowing whether or not that was true. The most that we can say is that, because the narratives were passed on within Christian communities which celebrated the eucharist, their liturgical experience appears, not surprisingly, to have had some effect on the way in which they told the story of the Last Supper.

Passover and Last Supper

Whether or not the Last Supper was a Passover meal has also been a topic of great debate. Some scholars accept as genuine the claim made in the synoptic Gospels that it was indeed a Passover meal, and regard the different chronology of the Fourth Gospel (which situates the Supper on the day before the Passover) as an adjustment made by the Evangelist for a theological purpose — so that the death of Jesus would coincide with the very time that the Passover lambs were being sacrificed in the Temple. Others note a number of details in the synoptic versions which do not seem to fit with the Passover explanation, and so prefer to accept John's chronology as historical.[71] Some have even tried to solve the apparent contradiction by ingenious

[69] *The Lord's Supper according to the New Testament.* See also Paul Neuenzeit, *Das Herrenmahl. Studien zur paulinischen Eucharistieauffassung,* Munich 1960.

[70] *Sharing the Eucharistic Bread,* New York 1987; see especially pp. 82–5, 96–8, 158–9.

[71] The various arguments are set out fully by Jeremias, *The Eucharistic Words of Jesus,* pp. 15–88, who supports the idea that the supper was a Passover meal; cf. Léon-Dufour, *Sharing the Eucharistic Bread,* pp. 306–8, who reaches the opposite conclusion.

attempts at harmonization. Annie Jaubert, for example, suggested that Jesus ate the Passover meal on Tuesday evening, following the solar calendar current among the Essenes, and died on Friday, the day of the Passover according to the official calendar.[72] I. Howard Marshall has more recently resurrected the explanation originally put forward by Paul Billerbeck, that the different methods of calendrical reckoning adopted by the Pharisees and the Sadducees led to the former keeping the Passover on Thursday (the practice followed by Jesus and recorded in the synoptic Gospels) and the Sadducees observing it on Friday (as the Fourth Gospel reports).[73]

Those who reject the notion that the Last Supper was a Passover meal have not been slow to offer alternative hypotheses for the occasion. Since the end of the nineteenth century a number of scholars have espoused the theory that it was a '*kiddush* meal'. Jeremias, however, has conclusively argued that there never was such a thing: a *kiddush* was simply a special blessing pronounced at the beginning of each Sabbath or festival, and 'the idea of a passover *kiddush* which takes place twenty-four hours before the beginning of the feast is *pure fantasy*; not one shred of evidence can be adduced for it'.[74] Others, including Gregory Dix,[75] have followed Hans Lietzmann in describing it as a *haburah* meal—a Jewish meal, 'invested with religious solemnity, which might be held by a company of friends'.[76] Once again Jeremias has pointed out the total lack of evidence for such an institution: the meals of the *haburot mishwah*, which did exist, were exclusively in connection with obligations such as circumcisions, weddings, and funerals; and, moreover, every Jewish meal had 'religious solemnity', whether it was taken alone or in company.[77] This, of course, does not deny the possibility that Jesus

[72] *La date de la Cène*, Paris 1957 = *The Date of the Last Supper*, New York 1965.

[73] *Last Supper and Lord's Supper* (Exeter 1980/Grand Rapids 1981), pp. 71—5.

[74] *The Eucharistic Words of Jesus*, pp. 26—9 (emphasis in original).

[75] *The Shape of the Liturgy*, pp. 50ff.

[76] *Messe und Herrenmahl*, Bonn 1926 = *Mass and Lord's Supper* (Leiden 1953—1978), pp. 170—1, 185.

[77] *The Eucharistic Words of Jesus*, pp. 29—31.

ate a meal with his friends which was not the Passover, but only that this would not have been a part of the tradition of the *haburot mishwah*.

Another possible connection which has been explored by some scholars is with the communal meals of the Essene movement at Qumran. Although only a few would see the Supper itself as having been directly influenced from this source, others suggest that early Christian eucharistic practice, and hence the accounts of the Supper, may have been affected by experience of such meals. But the similarities are only in elements common to all Jewish festal meals and not in elements unique to the Essenes.[78] Likewise, attempts to see a link with the Jewish tale of Joseph and Asenath fail to be convincing, not least because of uncertainties with regard to the date and provenance of that text.[79]

The most recent proposal for an alternative to the Passover meal as the source of Christian eucharistic practice has been the *zebah todah* ('sacrifice of praise/thanksgiving') —a cultic thank-offering by an individual or a group for divine deliverance, which in addition to the sacrifice itself involved a joyful hymnic proclamation (*todah*) of what God had done and a communion meal including, among other things, the consumption of leavened bread (Lev. 7.12–15).[80] Only Hartmut Gese has gone as far as to suggest that the Last Supper itself was intended by Jesus as a *todah*-meal, eaten in anticipation of his own imminent sacrificial death.[81] Other scholars have proposed either that the Christian eucharist came into being as a *todah*-meal in thanksgiving for the deliverance wrought by Jesus or merely that early eucharistic prayers were influenced in their form by the *todah*.[82] To a great extent these theories have been occasioned

[78] ibid., pp. 31–6.

[79] See Christoph Burchard, 'The Importance of Joseph and Aseneth for the Study of the New Testament: A General Survey and a Fresh Look at the Lord's Supper', *NTS* 33 (1987), pp. 102–34.

[80] See further Henri Cazelles, 'L'Anaphore et l'Ancien Testament', in *Eucharisties d'Orient et d'Occident* I (Paris 1970), pp. 11–21.

[81] 'Die Herkunft des Abendmahles', *Zur biblischen Theologie* (Munich 1977), pp. 107–27 = 'The Origin of the Lord's Supper', *Essays on Biblical Theology* (Minneapolis 1981), pp. 117–40.

[82] See Léon-Dufour, *Sharing the Eucharistic Bread*, pp. 41–5, and the works cited in n. 46 there. Cf. also below, pp. 151, 153.

by the need to explain why it is that later eucharistic prayers did not retain the *berakah* form thought to have been standard in first-century Jewish meal-prayers, but apparently show a preference for the *hodayah/eucharistia* form supposedly characteristic of the *todah*. If, however, as we have suggested in the preceding chapter,[83] Jewish meal-prayers were not standardized in the first century and the *hodayah* could be used in contexts other than the *zebah todah*,[84] then these hypotheses are rendered largely unnecessary. In any case, they do not account very satisfactorily for the Last Supper itself, nor for the strongly eschatological emphasis in the tradition.[85]

From the point of view of liturgical scholars, the question of whether the Last Supper was a Passover meal is not particularly crucial. Even if it *were* a Passover meal, no exclusively paschal practices seem to have been retained in the primitive Church's eucharistic celebrations; and even if it *were not* a Passover meal, it still took place within a Passover atmosphere and context. In any case, we are far from certain about the precise details of the Passover meal in the first century, and it is probable that it was considerably different from the form that it took after the destruction of the Temple. To cite just one example, it seems likely that it did not become a true family meal until the Passover ceased to be a Jerusalem pilgrimage festival after 70 C.E.[86]

Breaking of bread and eucharist

In his monumental work, *Messe und Herrenmahl*, Lietzmann developed a theory originally advanced by Friedrich Spitta at the end of the nineteenth century[87] that there were from the first two quite different types of eucharistic liturgy in the Church.

[83] See above, pp. 15−17, 24−6.

[84] As Léon-Dufour himself admits: *Sharing the Eucharistic Bread*, p. 42.

[85] See further Paul F. Bradshaw, 'Zebah Todah and the Origins of the Eucharist', forthcoming in *Ecclesia Orans*.

[86] See Baruch M. Bokser, *The Origins of the Seder*, Berkeley/Los Angeles 1984; J. B. Segal, *The Hebrew Passover from the Earliest Times to A.D. 70*, London/New York 1963.

[87] *Zur Geschichte und Litteratur des Urchristentums* (Göttingen 1893) I, pp. 207−337.

One was the joyful fellowship meal of the early Jewish-Christian communities, the 'breaking of bread' as in Acts 2.42; the other arose within the Pauline churches and was dominated by the theme of the memorial of the death of Christ. According to Lietzmann, the former type was a continuation of the meals shared by the disciples with Jesus during his earthly ministry and was not related to the Last Supper; it had no narrative of institution, did not involve the use of wine, and had a strong eschatological dimension, being the anticipation of the messianic banquet. The second type arose from Paul's belief that Jesus intended the Last Supper to be repeated as a liturgical rite ('Do this in remembrance of me' —found only in 1 Cor. 11.24, 25 and Luke 22.19); it was characterized by Hellenistic sacrificial concepts and eventually supplanted the former type everywhere.

Several other scholars adopted variations of this thesis. Ernst Lohmeyer differentiated between a Galilean tradition of bread-breaking stemming from the meals of Jesus with the disciples and a Jerusalem tradition descended from the Last Supper which evolved into the Pauline memorial rite.[88] Cullmann defended Lietzmann's original hypothesis, but with the qualification that the common origin of both types was to be sought in the historical Last Supper, 'even if only indirectly in the case of the first type'.[89] The direct origin he attributed to the post-resurrection meal appearances of Jesus. While earlier scholars from Spitta onwards[90] had seen a possible connection between the eucharist and these Christophanies, they had usually viewed the eucharistic experiences of the early Christians as having been responsible for the emergence of the stories, or at least as having influenced their form. Hence Cullmann appears to have

---

[88] 'Vom urchristlichen Abendmahl', *Theologische Rundschau* 9 (1937), pp. 168 — 227, 273 — 312; 10 (1938), pp. 81 — 99; 'Das Abendmahl in der Urgemeinde', *JBL* 56 (1937), pp. 217—52.

[89] 'La signification de la Sainte-Cène dans le christianisme primitif', *Revue d'histoire et de philosophie religieuses* 16 (1936), pp. 1—22 = 'The Meaning of the Lord's Supper in Primitive Christianity', in O. Cullmann & J. Leenhardt, *Essays on the Lord's Supper* (London/Richmond VA 1958), pp. 5—23; see also his *Early Christian Worship*, p. 17, n. 1.

[90] *Zur Geschichte und Litteratur des Urchristentums* I, pp. 292f.

been the first to explore the opposite idea, that the resurrection events themselves gave rise to the eucharistic practice. This approach has since been followed by some other scholars, including Willy Rordorf,[91] but has also met with criticism.[92]

The majority of scholars, however, have rejected Lietzmann's theory of a dual origin of the eucharist as being based on extremely tenuous evidence and as making the improbable assumption of a radical dichotomy between the thinking and practice of the primitive Jerusalem church and the Pauline communities. Nevertheless, there has been a growing acknowledgement of the existence of what R. H. Fuller has called a 'double strand' in the Supper tradition — the eschatological focus and the interpretative words over the bread and cup.[93] While there may still be disagreement as to whether or not the interpretative words go back to the historical Last Supper, there seems to be a general consensus that in the earliest period of the Church's existence it was the eschatological theme which dominated eucharistic practice, but that it became combined with the remembrance of the death of Christ in the early Palestinian tradition.

So, for example, while A. J. B. Higgins supported the essentials of Cullmann's position, he disputed the notion that the pre-Pauline type would not have involved the use of wine. As for the remembrance of Christ's death,

> although to be sure it is not actually mentioned any more than the partaking of wine, it must long have been present in the *Palestinian* as well as in the Hellenistic communities. It is very probable, especially in view of the dependence of both so-called types of Eucharist on the Last Supper, that what Paul did was to lay a renewed emphasis on the remembrance of the death of Christ which was already present, but which at Corinth was in danger of being forgotten. . . .[94]

[91] *Sunday*, pp. 215–37. See below, p. 192–3.

[92] See Gese, 'The Origin of the Lord's Supper', p. 128; Léon-Dufour, *Sharing the Eucharistic Bread*, pp. 39–40.

[93] 'The Double Origin of the Eucharist', *Biblical Research* 8 (1963), pp. 60–72.

[94] *The Lord's Supper in the New Testament* (London 1952), pp. 56–63 (emphasis in original).

Eduard Schweizer similarly observed that the eschatological sayings in the Last Supper narratives were always attached to the wine and not the bread, and concluded that it was

> impossible to establish the existence of two wholly distinct and independent types of the Lord's Supper in the early church. . . . If these two factors — the eschatological joy connected with the presence of the Lord at the table and his imminent return, and the proclamation of Jesus' death connected with the granting of the salvation wrought in this death — did not belong together from the very beginning, they must certainly have merged very early in the Palestinian church.[95]

More recently Léon-Dufour has spoken of the double tradition not in terms of the difference of its content but on the basis of its literary form. He believes that there was what he describes as a 'cultic' tradition about the Last Supper and a non-cultic or 'testamentary' tradition, which belonged to the genre of the 'farewell discourse'.[96]

Because of the sparsity of the evidence, it is extremely difficult to draw many conclusions about the form of the eucharistic celebrations of the early Christians. We need not assume that the eucharist everywhere took the shape implied by Paul's references to it in 1 Cor. 11. In any case, there is uncertainty whether the description of the informal ministry of the word in 1 Cor. 14.26f. refers to the same occasion as the Lord's Supper or not, and even if it does, whether the meal preceded or followed that event. In the light of the pluriformity of primitive Christianity, it seems probable that there was considerable variation not only in the theological emphases within the different traditions[97] but also in the structural details of the rite, and perhaps even in the frequency of its celebration.[98] Although the adoption of the term 'breaking of bread' by some early Christians certainly does not preclude the use of wine, it is still perfectly possible that in some traditions wine was not always a

---

[95] *The Lord's Supper according to the New Testament*, p. 25.

[96] *Sharing the Eucharistic Bread*, pp. 90ff.

[97] See, for example, Jerome Kodell, *The Eucharist in the New Testament* (Wilmington 1988), pp. 71−132; Léon-Dufour, *Sharing the Eucharistic Bread*, pp. 181−277.

[98] See Dennis E. Smith & Hal Taussig, *Many Tables: The Eucharist in the New Testament and Liturgy Today* (London/Philadephia 1990), chs. 2 & 3.

part of the ritual meal.[99] In some places the eucharistic action proper may have become detached from the meal at an early stage; in others the two may have remained united for a considerable time.[100]

Conclusion

This chapter has offered many more questions than answers, and that indeed was its purpose. Too often in the past over-confident assertions have been made about the nature of Christian worship in the first century on the basis of false assumptions and methods or of dogmatic rather than historical criteria. There is relatively little about which we can be sure with regard to this subject, and so the New Testament generally cannot provide the firm foundation from which to project later liturgical developments that it has frequently been thought to give. We must therefore be content to remain agnostic about many of the roots of Christian worship practices which we observe clearly for the first time in the following centuries.

[99] See Jeremias, *The Eucharistic Words of Jesus*, p. 115; Léon-Dufour, *Sharing the Eucharistic Bread*, p. 176.

[100] It is often assumed that 1 Cor. 11.17ff. represents a half-way stage, in which the meal immediately preceded the celebration of the eucharist proper, but this discounts the possibility that at Corinth the eucharist, whatever its *meaning*, may have been very little different in *appearance* from a normal communal meal: cf. also G. Theissen, *The Social Setting of Pauline Christianity* (Philadelphia 1982), pp. 151ff.

3. Ten Principles for Interpreting Early Christian Liturgical Evidence

As is the case with Jewish liturgy, extant liturgical manuscripts from the Christian tradition are nearly all of relatively recent date, beginning around the eighth century C.E. Sources for a knowledge of the practice of worship prior to that time are fragmentary, consisting chiefly of brief, and often partial, descriptions of rites in letters and sermons; of even briefer, and less easily interpreted, allusions that appear in writings dealing with some quite different subject; of pieces of legislation affecting liturgical matters that occur among the canons produced by various councils and synods; of some fragments of what seem to be the texts of individual prayers; and last, but not least, of the prescriptions concerning worship in an extremely enigmatic genre of early Christian literature, the pseudo-apostolic church orders.

All these are, in effect, little more than a series of dots of varying sizes and density on a large sheet of plain paper. To the liturgical historian, therefore, falls the task of attempting to join up those dots and so create a plausible picture that explains how, and more importantly why, Christian worship evolved in the way that it did. Because, however, the dots on this sheet of paper are not pre-numbered, and so the connections which should be made between them are by no means obvious, the assumptions and presuppositions with which one begins such an operation are vitally important in determining its outcome. If one adopts, for example, the axiom that the primary connections must always run between the dots that lie closest to one another on the paper, then one will get a very different picture than if one starts by joining up all the largest dots first and then proceeding to the smaller ones in relative order, no matter how many times one's pencil has to criss-cross the page.

Strangely enough, while conscious reflection on the methodologies appropriate to the discipline has constituted a significant element in scholarly research in such areas as biblical studies and ecclesiastical history in the course of recent decades, the same has not really been true in the field of liturgical history.

There has been very little critical discussion of the particular methods which are applicable to this subject and few serious attempts to formulate principles for the interpretation of primary sources which ought to guide ongoing research.

Anton Baumstark (1872–1948)

Baumstark constitutes an important exception. Over fifty years ago, in what became a classic work in the field, *Liturgie comparée*,[1] he did attempt to define an appropriate methodology for the study of liturgical history by applying to the discipline an approach which was widely used in the latter half of the nineteenth century for the study of culture —the comparative method. Although it is commonly assumed that his work was inspired by the comparative study of language (and indeed Bernard Botte makes this assertion in his foreword to the third edition of Baumstark's book), Frederick West has shown that the ultimate source of all the comparative sciences was nineteenth-century biological thought, as articulated in the *Naturphilosophen* of Germany, the comparative anatomy of Georges Cuvier, and the evolutionary theory of Charles Darwin.[2] From here comparative linguists and the other practitioners of the comparative sciences of culture derived both a model and a method. The model was the living organism. The method was systematic comparison and consequent classification on the basis of a supposed line of descent from the origin of the species.

The basic flaw in this approach was a failure to recognize the essential difference between nature and culture: whereas nature is generated genetically, culture is transmitted socially. As the French anthropologist Claude Lèvi-Strauss has observed, 'the historical validity of the naturalist's reconstruction is guaranteed, in the final analysis, by the biological link of reproduction. An axe, on the contrary, does not generate an axe.'[3] Since the

[1] Chevetogne, Belgium, 1940, 3rd edn, rev. Bernard Botte, 1953; English translation: *Comparative Liturgy*, London/Westminster MD 1958.

[2] Frederick Sommers West, 'Anton Baumstark's Comparative Liturgy in its Intellectual Context', unpublished Ph.D. thesis, Notre Dame 1988. In what follows, I am greatly indebted to this important work.

[3] *Structural Anthropology* (New York 1963), p. 4.

cultural objects of study were not truly 'organic', they were not in reality subject to the same laws of development as other organisms, and hence the exact analysis and predictive power of the natural sciences was simply not possible in these cases. Even so, since the evolutionary theory of the period maintained that development always progressed from simplicity to complexity, the same pattern was imposed upon the cultural data: the simple must be primitive; the complex must belong to a later period of time. Moreover, while in the study of language continuing structure provided the parameters to the field of comparison and made it possible to discern patterns of evolution, other aspects of culture exhibited no such evident structure. As a result, fields of cultural comparison tended to be defined on the basis of some *a priori* presumed 'essence' linking together the diverse phenomena, which the subsequent classification of 'genus' and 'species' merely served to reinforce.

Baumstark was not the first liturgical scholar to utilize analogies from the world of science. Edmund Bishop (1846–1917) had compared the rigour of the methods of the physical sciences to those of the liturgical historian;[4] and Fernand Cabrol (1855– 1937) had viewed the relationship of *the* liturgy to the various liturgical families as resembling that of a genus to its various species, and conceptualized the processes operative in liturgical history in terms of laws.[5] But Baumstark went further, both in his use of the comparative method as a tool of analysis and in his conviction that its conclusions could rival the certainty thought to be attainable by the exact sciences:

> It is the forms of liturgical action and the liturgical texts of a given age which by their structure and rubrics can best teach us how their historical development came about, just as geology draws its conclusions from the observable stratifications of the earth's crust. . . . It is this abundance of forms which makes possible a comparative study of Liturgies, by using methods similar to those employed in comparative linguistics and comparative biology. . . . In its method, then, the Comparative Study of Liturgies approximates to that of the natural sciences. This method, as we know, is of

[4] 'History and Apologetics', in *Proceedings of the Rota* (London 1900), pp. 1–7; reprinted in Thomas Michael Loome, *Liberal Catholicism, Reform Catholicism, Modernism* (Mainz 1979), pp. 373–81.
[5] *Les origines liturgiques* (Paris 1906), pp. 23–44.

necessity an empirical one; for it is only by setting out from exact results and precise observations that right conclusions will be reached.[6]

Adopting the linear and unidirectional understanding of historical development which was a common characteristic of the comparative sciences of culture, Baumstark maintained that the direction of liturgical evolution ran (a) from earlier variety to later uniformity, and (b) from austerity or simplicity and brevity to richness and prolixity. Yet he was forced by the realities of the historical data to qualify both these claims by acknowledging the existence of a 'retrograde movement' in each case: the movement towards uniformity was constantly being interrupted by a tendency towards local variation; that towards prolixity by a tendency towards abbreviation.[7]

This admission that liturgical development might in fact proceed in either direction, even though Baumstark wanted to label one of them 'secondary' and 'retrograde', robs his classification of any predictive power. We cannot judge a liturgical phenomenon 'primitive' simply because it exhibits variety, nor 'late' simply because it exhibits prolixity, since each of these may in fact be an instance of the alleged 'retrograde movement'. Nonetheless, Baumstark confidently stated, 'By the law which *requires* that liturgical evolution *should* proceed from the simpler to the more complex, we shall deem the more austere the more primitive.'[8] He then proceeded implicitly to deny his basic premise that variety was a characteristic of early liturgy, by asserting instead that uniformity was a sign of antiquity:

Moreover, we shall have to regard as primitive [those] phenomena which are found with the same meaning, the same function, and in the same area, in all Christian Rites, or at least in a sufficiently large number of such Rites, and especially so if they have parallels in the Liturgy of the Synagogue. We shall pronounce the same verdict where anything has a Jewish parallel, even when it is limited to a few Christian Rites or it may be only to one. On the

[6] *Comparative Liturgy*, pp. 2—3.
[7] ibid., pp. 15—22. The latter he explained as being a consequence of 'the decline in religious zeal of which the sermons of the great Patristic age often offer us abundant testimony' (p. 23). We can observe here in Baumstark the continuing influence of (Pseudo-)Proclus, *On the Transmission of the Divine Liturgy*: see below, p. 132.
[8] ibid., p. 31 (emphasis added).

other hand, we shall consider as recent all phenomena peculiar to a single Rite or to a few Rites, but without parallel of any kind in the Synagogue. The same verdict must be pronounced on those which, although absolutely or almost universal, change their meaning, place or function from one Rite to another.[9]

Since Baumstark viewed the liturgy as an organic unity, he naturally regarded its historical evolution as being subject to certain laws, and claimed that two basic ones governed the process. The first was 'the Law of Organic Development', by which new additions to the liturgy at first took their place alongside more primitive elements, but in the course of time caused them to be abbreviated or even disappear completely.[10] The second law was 'that primitive conditions are maintained with greater tenacity in the more sacred seasons of the Liturgical Year',[11] in other words, that liturgical communities tend to preserve ancient customs on more solemn and significant occasions even though they may have disappeared from use at other times.

Later in the book, however, he enunciated four further, more specific laws, three of which had been formulated by his students. Fritz Hamm claimed both that 'the older a text is the less is it influenced by the Bible' and that 'the more recent a text is the more symmetrical it is'; Hieronymous Engberding proposed that 'the later it is, the more liturgical prose becomes charged with doctrinal elements'; while Baumstark himself added that 'certain actions which are purely utilitarian by nature may receive a symbolic meaning either from their function in the Liturgy as such or from factors in the liturgical texts which accompany them'.[12]

While all these statements may contain a considerable measure of truth, it is their elevation to the status of scientific

[9] ibid., pp. 31–2.

[10] ibid., pp. 23ff.

[11] ibid., pp. 27ff. He had acknowledged in an earlier article, 'Das Gesetz der Erhaltung des Alten in liturgischen hochwertiger Zeit', *Jahrbuch für Liturgiewissenschaft* 7 (1927), p. 8, that this law arose from an observation by Adrian Fortescue, *The Mass* (London/New York 1912), p. 270, concerning 'the constant tendency of the greatest days to keep older arrangements'.

[12] *Comparative Liturgy*, pp. 59–60, 130.

laws that is their undoing. Both of Baumstark's students in fact disassociated themselves from the absolute character which he attributed to these laws,[13] and his editor, Bernard Botte, also entered a number of caveats in his foreword to the third edition. Although he believed that Baumstark's ideas were 'fundamentally right, even if he sometimes gave them too rigid a form and occasionally made unwarranted use of them', Botte warned of a number of pitfalls to be avoided:

The first is that of being duped by words. While it is legitimate to investigate the tendencies which have guided the evolution of the liturgy and even to give these tendencies the name of laws, it must also be remembered that this method is only a convenient device. The analogy with the natural sciences must not deceive us. These last set out from the postulate that phenomena are wholly determined, a presumption apart from which such sciences would not be possible. But when we pass to linguistics, this determinism is already mitigated. . . . When we pass to history in which free-will plays an even greater part, the element of determinism is still weaker, and here we need much circumspection if we are not to give the word 'law' too narrow a sense. There is a risk of confining what happens in history within an artificial framework which does violence to the facts. The first duty of the historian is always to respect the factual *datum* even when no place for it can be found in the scheme of a preconceived theory.

The second danger . . . is to take a logical construction as though it were a historic reality. The sciences do not always end in certainty. Induction may sometimes, indeed, lead to certain conclusions, but it often leads only to probabilities or even to provisional hypotheses. . . . And so it is with history. When documents are wanting or too fragmentary, we must guard against too absolute conclusions. And it is here that we meet with the chief limitation of Baumstark. He did not always see where to draw the line between his hypotheses and historical reality. Hence it will be no matter for surprise if parts of his work must be abandoned. While some of his constructions were interesting and suggestive and have done good duty as working hypotheses, it would be a mistake to take them for historic truths scientifically demonstrated.[14]

All this is not to deny the value of the comparative approach advocated by Baumstark in helping us reconstruct liturgical history. Indeed, some form of comparison must necessarily be a

[13] Fritz Hamm, *Die liturgischen Einsetzungsberichte im Sinne vergleichender Liturgie Forschung untersucht* (Münster 1928), p. 97; Hieronymous Engberding, 'Neues Licht über die Geschichte des Textes der Ägyptischen Markusliturgie', *Oriens Christianus* 40 (1956), p. 46, n. 32.

[14] *Comparative Liturgy*, pp. viii–ix.

part of any attempt to bridge the gaps in our knowledge; and a whole school of comparative liturgists has subsequently emerged which includes in its number such leading scholars as Engberding himself, Juan Mateos, and Robert Taft.[15] Their work, however, is much more cautious and sophisticated in its methodology: Taft, for example, insists on the importance of 'a constant dialectic between structural analysis and historical research'.[16] It proceeds from a close comparison of the similarities *and differences* between liturgical practices in different geographical regions, temporal periods, or ecclesiastical traditions to a hypothesis which attempts to account satisfactorily for the origin and development of those practices both in the light of the tendencies already observed in the evolution of other liturgical phenomena and within the context of their known historical circumstances. Obviously, such a process works better for periods when historical data is more plentiful, and especially after the emergence of actual liturgical texts, than it does in the less clearly defined world of the first three or four centuries of Christian history.

For this earlier time what we most need are not so much laws which tell us how the liturgy itself must have developed, nor even the 'observable tendencies' in liturgical evolution which Baumstark's so-called laws actually offer us —useful though they are —but rather some reliable guidelines to assist us in our efforts to interpret the fragmentary and often confusing primary sources on which any attempted reconstruction of primitive liturgical practice has to be based. What follows, then, is a brief critique of certain methodological presuppositions which have tended to be followed in traditional study of the origins of Christian worship, some indications as to how these are already changing —or in some cases ought to be changing, even if they are as yet not doing so —and the effect that this altered per-

[15] See especially Taft's important studies, 'The Structural Analysis of Liturgical Units: An Essay in Methodology', *Worship* 52 (1978), pp. 314—29; and 'How Liturgies Grow: The Evolution of the Byzantine Divine Liturgy', *Orientalia Christiana Periodica* 43 (1977), pp. 355—78. Both articles are reproduced in his *Beyond East and West* (Washington DC 1984), pp. 151—92.

[16] 'The Structural Analysis of Liturgical Units', p. 316 = *Beyond East and West*, p. 153.

spective has on our picture of early liturgical practice. It takes
the form of a decalogue of proposed interpretative principles.

**1. What is most common is not necessarily most ancient, and
what is least common is not necessarily least ancient.**
As we shall see in later chapters, the traditionally dominant
presuppositions among liturgical scholars concerning the origins
of Christian liturgy, and especially of the eucharist, have been
not very dissimilar to those which we observed in earlier Jewish
liturgical scholarship,[17] since both disciplines were built upon
the same foundation of comparative philology. Chief among
these assumptions were that the many varied forms found in different geographical regions in later centuries can all be traced
back to a single common root in their institution by Jesus; and
that variety tended to increase in the course of time as the
Church developed and these practices were subject to differing
local influences and emphases. Thus, it has been thought, what
is common to most or all of these later forms must represent the
very earliest stratum of Christian worship, while what is found in
just a few instances, or merely one, is a later development.[18]

Such views cannot really be sustained any longer in the light
of recent scholarship. Those propounding the traditional theory
always did have considerable difficulty in demonstrating how
such very diverse later practices could all have arisen from a
single source, and in the course of their defence frequently had
to resort to eliminating from consideration in one way or
another awkward pieces of evidence which did not fit the theory,
as, for example, the 'eucharistic' rite of *Didache* 9−10 or the
apparent absence of 'confirmation' from the early Syrian tradition.[19] Now, however, there are the added complications which
we have already observed, that first-century Jewish liturgy, from
which Christian worship took its departure, was not nearly so
fixed or uniform as was once supposed, and that New Testament
Christianity was itself essentially pluriform in doctrine and practice.

[17] See above, pp. 2−4.
[18] See, for example, the quotation from Baumstark above, pp. 59−60.
[19] See below, pp. 132ff., 163ff.

Thus, it does not necessarily follow that what is common in later Christian liturgical practice is what is most primitive. It certainly *may* be so, but it is also equally possible that similarities that exist between customs in different parts of the ancient world are the result of a conscious movement towards conformity. Similarly, what is unusual or unique is not necessarily a late development. Once again it *may* be so, but it is equally possible that the phenomenon is in fact the vestigial remains of what was once a much greater variety of forms of worship than we can now see in the surviving evidence. It may be an ancient local custom that somehow managed to escape — or at least avoid the full effect of — a later process that caused liturgical diversity to contract its horizons.

For, as we shall see in later chapters, the true story of the development of Christian worship seems to have been a movement from considerable differences over quite fundamental elements to an increasing amalgamation and standardization of local customs. The beginnings of this trend can already be seen in the second century C.E., but it gathered much greater momentum in the fourth, as the Church expanded, as communication — and hence awareness of differences — between different regional centres increased, and above all as orthodox Christianity tried to define itself over against what were perceived as heretical movements; for in such a situation any tendency to persist in what appeared to be idiosyncratic liturgical observances was likely to have been interpreted as a mark of heterodoxy. As Robert Taft has written:

> This is the period of the unification of rites, when worship, like church government, not only evolved new forms, but also let the weaker variants of the species die out, as the Church developed, via the creation of intermediate unities, into a federation of federations of local churches, with ever-increasing unity of practice within each federation, and ever-increasing diversity of practice from federation to federation. In other words what was once one loose collection of individual local churches each with its own liturgical uses, evolved into a series of intermediate structures or federations (later called patriarchates) grouped around certain major sees. This process stimulated a corresponding unification and standardizing of church practice, liturgical and otherwise. Hence, the process of formation of rites is not one of diversification, as is usually held, but of unification. And what one finds in extant rites today is not a synthesis of all that went before, but

rather the result of a selective evolution: the survival of the fittest — of the fittest, not necessarily of the best.[20]

2. The so-called Constantinian revolution served as much to intensify existing trends as it did to initiate new ones.

The conversion to Christianity of the emperor Constantine early in the fourth century is usually portrayed as marking a crucial turning-point in the evolution of forms of worship; and it is undoubtedly true that a very marked contrast can be observed between the form and character of liturgical practices in the pre-Constantinian and post-Constantinian periods. For example, whereas the first Christians saw themselves as set over against the world and were careful to avoid any compromise with paganism and its customs, stressing rather what distinguished Christianity from other religions, in the fourth century the Church emerged as a public institution within the world, with its liturgy functioning as a *cultus publicus*, seeking the divine favour to secure the well-being of the state, and it was now quite willing to absorb and Christianize pagan religious ideas and practices, seeing itself as the fulfilment to which earlier religions had dimly pointed.[21]

Now, however, scholars are beginning to realize that one must be careful not to overstate this contrast between the two periods of ecclesiastical history. A number of developments, the genesis of which has traditionally been ascribed to the changed situation of the Church after the Peace of Constantine, are now shown as having roots that reach back into the third century, and in some cases even earlier still.

For example, the pattern of daily worship practised in the urban monastic communities which began to emerge in the early fourth century was not entirely a new creation of this movement. In some respects it was simply a conservative preservation of a very traditional style of prayer and spirituality. There are certainly some new features — such as the regular recitation of the Book of Psalms in its entirety and in its biblical order as the cornerstone of the spiritual life — but in other ways the monks

[20] 'How Liturgies Grow', p. 355 = *Beyond East and West*, p. 167.

[21] See, for example, J. G. Davies, 'The Introduction of the Numinous into the Liturgy: An Historical Note', *SL* 8 (1972), pp. 216–23.

and nuns of the fourth century were simply continuing to do what ordinary Christians of earlier centuries had once done. Their customs only appear peculiarly monastic because they had by now been abandoned by other Christians, who, in the more relaxed atmosphere of the Constantinian era, tended to be more luke-warm about their religious commitment than their predecessors in the age of persecution.[22]

Similarly, the interest in time and history that comes to the fore during this period is not something to which the Constantinian world gave birth, though it certainly suckled and nurtured it. It is simply not true, as earlier generations of liturgical scholars tended to conclude, that the first Christians could not possibly have been interested in discovering and commemorating the precise dates and times of the events of the life of Jesus or in establishing a rhythmical pattern of hours of prayer because they expected the end of this world to come at any moment with the return of their Lord.[23] On the contrary, an interest in time and eternity, history and eschatology, can coexist, and indeed the one can be an expression of the other. The early Christians established regular patterns of daily prayer-times not because they thought that the Church was here to stay for a long while, but precisely so that they might practise eschatological vigilance and be ready and watchful in prayer for the return of Christ and the consummation of God's kingdom.[24]

Hence, the interest in eschatology, which certainly declined when it appeared less and less likely that the world was going to end soon, was not simply replaced by a new interest in time and history. Rather, a pre-existent interest took on a new vigour in a new situation, and a multiplicity of feasts and commemorations began to emerge in the fourth century in a way they had not done earlier. This development was generated at least in part by apologetic factors. The Church now needed to communicate the tenets of its faith to a barbarian world which was willing to listen, and to defend its doctrinal positions against a variety of

[22] See below, p. 191.

[23] See, for example, Dix, *Shape of the Liturgy*, ch. XI: 'The Sanctification of Time'.

[24] See Bradshaw, *Daily Prayer in the Early Church*, pp. 37–9.

heretical attacks; and what better means could be found than the promotion of occasions that publicly celebrated aspects of what the Church believed?[25]

Thus, in instances like these, the so-called Constantinian revolution did not so much inaugurate new liturgical practices and attitudes as create conditions in which some pre-existent customs could achieve a greater measure of pre-eminence than others which were no longer considered appropriate to the changed situation of the Church.

3. Authoritative-sounding statements are not always genuinely authoritative.

Many ancient Christian writers in their allusions to liturgical practices make very emphatic statements about what is or is not the case, and traditional liturgical scholarship has been inclined to accept such remarks as truly authoritative declarations of the established doctrine and practice of the Church at the time that they were written, especially as many of those making these apparently *ex cathedra* pronouncements did actually occupy the office of a bishop.

So, to cite two early examples which actually concern the development of the ordained ministry rather than liturgy itself, the *First Epistle of Clement*, usually thought to have originated from the church at Rome *c*. 96 C.E., is a long and impassioned denunciation of the church at Corinth for dismissing its presbyters and replacing them with others; and the letters of Ignatius of Antioch, conventionally dated early in the second century, repeatedly insist on the necessity of obedience to the bishop and his fellow ministers. Both have generally been understood as expressing the agreed position of the Church on these issues — that ministers were always appointed for life and that episcopal government was the norm early in the second century. Recent study, however, has suggested that, since they were apparently having to argue the case at considerable length and with great vigour against opponents who seemingly did not share their conclusions, they must, on the contrary, represent only one view

[25] See further Robert F. Taft, 'Historicism Revisited', *SL* 14 (1982), pp. 97–109 = *Beyond East and West*, pp. 15–30.

among others at the time, a view which ultimately came to triumph but which did not achieve supremacy without a considerable struggle against alternative positions and practices.[26]

Authoritative-sounding statements therefore need to be taken with a pinch of salt. When some early Christian author proudly proclaims, for example, that a certain psalm or canticle is sung 'throughout the world', it probably means at the most that he knows it to be used in the particular regions he has visited or heard about: it remains an open question whether a similar usage obtained in other parts of the world.[27] Similarly, when some ancient bishop solemnly affirms that a certain liturgical custom is 'unheard of' in any church, he is almost certainly excluding from his definition of 'church' those groups of Christians whom he judges to be heretical and among whom the practice might well still be flourishing as it once had done in many other places in earlier times, in spite of our bishop's confident (though ignorant) assertion to the contrary.[28] Hence the development of ecclesiastical structures and liturgical practices seems to have been much slower than has traditionally been supposed. Though many things did emerge quite early in the life of the Church, they did not immediately achieve normative or universal status, however strongly some individuals might have thought that they should.

4. Legislation is better evidence for what it proposes to prohibit than for what it seeks to promote.

When attention is directed towards the decrees of ecclesiastical councils and synods in the search for information about the

[26] See further Paul F. Bradshaw, *Liturgical Presidency in the Early Church* (GLS 36, 1983), pp. 11—14.

[27] Caesarius of Arles, for example, makes this claim with regard to the use of Ps. 104 at the daily evening service (*Serm.* 136.1). He maintains that as a result it 'is so well known to everybody that the greatest part of the human race has memorized it'; whereas in reality its use at this service seems to have been restricted to parts of the West, and in the East Ps. 141 was instead the standard evening psalm.

[28] For example, Demetrius, patriarch of Alexandria in the third century, made such a claim with regard to the practice of preaching by those who were not ordained ministers, though the custom was defended by the bishops of Caesarea and Jerusalem, and seems to have left other traces of its former existence: see Bradshaw, *Liturgical Presidency in the Early Church*, pp. 18—20.

practice of worship in the early Church, there is a natural tendency to focus on the things that those decrees say shall or shall not be done. Thus, to cite a simple example, when the Council of Braga in 561 C.E. insists that 'one and the same order of psalmody is to be observed in the morning and evening services; and neither individual variations nor monastic uses are to be interpolated into the ecclesiastical rule', one might be tempted to conclude that liturgical practices in Spain must have been uniform thereafter. Such a conclusion, however, can be shown to be false by the fact that synods held in later years found it necessary to repeat over and over again this demand for a standardization in usage.[29] Just because an authoritative body makes a liturgical regulation does not mean that it was observed everywhere or ever put into practice anywhere at all. Conservatism in matters liturgical is notoriously intractable, and, as we all know well, canonical legislation from even the highest level is frequently unable to dislodge a well-established and much-loved local custom.

This does not mean, however, that such pieces of legislation are entirely valueless in the search for clues to the liturgical customs of the early Church. Indeed, quite the opposite is the case: regulations provide excellent evidence for what was actually happening in local congregations, not by what is decreed should be done but by what is either directly prohibited or indirectly implied should cease to be done. That such regulations were made at all shows that the very opposite of what they were trying to promote must have been a widespread custom at that period. Synodical assemblies do not usually waste their time either condemning something that is not actually going on or insisting on the firm adherence to some rule that everyone is already observing. Thus, for example, the decree by the Council of Vaison in 529 C.E. that the response *Kyrie eleison* should be used does not prove that this foreign innovation was quickly accepted in that part of Gaul — and indeed we have virtually no trace of its subsequent adoption there — but it does show that prior to this time that response was not a common part of the worship of that region.

[29] See further Bradshaw, *Daily Prayer in the Early Church*, p. 115.

The same is true of the liturgical comments that are found in many of the writings and homilies of early Christian theologians and bishops. We generally cannot know whether the practices and customs that they advocated were ever adopted by their congregations, or just politely listened to and then ignored, as the pleas of preachers often are; but we can conclude that there must have been some real foundation to the contrary custom or practice which is either directly criticized or implicitly acknowledged in the advice being given. Such writers may sometimes be suspected of hyperbole in the things they say, but they do not usually tilt at non-existent windmills. So, for example, when John Chrysostom describes those who fail to stay for the reception of communion at the celebration of the eucharist as resembling Judas Iscariot at the Last Supper,[30] we do not know if he had any success in reforming the behaviour of his congregation, but we can safely assume that what he is complaining about was an observable feature at that time.

5. When a variety of explanations is advanced for the origin of a liturgical custom, its true source has almost certainly been forgotten.
One frequently encounters in early Christian writings not only a partial description of some liturgical practice but also an explanation as to how it originated. Sometimes it is very easy to detect when such an explanation seems to be no more than the product of a pious imagination. When one reads, for example, in Coptic tradition that it was Theophilus, patriarch of Alexandria in the fourth century, who introduced baptismal chrism into Christian usage in response to the instruction of an angel to bring balsam trees from Jericho, plant them, extract the balsam, and cook the spices,[31] one may well have serious doubts about the veracity of the claim. But in other cases it is less clear whether the author has access to a reliable source of information or not. Sometimes several writers will allude to the same custom but offer widely differing stories as to its true meaning or origin. This is the case, to cite just two examples, with regard to

[30] John Chrysostom, *De Baptismo Christi* 4.
[31] See Louis Villecourt, 'Le livre du chrême', *Muséon* 41 (1928), pp. 58–9.

the times of daily prayer commonly observed in the third century, and with regard to the custom, first evidenced in Syria in the late fourth century, of placing the book of the Gospels on the head of a bishop during his ordination.

It is tempting in such instances to opt for the explanation that one finds most congenial to one's point of view and to discount the rest. This is in fact what scholars have generally done with respect to the explanations for the customs just mentioned,[32] but there seems no particular reason to suppose that any one of the ancient commentators had access to a more authoritative source of information than the others. Indeed, the very existence of multiple explanations and interpretations is itself a very good indication that no authoritative tradition with regard to the original purpose and meaning of the custom had survived, and hence writers and preachers felt free to use their imaginations. This is not to say that the real origin can never be unearthed by modern scholarship, with its access to sources and methods not known to the ancients, or that sometimes one of those early writers may not have hit upon the right solution. But it does suggest that in such situations it may often be necessary to look for the real answer in a quite different direction from that of the conventional accounts.

6. Ancient church orders are not what they seem.

Within early Christian literature is a group of documents that look very like real, authoritative liturgical texts, containing both directions for the conduct of worship and also the words of prayers and other formularies. Since these documents claim in one way or another to be apostolic, they have generally been referred to as apostolic church orders. But they are not what they seem. Not only is their claim to apostolic authorship spurious—a judgement that has been universally accepted since at least the beginning of the twentieth century—but they are not even the official liturgical manuals of some third- or fourth-century local church, masquerading in apostolic dress to lend

[32] For further details see Bradshaw, *Daily Prayer in the Early Church*, pp. 48–62, and idem, *Ordination Rites of the Ancient Churches of East and West*, pp. 39–44.

themselves added authority —a judgement that is still not always fully appreciated by all contemporary scholars.

It is usually recognized that at least some, especially those dated later in the sequence, were in part the products of the imagination and aspirations of their compilers —armchair liturgists dreaming up what the perfect liturgy might be like if only they had the freedom to put into practice what their idiosyncratic tastes and personal convictions longed for. Even so, there has still been a tendency to want to hold on to at least one or two of them as reliable descriptions of the real liturgy of the local church from which they seem to derive. Indeed, the prayers contained in one of them, the so-called *Apostolic Tradition* of Hippolytus, have been reproduced for use in the modern service-books of a considerable number of Christian churches in the last few years, so convinced have the revisers been that here we are in touch with the authentic liturgy of the early Church and can now say the same words that ancient Christians once did when we celebrate the eucharist, ordain a bishop, or initiate a new convert.

As we shall see in somehat greater detail in the next chapter, however, there is no reason to suppose that this document is a more, or a less, reliable guide to what early Christians were really doing in their worship than any of the other church orders, especially as there is also some uncertainty as to what part of the ancient world it comes from and what its original text actually said, since all we have extant are various translations and reworkings of it. This does not mean that these church orders are of no value in attempting to recover the liturgical practices of the early Church. They may indeed present evidence for what was actually going on in the churches from which they came, but that evidence can only be disentangled with difficulty and caution from both the idiosyncratic idealizing of the individual authors and the corrections and updating to which the documents tend to have been subjected in the course of their subsequent transmission. Without corroborative evidence from another source it is dangerous to claim that any particular prayer-text in them was typical of the worship of the period, and it is still more unwise, on the doubtful presumption of its once-authoritative status, to ask twentieth-century congregations to make it their own.[33]

7. Liturgical manuscripts are more prone to emendation than literary manuscripts.

F. L. Cross once observed:

> Liturgical and literary texts, as they have come down to us, have a specious similarity. They are written in similar scripts and on similar writing materials. They are now shelved shoulder to shoulder in our libraries and classified within the same system of shelfmarking. . . . But these similarities mask a radical difference. In the first place, unlike literary manuscripts, liturgical manuscripts were not written to satisfy an historical interest. They were written to serve a severely practical end. Their primary purpose was the needs of the services of the Church. Like timetables and other books for use, liturgical texts were compiled with the immediate future in view. Their intent was not to make an accurate reproduction of an existing model.[34]

In other words, copyists or translators of ancient material dealing with liturgical matters did not normally expend considerable time and energy on their work merely out of a general desire to preserve antiquity for its own sake but because they believed that the document legitimized as traditional the worship practices of their own day. What were they to do, then, when they encountered in a text something which did not correspond with their own experience —for instance, injunctions which advocated practices contrary to those of their own tradition, or the omission of some element which they regarded as important or essential? They could only conclude that the text before them really ought to accord with that with which they were familiar, that the traditions of their own church *must* be those which had been prescribed in ancient times and had simply been omitted by accident from the document or had fallen out in the course of its transmission. It was then only the

[33] On this point, see also Paul F. Bradshaw, 'The Liturgical Use and Abuse of Patristics', in Kenneth Stevenson, ed., *Liturgy Reshaped* (London 1982), pp. 134−45.
[34] 'Early Western Liturgical Manuscripts', *JTS* 16 (1965), pp. 63−4.

work of a few moments to restore what they thought was the original reading and bring it into line with current practice.

Liturgical manuscripts are not unique in this respect. They belong to a genre which may be called 'living literature'.[35] This is material which circulates within a community and forms a part of its heritage and tradition but which is constantly subject to revision and rewriting to reflect changing historical and cultural circumstances. It would include such diverse specimens as folk tales, the pseudo-apostolic church orders,[36] and even some scriptural material, all characterized by the existence of multiple recensions, sometimes exhibiting quantitive differences (i.e., longer and shorter versions) and sometimes qualitive differences (i.e., various ways of saying the same thing, often with no clear reflection of a single *Urtext*), and sometimes both.[37]

This is a very different situation from, say, the copying of the works of Augustine or some other patristic writer, when the desire was precisely to preserve antiquity and make an accurate reproduction of the original. Although such literary manuscripts might also be subject to occasional attempts to correct what were perceived as lapses from doctrinal orthodoxy in the text, these emendations are relatively rare and much easier to detect than in liturgical manuscripts, where the risk of a passage being updated and modified to fit a changed situation is far greater. Hence one should not easily assume that the received version of any liturgical document necessarily represents what the author originally wrote, especially when it has been subsequently translated from one language to another. The careful disentangling of the various strata present in such texts can often not only point to a very different reading in the original but also tell a fascinating story of how later liturgical practice evolved.

[35] An expression used in reference to the *Didache* by Stanislas Giet, *L'Énigme de la Didachè* (Paris 1970), p. 257. For the *Didache*, see below, pp. 84–6.

[36] See below, pp. 101ff.

[37] For some examples, see Robert A. Kraft, 'Reassessing the "Recensional Problem" in Testament of Abraham', in George W. E. Nickelsburg, ed., *Studies on the Testament of Abraham* (Missoula MT 1976), pp. 121–37.

8. Liturgical texts can go on being copied long after they have ceased to be used.

This principle serves as an important counter-balance to the previous one, in that we should be cautious about concluding that everything which appears in an ancient source must have been in active use in the communities through which that document is thought to have passed. We are all doubtless familiar in our own experience with certain prayer-texts, or hymns, or complete orders of service that go on appearing in successive editions of an official book of liturgies for years and years without ever being used by anyone. They were appropriate or fashionable in some earlier generation, perhaps at a particularly sensitive point in the history of that religious tradition, but have since become out of date. Yet nobody has the courage to say, 'Let's drop this from our formularies', since to do so would appear to be somehow a betrayal of our heritage, a reneging on our ancestors in the faith, or a wanton disregard for tradition. So it goes on appearing in the book, and everyone knows that when you reach it in the order of worship, you simply turn the page and pass over it to the next prayer or whatever.

Thus, while it is true that liturgical manuscripts were generally copied in order to be used, yet Christians of earlier generations were quite as capable as we are of carrying some excess liturgical baggage along with them, of copying out primitive and venerable texts into later collections of material just because they were primitive and venerable and not because of any real intention of putting them into practice. The problem is that they knew which of their texts were to be used and which passed over, while we are left to guess at it with whatever assistance other sources can give us. So, for example, while all who have studied the matter are agreed that in book 7 of the fourth-century church order, the *Apostolic Constitutions*, a number of the prayers have a strongly Jewish character, nobody can be sure what conclusions should be drawn from it.[38] Does it mean that Judaism was still exercising a strong influence on Christian worship at this late date, or it is just another piece of

[38] See below, p. 103, n. 63.

what Robert Taft has called 'liturgical debris', carried down by the tide of tradition from former times?

9. Only particularly significant, novel, or controverted practices will tend to be mentioned, and others will probably be passed over in silence; but the first time something is mentioned is not necessarily the first time it was practised.

It is dangerous to read any ancient source as though it were a *verbatim* account of any liturgical act. This is obviously so in the case of the brief allusions to Christian worship that crop up in writings dealing with some quite different topic. We cannot there expect the authors to be describing in exact and full detail all the aspects of the custom to which they are referring, for they are naturally only choosing to mention what is germane to the point they are making. It is important to remember, however, that the same is also true of other early sources. Even the fourth-century sets of homilies delivered to new converts to Christianity and intended to instruct them in the meaning of the liturgies of baptism and the eucharist cannot be presumed to be mentioning everything that was said or done in those services. The authors will have highlighted those parts of the liturgy which seemed to them especially significant or containing something they judged it important for the neophytes to know, but they probably will have passed over other parts which they thought less significant or lacking a relevant lesson.

What is more, the same selectivity can be expected even in sets of directions for the conduct of worship, such as we find in the ancient church orders, in conciliar decrees, or in early monastic rules. At first sight, they may look like a complete list of instructions, but one has only to consider for a moment the twentieth-century equivalents of these texts to realize how much is always left unsaid because it is presumed to be familiar to the readers. Indeed, many amusing stories can be told of groups attempting to replicate solely on the basis of the printed rubrics liturgical rites which they have never seen, for even the clearest of instructions always contain an element of ambiguity for those unfamiliar with the tradition. Thus, directions do not generally deal with accepted and customary things, but only with new, uncertain, or controverted points: everything else will tend either to be passed over in silence or to receive the briefest of allusions. This leads to the infuriating situation for the liturgical scholar of passages which give the reader an instruction like 'say the customary psalms' or 'do what is usual everywhere on this day', since it is precisely those things that were known to every-one of the period and so were never written down that are con-sequently unknown to us and of greatest interest in our efforts to comprehend the shape and character of early Christian worship.

On the other hand, we ought not to rush to draw the opposite conclusion and assume that the first time something is men-tioned was the first time it had ever occurred. As Joachim Jeremias has said, 'In investigating a form of address used in prayer we must not limit ourselves to dating the prayers in which it occurs; we must also take into account the fact that forms of address in prayer stand in a liturgical tradition and can therefore be older than the particular prayer in which they appear.'[39]

All this naturally makes the task more difficult. We cannot assume that just because something is not mentioned it was not being practised. Equally, arguments from silence are notoriously unreliable. Earlier generations of liturgical scholars frequently attempted to reconstruct the worship of the first and second centuries by reading back customs which were described for the first time only in the fourth century, especially if they bore the slightest resemblance to Jewish customs which were, rightly or wrongly, thought to have been current in the first century C.E., for it was concluded that the one was directly descended from the other and so must have been practised by Christians in unbroken continuity in the intervening years. In many cases, more recent investigation of either the Christian or the Jewish custom has often shown such conclusions to be mistaken.

10. Texts must always be studied in context.
This principle is in effect a summary of many of the others, for knowledge of the true nature of a document is vital to its correct interpretation, and the temptation to 'proof-text' sources must be resisted as much here as in biblical study. For example, whether or not it is significant that something is mentioned or

[39] *The Prayers of Jesus* (London 1967), p. 26.

omitted will depend to a considerable extent upon the type of material with which one is dealing: the same treatment of a subject should not be expected in, say, a mystagogical catechesis as in monastic directions for reciting the divine office. Even historically inaccurate statements, like the Theophilus story referred to in principle 5 above, can continue to yield useful evidence for the period in which they originated, once their *Sitz im Leben* is properly appreciated.[40] Contextual study, however, involves more than just source- or form-criticism. It also requires the search for another point of reference besides the text itself, whether this is a further document or archaeological remains or whatever, so that any conclusion drawn may be based not upon the unsubstantiated testimony of one witness but upon some form of triangulation.

Conclusion

These, then, are ten principles or guides that may be of assistance in the task I described at the beginning as that of joining up the dots, connecting the scattered pieces of possible evidence for the ways in which Christians were worshipping in the early centuries of the Church's existence. I make no claim that these ten constitute a definitive or comprehensive set of principles, and more could doubtless be added to them. But perhaps my ten will suffice as a starting-point for the operation.

On the other hand, in the light of all the caution and uncertainty which I have stressed in the course of my journey through them, some readers may feel that the whole attempt to reconstruct patterns of ancient Christian worship is doomed to failure, that it is not simply a matter of joining up dots on a sheet of plain paper as I advertised at the beginning, but rather of finding the dots in the first place, buried as they are among countless others of different shades and hues, and of doing so with a blindfold over one's eyes. I can sympathize with some of that trepidation: the task is certainly not as easy as former generations often judged it. Yet, while we cannot hope to learn

[40] See Paul F. Bradshaw, 'Baptismal Practice in the Alexandrian Tradition, Eastern or Western?', in Paul F. Bradshaw, ed., *Essays in Early Eastern Initiation* (A/GLS 8, 1988), pp. 5—17.

everything we would like to know about the Church's early worship, it is not wholly impossible to say, even if only in a provisional way, a certain amount about how that worship began and developed in the first few centuries of the Christian tradition. When the dots are carefully joined, a faint picture can indeed emerge.

4. Ancient Church Orders: A Continuing Enigma

Ancient church orders constitute one of the more fascinating *genres* of early Christian literature, purporting to offer authoritative 'apostolic' prescriptions on matters of moral conduct, liturgical practice, and ecclesiastical organization and discipline. What these pseudo-apostolic texts have to say about the apostolic age itself may be of little interest, but they are potentially valuable sources of evidence for the thought and practices of the periods in which they were composed. Although they were apparently originally written in Greek, in some cases all that has survived are translations into other languages.

Their discovery
Prior to 1800 only one such document was generally known, the *Apostolic Constitutions*, first published in 1563. Although its authenticity did not go entirely unchallenged, it was accepted by many as a genuinely apostolic work in the centuries which followed its discovery. During the nineteenth century, however, discoveries of other church orders came thick and fast. In 1843 J. W. Bickell published the Greek text of a short treatise which he called 'the Apostolic Church Order'.[1] In 1848 Henry Tattam produced an edition of what turned out to be a translation into the Bohairic dialect of Coptic, made as recently as 1804, of a composite work comprising three elements — Bickell's *Apostolic Church Order*; another previously unknown document, which for want of a better title was later designated by Hans Achelis as 'the Egyptian Church Order'; and a different recension of the final book 8 of the *Apostolic Constitutions*.[2] This collection is usually called the Clementine Heptateuch or Alexandrine Sinodos.

In 1854 Paul de Lagarde edited a Syriac version of a document generally referred to as the *Didascalia Apostolorum*;[3] and

[1] *Geschichte des Kirchenrechts* I (Giessen 1843), pp. 107–32.
[2] *The Apostolical Constitutions or the Canons of the Apostles in Coptic with an English Translation*, London 1848.
[3] *Didascalia Apostolorum syriace*, Leipzig 1854 = Osnabruck-Wiesbaden 1967.

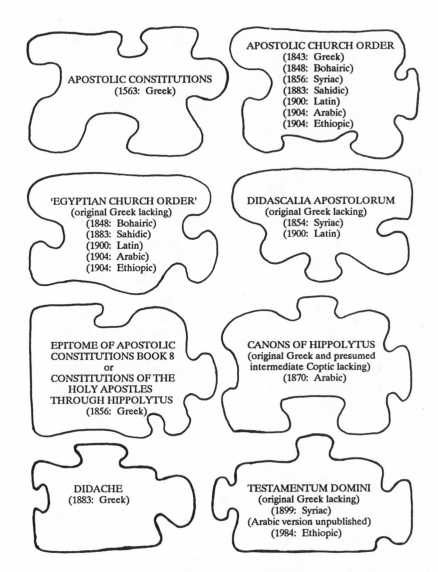

TABLE 1: THE PUBLICATION OF THE PIECES OF THE PUZZLE

in 1856 he published a Syriac translation of the *Apostolic Church Order* and the Greek text of a work known as the *Epitome* of *Apostolic Constitutions* 8, or alternatively by the title which appears in some manuscripts, 'the Constitutions of the Holy Apostles through Hippolytus'.[4] In 1870 Daniel von Haneberg

---

[4] *Reliquiae iuris ecclesiastici antiquissimae* (Leipzig 1856), pp. 1—23.

produced the Arabic text of what claimed to be the *Canons of Hippolytus*;[5] and in 1875 Philotheos Bryennios discovered the only known Greek text of the *Didache*, or 'Teaching of the Twelve Apostles', which he published in 1883.[6] In the same year Lagarde disclosed the existence of a Sahidic dialect version of the Bohairic collection earlier published by Tattam,[7] and in 1899 Ignatius Rahmani produced a Syriac document, the *Testamentum Domini*, which capped all other apostolic claims by feigning to be the words of Jesus himself to the apostles after his resurrection.[8] In 1900 Edmund Hauler edited a fifth-century palimpsest from Verona which contained — unfortunately with many lacunae — Latin translations of the *Didascalia*, the *Apostolic Church Order*, and the 'Egyptian Church Order'.[9] Finally, in 1904 George Horner contributed Arabic and Ethiopic versions of the Alexandrine Sinodos to the Bohairic and Sahidic texts earlier published by Tattam and Lagarde.[10]

Although no new church orders have been added to the list of discoveries since the beginning of the twentieth century, some new manuscripts of various recensions have been found, including in some cases a few small fragments of otherwise missing Greek originals. These have affected the task of establishing the text, and consequently better editions have since been produced for most of the individual documents.

Their relationship

As the various church orders began to appear, it rapidly became obvious that they were more than merely parallel examples of a particular type of literature. Parts of the different documents exhibited such a marked similarity to one another that it clearly pointed to a direct literary relationship. But what was that rela-

---

[5] *Canones S. Hippolyti arabice*, Munich 1870.

[6] *DIDACHE TON DODEKA APOSTOLON*, Constantinople 1883.

[7] *Aegyptiaca* (Göttingen 1883 = 1972), pp. 209—91.

[8] *Testamentum Domini nostri Jesu Christi*, Mainz 1899 = Hildesheim 1968.

[9] *Didascaliae apostolorum fragmenta Veronensia latina. Accedunt canonum qui dicuntur apostolorum et aegyptiorum reliquiae*, Leipzig 1900.

[10] *The Statutes of the Apostles or Canones Ecclesiastici*, London 1904; later edition of the Arabic by Jean & Augustin Périer, *Les 127 Canons des Apôtres*, PO 8/4, Paris 1912.

tionship? How did these various pieces of the jigsaw puzzle fit together?

There was no shortage of theories, and almost every possible combination was suggested. Thus in 1891 Achelis proposed that the genealogy ran from the *Canons of Hippolytus* through the so-called 'Egyptian Church Order', and also another work subsequently lost, to the *Epitome* and then to *Apostolic Constitutions* 8;[11] while in the same year F. X. Funk suggested almost exactly the opposite order: *Apostolic Constitutions* 8 → *Epitome* → 'Egyptian Church Order' → *Canons of Hippolytus*.[12] When Rahmani published the *Testamentum Domini* in 1899, he claimed that it was a second-century work from which *Apostolic Constitutions* 8 and the 'Egyptian Church Order' were both derived, with the *Canons of Hippolytus* in turn being dependent upon the latter. In 1901 John Wordsworth propounded the theory that there was a lost church order from which all the known ones had emanated.[13]

What is ironical to later eyes is that at this stage nobody proposed a combination which would have put the 'Egyptian Church Order' first in this line. Instead, it was unanimously judged to be descended from one or other of the documents to which it had close similarity. It was not until 1906 that Eduard von der Goltz suggested that this anonymous text might in reality be a genuine work by Hippolytus of Rome, the *Apostolic Tradition*, previously believed to have been lost.[14] This theory was taken up and elaborated, first by Eduard Schwartz in 1910, and then quite independently and much more fully by R. H. Connolly in 1916.[15] Although a few scholars still entertain doubts about its attribution to Hippolytus or its Roman origin

[11] *Die Canones Hippolyti*, Texte und Untersuchungen 6/4, Berlin 1891.

[12] F. X. Funk, *Die apostolischen Konstitutionen, eine litterar-historische Untersuchung*, Rottenburg 1891 = Frankfurt 1970.

[13] *The Ministry of Grace* (London 1901), pp. 18–21. A similar view was taken by A. J. Maclean, *The Ancient Church Orders* (Cambridge 1910), pp. 141–73.

[14] 'Unbekannte Fragmente altchristlicher Gemeindeordnungen', *Sitzungsberichte der Preussischen Akademie der Wissenschaften* (1906), pp. 141–57.

[15] Eduard Schwartz, *Über die pseudoapostolischen Kirchenordnungen*, Strasbourg 1910; R. H. Connolly, *The So-called Egyptian Church Order and Derived Documents*, Cambridge 1916 = 1967.

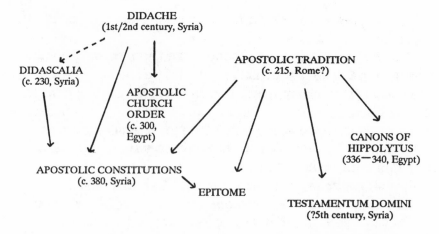

TABLE 2: THE RELATIONSHIP BETWEEN THE INDIVIDUAL CHURCH ORDERS

(about which more will be said later), it is now universally accepted that this document is the original source of the other church orders from which it was formerly presumed to be derived.

Thus, as can be seen from Table 2, a family tree can now be established for the whole collection of church orders with a high degree of certitude. Because they claim to be apostolic, they reveal neither the names of their true authors nor the place and date of their real origin, and hence such questions usually have to be answered largely on the basis of the internal evidence of the documents themselves.

The individual documents
1. The Didache
The first part of this church order (chs 1–6) is usually known as the 'Two Ways' because it presents moral teaching in the form of the way of life and the way of death. Then follow brief instructions about baptism (7),[16] the practices of twice-weekly fasting (on Wednesdays and Fridays) and thrice-daily prayer (8),[17] forms of prayer for use at either an agape or a eucharist (9–10),[18] the treatment of 'apostles and prophets' (11–13), the

[16] See below, p. 170.
[17] For these, see below, pp. 190, 194.
[18] For this heavily debated issue, see below, pp. 132ff.

celebration of the eucharist 'on the Lord's Day of the Lord' (14),[19] and the appointment of bishops and deacons (15).[20] It concludes with an admonition to eschatological vigilance (16).

At first the only witness to the original was the Greek text discovered by Bryennios, but subsequently other Greek fragments were discovered at Oxyrhynchus and also parts of translations into Ethiopic and Coptic (although whether the latter is translated directly from the Greek or from Syriac is uncertain). A complete translation into Georgian has also been found, but scholars are divided over its antiquity: while the manuscript itself dates only from the nineteenth century, some think the translation may have been made in the fifth century. Also of assistance in determining the reading of the original is the use of the *Didache* in the *Apostolic Church Order* and in *Apostolic Constitutions* 7.[21] The most recent edition of the text is by Willy Rordorf and André Tuilier.[22]

Although the *Didache* is generally accepted as having originated in Syria, estimates of its date have varied widely. Some place it in the second century,[23] others assign it to the first century, and some argue that it antedates many of the New

[19] C. W. Dugmore, 'The Lord's Day and Easter', in *Neutestamentica et Patristica* (Festschrift for Oscar Cullmann, Supplements to Novum Testamentum 6, Leiden 1962), pp. 272–81, thought that this was a reference to Easter, but Rordorf (*Sunday*, pp. 209–10) rightly denied this and affirmed that it was speaking of Sunday.

[20] Among recent studies of the question of ministry within the *Didache* are André de Halleux, 'Les ministères dans la Didachè', *Irénikon* 53 (1980), pp. 5–29; Hermann A. Stempel, 'Der Lehrer in der "Lehre der zwolf Apostel" ', *Vigiliae Christianae* 34 (1980), pp. 209–17.

[21] Some scholars have thought that the latter may give evidence of a better text than the Bryennios ms. at some points. For example, they would accept as part of the original the prayer over *myron* ('ointment') found both in the Coptic version and in *Apostolic Constitutions* 7: see below, p. 170.

[22] *La doctrine des douze apôtres*, SC 248, 1978 (bibliography of secondary literature, pp. 129–35). See also W. Rordorf, 'Une nouvelle édition de la Didachè (problèmes exégetiques, historiques et théologiques)', *SP* 15 (1984), pp. 26–30; A. Tuilier, 'Une nouvelle édition de la Didachè (problèmes de méthode et de critique textuelle)', *SP* 15 (1984), pp. 31–6. For an English translation of the text, see R. A. Kraft, *The Apostolic Fathers 3: The Didache and Barnabas*, New York 1965.

[23] See, for example, R. H. Connolly, 'Agape and Eucharist in the Didache', *Downside Review* 55 (1937), pp. 477–89.

Testament writings. Perhaps the most extreme claim in this direction was that made by Joan Hazelden Walker, who asserted that the *Didache* reflects a less sophisticated eucharistic theology than that of the canonical Gospels, and so must have been composed before they were written.[24] But her conclusion is flawed, since it cannot be assumed that Christianity developed at the same speed in every place, and hence a more primitive theology does not necessarily mean an earlier date.[25]

Obviously, the literary dependence of the *Didache* on other early Christian writings could be a significant point in establishing its date, but once again there has not been any scholarly consensus as to which, if any, of the New Testament books may have been known to the author.[26] Some scholars have argued that the author of the *Didache* knew the Fourth Gospel, chiefly on the basis of the belief that the word *klasma* ('broken bread') in *Didache* 9.4 was dependent on John 6.3 and 11.52. This theory was strongly challenged by Arthur Vööbus, who argued that the other versions of the document clearly revealed that the original reading of *Didache* 9.4 was *artos* ('bread') and not *klasma*, and that in any case the sequence of ideas in the *Didache* was very different from those in John's Gospel. He also believed that its trinitarian baptismal formula was a later addition to the text, the original being simply baptism into the name of the Lord.[27]

[24] 'A pre-Marcan Dating for the Didache: Further Thoughts of a Liturgist', *Studia Biblica 1978* III (Sheffield 1980), pp. 403−11.

[25] The same criticisms can be levelled against Enrico Mazza, 'Didachè IX−X: elementi per una interpretazione eucaristica', *EL* 92 (1978), pp. 393−419; 'L'Eucaristia di 1 Corinzi 10, 16−17 in rapporto a Didachè 9−10', *EL* 100 (1986), pp. 193−223, who postulates an extremely early date for the prayer material in *Didache* 9−10.

[26] Recent studies include John M. Court, 'The Didache and St Matthew's Gospel', *SJT* 34 (1981), pp. 109−20; John S. Kloppenborg, 'Didache 16.6−8 and special Matthean tradition', *ZNW* 70 (1979), pp. 54−67.

[27] *Liturgical Traditions in the Didache* (Stockholm 1968), pp. 35−9, 137−57; 'Regarding the Background of the Liturgical Traditions in the Didache: The Question of the Literary Relation between Didache ix, 4 and the Fourth Gospel', *Vigiliae Christianae* 23 (1969), pp. 81−7. Jean Magne, 'Klasma, sperma, poimnion. Le voeu pour la rassemblement de Didachè ix, 4', in *Mélanges d'histoire des religions offerts à Henri-Charles Puech* (Paris 1974), pp. 197−208, went further and proposed that *Didache* 9.4 originally spoke of sheep, and only later was this changed, first to corn, and then to bread.

2. Didascalia Apostolorum

This church order is obviously modelled on the *Didache*, and begins with admonitions concerning the Christian life (1−3). It continues with a lengthy section on the qualifications, conduct, and duties of a bishop (4−11). Here, and at other points, the possibility of the remission of serious post-baptismal sins after a period of penance is presupposed, including adultery and apostasy: this contrasts with the more rigorist approach which tended to be taken in the West at this period. The physical disposition of bishop, presbyters, deacons, lay men, lay women, and children in the church building is dealt with next (12), and the people are exhorted to be constant in their attendance at church, and to avoid heretical assemblies and pagan festivities (13). Then follow injunctions concerning widows (14−15), male and female deacons (16), and the adoption of orphans (17). Bishops and deacons are forbidden to accept alms from those leading evil lives or following unacceptable occupations (18), and all Christians are exhorted to care for those who are imprisoned for the faith, and to be ready to face persecution and death themselves, comforted by the hope of the resurrection (19−20). Every Wednesday and Friday in the year, and the six days prior to Easter, are to be observed as days of fasting (21), and the treatise then moves on to refer to the upbringing of children (22), and to denounce heresy and schism (23). Chapters 24 and 25 purport to describe the composition of the work by the Apostles as a defence against heresy, and the final lengthy chapter (26) argues strongly for the freedom of Christians from the ritual legislation of the Old Testament.

With the exception of a small fragment of ch. 15 and a reworked form of the document in *Apostolic Constitutions* 1−6, the original Greek has been lost, and our main knowledge of the text therefore has to rest on two early translations, one into Latin and the other into Syriac. The Latin is known only from the Verona palimpsest, which preserves about two-fifths of the work. The Syriac, which thus constitutes the sole witness to the complete text, is preserved wholly or partially in a number of manuscripts, the oldest of which dates from the eighth century. The fourth century has been proposed as a possible date for this translation, but certain features of it might suggest a somewhat later period.[28] Arabic and Ethiopic versions of the *Didascalia* are dependent on *Apostolic Constitutions* 1–6.

The *Didascalia* was almost certainly composed in North Syria during the first half of the third century, probably *c.* 230. From the prominence that it gives to the episcopate, it has been concluded that its author may himself have been a bishop, and because he exhibits some medical knowledge, some have supposed that he may also have been a physician. Claims sometimes made that he was a convert from Judaism seem to have little justification, as interest in the relationship between Christianity and the Old Testament Law, which figures in this church order, was something which concerned other Christians too.

3. Apostolic Church Order

This small treatise was given this name when it was first published in 1843 by J. W. Bickell, though it has also received other appellations, among them 'The Ecclesiastical Constitution of the Apostles'. The title which appears in the Greek text is 'The instructions through Clement and ecclesiastical canons of the holy Apostles'. After a short introduction (1–4), the first half (5–14) is an adaptation of *Didache* 1–4, and the second half (15–30) issues brief regulations for the appointment of bishops, presbyters, readers, deacons, and widows, and directives concerning the duties of deacons, lay men, and lay women.[29] Only one manuscript, of the twelfth century, contains the entire text of the Greek original, though an excerpt from the first part is extant in four other codices, and there are Latin, Syriac, Sahidic, Bohairic, Arabic, and Ethiopic translations. It appears to have

[28] Latest edition, with English translation: Arthur Vööbus, *The Didascalia Apostolorum in Syriac*, Corpus Scriptorum Christianorum Orientalium 401, 402, 407, 408; Scriptores Syri 175, 176, 179, 180, Louvain 1979; English extracts in Sebastian Brock & Michael Vasey, *The Liturgical Portions of the Didascalia*, GLS 29, 1982; bibliographies of secondary literature in B. Altaner, *Patrologie* (9th edn, Freiburg 1978), pp. 85, 558; Paul F. Bradshaw, 'Kirchenordnungen I: Altkirchliche', *Theologische Realenzykopädie* 18 (Berlin 1989), p. 666.

[29] There is no recent edition, and the only recent studies are by Alexandre Faivre, 'Le texte grec de la Constitution ecclésiastique des apôtres 16–20 et ses sources', *RevSR* 55 (1981), pp. 31–42; and Arthur Vööbus, 'Die Entdeckung der alteste Urkunde für die syrische Ubersetzung der Apostolische Kirchenordnung', *Oriens Christianus* 63 (1979), pp. 37–40. For older editions and studies, see Bradshaw, 'Kirchenordnungen', pp. 666–7.

been written in Egypt, although some scholars would assign it to Syria, and in its final form it dates very probably from the end of the third century.

4. *Apostolic Tradition*

After a very brief prologue this church order begins with directions for the ordinations of a bishop, presbyter, and deacon, and provides an ordination-prayer for each one. In the case of the episcopal ordination it also sets out a specimen form of eucharistic prayer for the new bishop to use, although permitting him to substitute his own words if he wishes. This prayer consists of an opening dialogue, extensive thanksgiving for the work of Christ, leading into the narrative of institution and an anamnesis/offering section ('Remembering, therefore, his death and resurrection, we offer to you the bread and the cup'), a brief thanksgiving for having made us worthy, a petition for the sending of the Holy Spirit on the oblation (epiclesis), and a supplication for the communicants, ending with a doxology. The church order then proceeds to the appointment of widows, readers, virgins, subdeacons, and those with the gift of healing. Lengthy instructions follow concerning the process of Christian initiation, beginning with the procedure for admission to the catechumenate and a list of occupations forbidden to prospective Christians, and continuing with the baptismal rite itself, which is intended for both adults and children and leads into the first communion of the neophytes. The final part of the work deals with other liturgical matters, among them the conduct of an agape, the observance of a two-day fast before Easter, the times of daily prayer and instruction in the word, and the use of the sign of the cross.

Since a Greek text of the work has not survived, except in the form of a few isolated fragments, attempts have been made to reconstruct the original — principally by Gregory Dix and subsequently by Bernard Botte[30] — from the various extant transla-

---

[30] Gregory Dix, *The Treatise on the Apostolic Tradition of St Hippolytus*, London 1937, 2nd edn 1968 with preface and corrections by Henry Chadwick; Bernard Botte, *La Tradition apostolique de saint Hippolyte*, Münster 1963, 4th edn 1972. See also the edition by G. J. Cuming, *Hippolytus. A Text for Students*, GLS 8, 1976, and the massive documentation in J. M. Hanssens, *La Liturgie d'Hippolyte* I (Rome 1959, 2nd edn 1965), II (Rome 1970).

tions (which differ considerably from one another) and from the adaptations made of it in the other church orders. It is commonly assumed that these reconstructions present us — at least substantially — with what the author originally wrote. This assumption, however, is very much open to question, and at least some scholars have argued that parts of the original work may have been re-touched by later hands in order to bring it into line with current doctrine and practice.[31] Hence the task of establishing the original is by no means straightforward and there remains considerable uncertainty over the true reading of many parts of the text.

There are further doubts concerning its place of origin and authorship. The majority of scholars have supported the position that it originates from Rome and is the genuine work of Hippolytus, written *c.* 215, but this is far from sure.[32] The internal evidence of the document itself is of little help in settling the question. No existing manuscript bears a title for the work, and it was really the attribution to Hippolytus of two of the derived church orders, the *Epitome* of *Apostolic Constitutions* 8 and the *Canons of Hippolytus*, which encouraged the identification of this document with that author. The liturgical prescriptions of the text are certainly consistent with the traditional provenance, but are also equally consistent with other possible alternatives — Alexandria and even Syria having been suggested.[33] Apart

[31] See A. F. Walls, 'The Latin Version of Hippolytus' Apostolic Tradition', *SP* 3 (1961), pp. 155—62. With regard to the ordination rites, see the works cited in Bradshaw, *Ordination Rites of the Ancient Churches of East and West*, ch. 1, n. 3; with regard to the eucharistic prayer, see below, pp. 143—4; with regard to the post-baptismal ceremonies, see below, pp. 175—8; and with regard to the hours of daily prayer, see below, pp. 190—1.

[32] An extensive bibliography of secondary literature up to 1972 in chronological order is provided by Jean Magne, *Tradition apostolique sur les charismes et Diataxeis des saints Apôtres* (Paris 1975), pp. 193—225. See also Altaner, *Patrologie*, pp. 82—4, 557—8; Bradshaw, 'Kirchenordnungen', p. 668; Johannes Quasten, *Patrology* II (Utrecht 1953), pp. 180—94. The most recent case against Hippolytean authorship is presented by Marcel Metzger, 'Nouvelles perspectives pour la prétendue *Tradition apostolique*', *Ecclesia Orans* 5 (1988), pp. 241—59.

[33] Hanssens in *La Liturgie d'Hippolyte* championed the thesis that Hippolytus came to Rome from Alexandria, bringing with him the liturgy of his own country.

from the baptismal interrogations, the double post-baptismal unction, and the prayer over the oil for the sick,[34] there are no close parallels with the later Roman liturgy, and the document subsequently had much more influence in the East than in the West.[35]

The case for Rome rests mainly upon the supposition of Hippolytean authorship, and the case for his authorship in turn rests mainly upon the document's identification with an otherwise unknown treatise, the *Apostolic Tradition*, apparently included in a list of the works of Hippolytus inscribed on the base of a statue discovered in Rome in 1551. Not only does the statue itself have nearly as strange and complicated a history as the document,[36] but it is not entirely clear whether these lines of the inscription (*Peri Charismaton/Apostolike Paradosis*: 'Of Charisms/Apostolic Tradition') refer to one work or to two (one called 'Of Charisms' and the other 'Apostolic Tradition'),[37] nor exactly which Hippolytus is intended — a priest martyred after 235 and commemorated on 13 August, or the bishop of Portus Romanus, martyred after 253 and commemorated on 22 August, or some other person altogether.[38]

[34] See Eric Segelberg, 'The Benedictio Olei in the Apostolic Tradition of Hippolytus', *Oriens Christianus* 48 (1964), pp. 268—81.

[35] But for its later influence on ordination in the West, see below, n. 70.

[36] Recent research has revealed that it was in origin not a representation of Hippolytus at all but a female figure, which was restored in the sixteenth century as a male bishop because of the list of works inscribed on its base, using parts taken from other statues. See Margherita Guarducci, 'La statua di "Sant'Ippolito" ', in *Ricerche su Ippolito* (Studia Ephemeridis 'Augustinianum' 13, Rome 1977), pp. 17—30. For further details concerning the statue and inscription, see Hanssens, *La Liturgie d'Hippolyte* I, pp. 217—31.

[37] Magne in *Tradition apostolique* espoused the former view, that 'Apostolic Tradition on Charisms' was the title of a single work by Hippolytus, but he argued that this document was not it. Instead he thought that *Apostolic Constitutions* 8.1—2 contained the genuine work by Hippolytus. See also Magne, 'Un extrait de la "Tradition apostolique sur les charismes" d'Hippolyte sous les gloses du Constituteur, et les "Diataxeis des saints Apôtres" ', in F. Paschke, ed., *Uberlieferungsgeschichtliche Untersuchungen* (Berlin 1981), pp. 399—402. Botte, 'Le traité des charismes dans les Constitutions apostoliques', *SP* 12 (1975), pp. 83—6, responded with the assertion that this section of *Apostolic Constitutions* was an adaptation by its compiler of a treatise about signs and miracles which was not the work of Hippolytus.

[38] See the extensive discussion in Hanssens, *La Liturgie d'Hippolyte* I, pp. 283—340.

This church order therefore deserves to be treated with greater circumspection than has generally been the case, and one ought not automatically to assume that it provides reliable information about the life and liturgical activity of the church in Rome in the early third century.

5. Canons of Hippolytus

Although attention had been drawn as early as the seventeenth century to this Arabic collection of thirty-eight canons with a concluding sermon, Haneberg's 1870 edition was the first published text, and it was from this that Achelis made his 1891 translation into Latin, containing many doubtful conjectures. As indicated above, Achelis accepted the attribution to Hippolytus as genuine and arrived at the conclusion that this was the original from which all the other church orders containing similar material were derived. As a consequence, interest was aroused in the document among liturgical scholars, but after the researches of Schwartz and Connolly had demonstrated that it was in reality merely a derivative of the *Apostolic Tradition*, it came to be considered as the latest of the group of related church orders, dating from the fifth or sixth century, and interest in it declined.

However, in 1956 Bernard Botte suggested that it had been composed in Egypt around the middle of the fourth century,[39] and in 1966 René-Georges Coquin, in the first and only proper critical edition of the text, followed up and amplified Botte's arguments, proposing on the basis of internal evidence a date between 336 and 340 for the work.[40] This makes it not the latest but the earliest known derivative of the *Apostolic Tradition*. It thus warrants more attention than it has hitherto received, both because it constitutes an important source for our knowledge of early fourth-century Egyptian church life, about which we have relatively little other evidence, and because it may actually have

[39] 'L'origine des Canons d'Hippolyte', in *Mélanges en l'honneur de Mgr Michel Andrieu* (Strasbourg 1956), pp. 53—63.

[40] *Les Canons d'Hippolyte*, PO 31/2, 1966; English translation of the text based on this edition in Paul F. Bradshaw, *The Canons of Hippolytus*, A/GLS 2, 1987.

something to contribute to the reconstruction of the original text of the *Apostolic Tradition*. Although the author seems to have freely paraphrased, supplemented, and adapted that source in the light of his own ecclesiastical situation and liturgical tradition, yet at least a few of these apparent drastic recastings may not be that at all, but rather points at which he alone has retained primitive readings which have been revised by the other later witnesses to the text.

Although it is now extant only in Arabic, there is general agreement that this text is derived from a lost Coptic version, which was in turn a translation of an original Greek text. Coquin considered that it had been written by a priest rather than a bishop—though his arguments are not totally convincing[41]—and that its place of composition was Alexandria: this latter view has since been challenged by Heinzgerd Brakmann, who has argued instead that it originates from elsewhere in northern Egypt.[42]

6. Apostolic Constitutions

This is a composite work, comprising the *Didascalia* (forming books 1–6 of the work), the *Didache* (book 7), and the *Apostolic Tradition* together with some other material (book 8)—all of the sources having been extensively reworked in the process. It is generally agreed that it was written in Syria, and probably in Antioch, between 375 and 380. It is unlikely to be much earlier than that, because it includes a reference to the feast of Christmas, which was only just beginning to make an appearance in eastern churches, and it is unlikely to be much later, because its doctrine of the Holy Spirit is incompatible with the definition agreed at the Council of Constantinople in 381. The identity and theological position of the compiler, on the other hand, have been long debated. Indeed, the orthodoxy of the document became suspect at an early date, and it was thought by the Trullan Synod (691–2) that heretics must have falsified the original apostolic work. Photius, the patriarch of Constantinople (d. 891),

---

[41] See Bradshaw, *The Canons of Hippolytus*, p. 8.

[42] 'Alexandreia und die Kanones des Hippolyt', *Jahrbuch für Antike und Christentum* 22 (1979), pp. 139–49.

criticized the whole compilation for its Arianism, although sub-sequently opinion was divided over this question.

Among modern scholars, Funk in his 1905 edition of the text (which has generally been treated as definitive) tended to play down the heterodoxy of the work by preferring orthodox variant readings wherever possible and by claiming that any suspect for-mulae came from the compiler's source and thus antedated the Arian controversy.[43] C. H. Turner criticized Funk's textual methods and argued strongly for an Arian compiler,[44] and Bernard Capelle later demonstrated that the text of the *Gloria in Excelsis* found in the *Apostolic Constitutions* was not the original form of the hymn, as had been thought, but that the compiler had changed a hymn addressed to Christ into one addressed to the Father.[45] Because of similarities of language with the longer recension of the letter of Ignatius of Antioch, scholars have usually concluded that the compiler of the *Apostolic Constitutions*, whatever his theological stance, was also the interpolator of these letters.[46]

The most recent contributions to the authorship debate are by Georg Wagner (who drew linguistic parallels with the writ-ings of Eunomius),[47] by Dieter Hageborn (who attributed the composition to an obscure bishop named Julian by a comparison of literary parallels),[48] and by Marcel Metzger, who built upon Hageborn's suggestion and concluded that, although Julian's commentary on Job is much more explicitly Arian than the more moderate subordinationism of the *Apostolic Constitutions*, this difference could be explained by the fact that the latter was a

---

[43] *Didascalia et Constitutiones Apostolorum*, Paderborn 1905 = 1979; English translation based on this edition by James Donaldson, *Constitutions of the Holy Apostles* (Edinburgh 1886/New York 1926), pp. 387−505.

[44] 'A Primitive Edition of the Apostolic Constitutions and Canons', *JTS* 15 (1913), pp. 53−65; 'Notes on the Apostolic Constitutions', *JTS* 16 (1914), pp. 54−61, 523−38; 21 (1920), pp. 160−8.

[45] 'Le texte du "gloria in exclesis" ', *Revue d'histoire ecclésiastique* 44 (1949), pp. 439−57.

[46] Bibliography of secondary literature in Altaner, *Patrologie*, p. 256.

[47] 'Zur Herfunkt der apostolischen Konstitutionen', in *Mélanges liturgiques offerts au R. P. Dom Bernard Botte OSB* (Louvain 1972), pp. 525−37.

[48] *Der Hiobkommentar des Arianers Julian* (Berlin 1973), pp. XXXVII−LVII.

liturgical work and so drew upon traditional material. Metzger did not think, however, that its compiler could be considered a strict Arian.[49] He has also recently published a new edition of the text, making use of a wider range of manuscripts and free from the orthodox bias of Funk's edition.[50]

The *Epitome* or 'Constitutions of the Holy Apostles through Hippolytus' seems to be a series of extracts from *Apostolic Constitutions* 8 (1−2, 4−5, 16−28, 30−4, 42−6),[51] but at two points —the prayer for the ordination of a bishop and the instructions for appointing a reader—it reproduces what appears to be the original Greek of the *Apostolic Tradition* in preference to the expanded version from the *Apostolic Constitutions*. Thus, whether in origin this was a first draft of *Apostolic Constitutions* 8 or —as seems more likely—a later condensation of it, it seems certain that the editor must also have had access to the *Apostolic Tradition* itself.

7. *Testamentum Domini*

This church order is a much enlarged version of the *Apostolic Tradition*, set within the context of instructions given by Jesus himself to his disciples before his ascension, and beginning with an apocalytic discourse. The author displays a somewhat perverse fidelity to his source: although he has retained much of its wording, he has interpolated so many words and phrases of his own that it frequently has an entirely different appearance and sense from the original. Thus all the various prayers are retained, but in a much expanded form, and others are added.

The original Greek text is lost, and reliance has usually been placed on the Syriac version published by Rahmani,[52] but here

[49] 'La théologie des Constitutions apostoliques par Clement', *RevSR* 57 (1983), pp. 29−49, 112−22, 169−94, 273−94.

[50] *Les Constitutions apostoliques*, SC 320, 329, 336, 1985−7; partial English translation based on this edition in W. Jardine Grisbrooke, *The Liturgical Portions of the Apostolic Constitutions: A Text for Students*, A/GLS 13−14, 1990.

[51] Text in Funk, *Didascalia et Constitutiones Apostolorum* II, pp. 72−96. For further details, see Botte, *Tradition apostolique*, pp. XXV−XXVI; Hanssens, *La Liturgie d'Hippolyte* I, pp. 78−9.

[52] English translation by James Cooper & A. J. Maclean, *The Testament of Our Lord Translated into English from the Syriac*, Edinburgh 1902; partial English translation and bibliography of secondary literature in Grant Sperry-White, *The Testamentum Domini: A Text for Students*, A/GLS 19, 1991.

there are two problems. First, his edition was based on only one family of manuscripts, while a different manuscript tradition seems to underlie the text of the *Testamentum Domini* found in the West Syrian Synodicon,[53] which may offer indications of better readings at some points. Second, even if the earliest text of the Syriac can be established, it is not certain that it always accurately reproduced the original Greek, especially as there are also extant Arabic and Ethiopic versions of the document with significantly different readings. These are both probably dependent upon a lost Coptic translation. Until recently any comparison with these versions was extremely problematic, as neither had ever been published, but Robert Beylot has now produced a critical edition of the Ethiopic,[54] which goes some way to meet the difficulty, though the quality of his work has been questioned.[55] Since both these versions are later than the Syriac, many differences can be dismissed as the emendations — intentional and unintentional — of translators and copyists, but at least at some points they may retain older readings. The doxologies in the Ethiopic, for example, have a much simpler — and hence seemingly more primitive — form than those in the Syriac.[56]

Most scholars believe that the work originates from Syria, though Asia Minor and Egypt have also been suggested, and it has usually been regarded as the last of the church orders to have been written, dating most probably from the fifth century. Grant Sperry-White, however, has recently proposed its origin as being in the second half of the fourth century.[57]

[53] Arthur Vööbus, ed., *The Synodicon in the West Syrian Tradition*, Corpus Scriptorum Christianorum Orientalium 367, 368; Scriptores Syri 161, 162, Louvain 1975. This is based on MS. 8/11 of the Syrian Orthodox Patriarchate of Damascus, 1204 C.E.

[54] *Le Testamentum Domini éthiopien*, Louvain 1984.

[55] See the review by the late Roger Cowley in the *Journal of Semitic Studies* 31 (1986), pp. 292−5.

[56] Compare the Syriac 'to you be praise and to your only-begotten Son our Lord Jesus Christ and to the Holy Spirit honorable and worshipped and life-giving and consubstantial with you, now and before all worlds and to the generation of generations and to the ages of ages' (Rahmani, p. 99) with the Ethiopic 'Glory to the Father, to the Son, and to the Holy Spirit, now and always and to the ages of ages' (Beylot, p. 206).

[57] *The Testamentum Domini*, p. 6.

The collections

That it has been possible to put these particular pieces together in what appears to be their correct order should not fool us into thinking that the whole church-order puzzle has been solved. It would be rather like thinking that once the literary relationship between Matthew, Mark, and Luke had been established, no further critical work on the synoptic Gospels was necessary. Other questions still remain with regard to the church-order literature, and it is to these that we now turn.

Until relatively recently no attention was paid to the fact that the majority of the church orders were known to us not as individual documents at all but only as part of larger collections of such material. Even now only two scholars in the last thirty years, Bernard Botte and J. M. Hanssens, have tried to explore the nature of that interrelationship. As can be seen from Table 3, there are four such collections:

(a) the *Apostolic Constitutions*;

(b) a Latin translation of three Greek works thought to have been made about the same time as the *Apostolic Constitutions*, but known to us only through one manuscript, a fifth-century palimpsest;[58]

(c) the collection known as the Alexandrine Sinodos, or the Clementine Heptateuch, found in several different language versions — in the two dialects of Coptic (Sahidic and Bohairic), in Arabic, and in Ethiopic — of which the Sahidic is the oldest and the others all in one way or another ultimately depend on it;

(d) what is known as the Clementine Octateuch, which is found in different forms in two different languages, Syriac and Arabic, neither of which has yet ever been published in full. It consists of the *Testamentum Domini*, followed by the material included in the Alexandrine Sinodos, except that the Syriac version differs from the Arabic in omitting the text of the *Apostolic Tradition* of Hippolytus, and consequently dividing the *Testamentum Domini* into two books in order to retain the eightfold form.

---

[58] Most recent edition by Erik Tidner, *Didascaliae apostolorum Canonum ecclesiasticorum Traditionis apostolicae versiones Latinae*, Texte und Untersuchungen 75, Berlin 1963.

APOSTOLIC CONSTITUTIONS (Greek)		
Books 1—6:	Book 7:	Book 8:
Didascalia	Didache	Apostolic Tradition
VERONA PALIMPSEST LV (53) (Latin)		
Didascalia	Apostolic Church Order	Apostolic Tradition

ALEXANDRINE SINODOS (Sahidic, Bohairic, Arabic, Ethiopic)			
	Apostolic Church Order	Apostolic Tradition	Apostolic Constitutions Book 8
CLEMENTINE OCTATEUCH (Syriac)			
Testamentum Domini (in 2 books)	Apostolic Church Order		Apostolic Constitutions Book 8
CLEMENTINE OCTATEUCH (Arabic)			
Testamentum Domini	Apostolic Church Order	Apostolic Tradition	Apostolic Constitutions Book 8

TABLE 3: THE COLLECTIONS OF CHURCH ORDERS

What is particularly interesting about these collections is that the various church orders tend to appear in them in the same sequence. Thus we have the *Didascalia*, the *Didache*, and the *Apostolic Tradition* in the *Apostolic Constitutions*; and the *Didascalia*, the *Apostolic Church Order* (which we saw earlier itself incorporates part of the *Didache*), and the *Apostolic Tradition* in the Latin palimpsest. The Alexandrine Sinodos retains the latter two works in the same order as in the Latin translation, but appends to them another version of *Apostolic Constitutions* 8. The same is true of the Octateuch, though here the

Testamentum Domini is prefixed. It appears impossible to dismiss all these similarities as merely coincidental, and it seems that there is a literary relationship between the collections as well as between the individual church orders.

One simple answer — that there is direct dependency — must be ruled out. The Latin translation is certainly not derived from the *Apostolic Constitutions*, nor is the latter a re-translation back into Greek from the Latin: its Greek is too close to that of the sources — where we can check it — for such an idea to be conceivable, and in any case, one has the *Didache* and the other the *Apostolic Church Order* as its middle document. It is equally difficult to imagine that the Sahidic version of the Sinodos obtained its material from anywhere except a Greek source, and the same is true of the Syriac version of the Octateuch: indeed the colophon attached to the *Testamentum Domini* in this collection explicitly affirms that it at least was translated from Greek into Syriac by James of Edessa in the seventh century.

Thus, we need to seek some other solution to their similarities. Botte proposed the existence of an early Greek 'tripartite collection', subsequently lost, which consisted of the *Didascalia*, the *Apostolic Church Order*, and the *Apostolic Tradition* — in that order.[59] This would mean that the Latin collection was a translation of that work, while the author of the *Apostolic Constitutions* would have been influenced by it with regard to his order, but for some reason preferred to replace the *Apostolic Church Order* with the *Didache*, since the two were similar to one another.

Botte's theory, however, still leaves a number of difficulties. It suffices to explain the relationship between two of the collections, but is not really adequate when it comes to the other two. If the author of the Sinodos had a triple collection in front of him, why should he discard the first of its three works but retain the other two? Botte suggested that it may have been because the *Didascalia* did not lend itself as easily as the others to the division into separate canons which we find in this collection. But, in any case, why should both the Sinodos and the Octateuch

[59] 'Les plus anciennes collections canoniques', *L'Orient syrien* 5 (1960), pp. 331—49.

have chosen to add to this supposed triple collection a version of *Apostolic Constitutions* 8? That cannot surely be put down to coincidence, especially as there is nothing to suggest that this particular extract ever circulated on its own. Moreover, at the very least we seem obliged to posit the existence of an earlier, Greek form of the Octateuch, from which both our present versions, the Syriac and the Arabic, are ultimately descended. The Arabic cannot be descended directly from the Syriac, because the Syriac lacks the *Apostolic Tradition* (presumably omitted because it was so similar to the material in the *Testamentum Domini*), and the Syriac was obviously aware of a previous eightfold form of its material, since it divided the *Testamentum Domini* into two in order to retain that structure after the omission the *Apostolic Tradition*.

It looks, therefore, as though we are forced to take seriously something like the more complicated theory put forward by Hanssens.[60] He held that originally only the *Apostolic Church Order* and the *Apostolic Tradition* circulated together in the fourth century. From this combination developed two further collections: one comprising the *Didascalia*, the *Apostolic Church Order*, and the *Apostolic Tradition*, from which the *Apostolic Constitutions* and the Latin translation were derived; the other made up of the *Apostolic Church Order*, the *Apostolic Tradition*, and a version of *Apostolic Constitutions* 8. This latter document would thus have constituted the original Greek collection of which the Alexandrine Sinodos was a translation; and our conjectured Greek Octateuch would then have been an expanded form of this, prefixed by the *Testamentum Domini*, since the supposed words of Jesus himself would naturally be placed before, and not after, what were then taken to be injunctions of the apostles.

Although the outlines of the process of transmission and aggregation of the various documents may thus be discerned, many questions of detail still remain unanswered. To give just one example, how are we to account for the existence of an Ethiopic version of the *Testamentum Domini*? Was it derived from our conjectured Sahidic Octateuch, and if so, why were the

---

[60] *La Liturgie d'Hippolyte* I, pp. 171ff.

rest of its contents not translated as well? Was it perhaps because they already existed in the Ethiopic version of the Sinodos, or does the Ethiopic *Testamentum* emerge by some other route?

'Living literature'

Even if we can begin to see *how* the various church orders were transmitted and combined, our puzzle is still far from complete. We may have been able to account for the process at a physical level, but that does not explain *why* it ever happened at all. Why should anyone take the time and trouble repeatedly to copy out these texts, translate and revise them, and combine them with others? What lies behind this gigantic spider's web?

Strange though it may seem, this is not a question which those who have made use of the documents as historical source-material have often stopped to ask. They have simply plundered what they wanted to fit the picture of the early Church that they were attempting to paint, without asking themselves why it ever came to be there in the first place, and what this might have to say about its value as historical evidence.

As suggested in the previous chapter, documents dealing with liturgical matters are particularly prone to editorial corrections so as to give authoritative status to current worship practices.[61] This development can be seen not only between the individual church orders in the series, as each one revised its predecessor, but also in the process of the copying of manuscripts, the translation from one language to another, and even the aggregation into collected works. At each step along the way, the aim was not simply to reproduce exactly the last example of the material but to amend and update it. Thus, these texts are not always copies or translations in the sense in which we usually mean those words, but are instead really versions of the original, and frequently differ markedly from one another. Prayer-texts may be modified, for example, or even entirely omitted, if they do not resemble the prayers with which the copyists or translators were familiar; and additional prayer-material from their own tradition may be inserted among that from the source-document.

[61] See above, pp. 73—4.

The church orders, therefore, should not be treated in the same way as other ancient works. When we encounter variant readings between different manuscript traditions, we are not always looking at accidental dislocation and copyists' errors. We are frequently seeing deliberate emendations designed to alter the sense of the text. This of course makes the task of restoring the original more difficult than it is in other types of literature. But we must also keep in mind that, in looking at this material, the original is not the only important historical source: we should be equally interested in the changes which were made by the first, second, and even third translators, as indicating something about the world in which each lived, about what had changed and what had remained the same in the ongoing life of the Church, about the matters which were of vital importance to each translator's generation and those issues which had now ceased to be of concern.

Perhaps the best way of thinking of this material is as 'living literature',[62] constantly growing, changing, and evolving as it moves from generation to generation, or from one ecclesiastical tradition to another, with each stage, and not just the first, offering valuable source-material for historical study. Indeed, we may even be mistaken in what we regard as the beginning of the process, as the original documents in the series. If we may vary the metaphor a little, and look upon the literature as a great river which is made up of a number of smaller tributaries, what we consider the sources of the streams may perhaps not be where the water first begins at all, but only where it bursts forth into our view from beneath the ground — another stage in its long journey and not the point at which it is formed.

Sources

There are certainly signs which suggest that at least some of the documents are made up of a number of different strata of material. They may have been drawing upon older sources which are otherwise unknown to us, or may themselves have gone through a number of different editions, as it were, being amplified and revised in response to changing situations, before

---

[62] See above, p. 74.

attaining the form which we mistakenly treat as 'the original text'.

For example, it is acknowledged that the *Apostolic Constitutions* probably made use of other sources besides the works known to us, especially in book 7, where prayer-texts of a strongly Jewish character are found.[63] It has also long been recognized that not only is the first half of the *Apostolic Church Order* dependent upon the first part of the *Didache* (or some earlier form of it), but part of the second half appears to imply a very primitive stage of the evolution of the Christian ministry and does not seem entirely consistent with what is written elsewhere in the document. Thus, this too may well be a composite work bringing together a number of earlier written sources.[64]

Most scholars now subscribe to the view that the *Didache* also evolved by stages, but are divided over the number of redactions, and the relative antiquity of different parts of the work.[65] At the very least, the first part of the document, the 'Two Ways', appears to have had a separate existence: it is also found in a Latin version, the *Doctrina Apostolorum*, and in parallel form in the later chapters of the second-century *Epistle of Barnabas*, though the precise relationship between the three documents is debated. The question is further complicated by the omission of a small section of this part of the *Didache* (1.3b–2.1) both from the *Doctrina Apostolorum* and from the *Apostolic Church Order*. Is this section a later interpolation? And what are we to make of the fact that both Pseudo-Cyprian, *adversus Aleatores*, and Augustine knew the whole *Didache* in Latin, including this 'interpolation'?[66] The 'Two Ways' material is often thought to

---

[63] See the recent study by David A. Fiensy, *Prayers Alleged to be Jewish: An Examination of the Constitutiones Apostolorum*, Brown Judaic Studies 65, Chico CA 1985.

[64] See Adolf Harnack, *Die Quellen der sog. apostolischen Kirchenordnung*, Berlin 1886; Faivre, 'Le texte grec de la Constitution ecclésiastique des apôtres 16–20 et ses sources'.

[65] For a discussion of some recent theories, see F. E. Vokes, 'The Didache still Debated', *Church Quarterly* 3 (1970), pp. 57–62. See also Giet, *L'énigme de la Didachè*.

[66] See Willy Rordorf, 'Le problème de la transmission textuelle de Didachè 1,3b–2,1', in Paschke, *Uberlieferungsgeschichtliche Untersuchungen*, pp. 499–513.

be of Jewish origin, but this is less sure than is commonly supposed: although the Qumran Manual of Discipline has shown that there existed a Jewish arrangement of moral teaching in the form of 'Two Ways' (1 QS 3.13−4.14), this does not prove a direct literary relationship with the material found in the *Didache*.

Some scholars have begun to suggest that a similar process of evolution may also be true in the case of the *Apostolic Tradition*. It would appear from the Latin translation that at one time it circulated in at least two different forms, one with a longer and the other with a shorter ending, and there are other signs in the text which may point to more extensive revisions —statements which do not quite harmonize, practices described twice, and so on. However, it is difficult to know how many of these should be attributed to the actions of the author himself, bringing together older written sources which did not cohere with one another, and how many should be attributed to subsequent copyists and translators revising the original text.[67]

Indeed, it would perhaps be better to think of the various church orders not as works by a single author at all, but rather as having had a succession of editors who shaped the stream of tradition which came down to them, both before and after it emerges to our sight in documentary form.

Fact or fantasy?

Viewed in this light, therefore, can any overall trends be discerned in the development of this material? Why were the different editors modifying it?

As A. F. Walls has pointed out,[68] there is a change in the way in which the term 'apostolic' seems to be understood as the literature evolves. In the earlier documents it appears to have a more dynamic sense, meaning 'that which is in accordance with the witness and teaching of the apostles', whereas the later documents become pseudepigraphical, with the various injunctions explicitly attributed to the apostles themselves, either collec-

[67] See the references given in n. 31 above.

[68] 'A Note on the Apostolic Claim in the Church Order Literature', *SP* 2 (1957), pp. 83−92.

tively or individually. Thus, beyond the title, 'The teaching of the twelve apostles', the *Didache* makes no other claims concerning the source of its material, and the same is true of the *Apostolic Tradition*, and even of the *Canons of Hippolytus*. These works claim that what they are teaching is in accordance with the apostolic tradition which has come down to them, but do not suggest that it derives verbatim from the mouths of the original twelve disciples.

Not so, however, with the *Didascalia*: although this starts out in a similar way to the other church orders mentioned above, just before the last chapter of the work, and immediately after a robust attack on heretics who pervert the truth, there is inserted an alleged account of the composition of the document by a council of the twelve apostles, who intended it as a defence against heresy. Then follows the final lengthy chapter which argues strongly that Christians are free from any obligation to obey the ritual legislation of the Old Testament, even though they are bound to follow its moral law. This arrangement of material would seem to suggest that this final point was a much controverted issue in the Christian community from which this church order came, and so at this stage in his work the author needed to bring out the biggest weapons he could find — the authority of the twelve apostles themselves — to defend his position against that of his opponents, although he had not found it necessary to do this for the earlier, and presumably less controversial, part of what he had written.

The author of the *Apostolic Church Order* goes one step further, and distributes everything he has to say between the twelve apostles, putting a different injunction into the mouth of each of them in turn — though he appears to regard Peter and Cephas as two separate individuals but manages to keep the total at twelve by excluding both Judas Iscariot and his successor Matthias. Like the *Didascalia*, he places the origin of his work in a meeting of the twelve, at which Martha and Mary are also said to be present — the main purpose for this addition being apparently to create an excuse for the apostles to give firm directions about what women are not to be allowed to do in the Church. As we have already mentioned, the *Testamentum*

Domini caps the whole process by attributing the teaching not just to the apostles but to Jesus himself.

Not only is there this change of form in the gradual develop-ment of the literature, but there is also a change of content. Most of the earlier documents — the *Didache*, the *Didascalia*, and the *Apostolic Church Order* — are principally concerned with the Christian life as a whole, with the moral conduct of the members of the Church. It is only in relation to the welfare of the whole community, therefore, that they deal with those who are its leaders, and consequently are naturally more concerned about the personal qualities which such ministers should display than with the process of their institution. The *Didache* devotes no more than a single sentence to their appointment, the *Apostolic Church Order* scarcely more than that, while the *Didas-calia* does not refer to it at all. Indeed the *Apostolic Church Order* contains no strictly liturgical material; the *Didascalia* merely alludes obliquely to liturgical practices; while the *Didache* includes only very brief liturgical directions together with prayer-texts for the eucharist or agape, all of which may be later additions to its original nucleus.

Alexandre Faivre, in an important study of the church order literature, would extend this trajectory further, and see the roots of the genre as being related to writings such as the Pastoral Epistles and the *Letter of Polycarp to the Philippians* which similarly offer moral exhortations to the community followed by the delineation of the qualities required in its ministers.[69] Indeed, there is another resemblance which should be noted between the Pastoral Epistles and some of the church orders: both are pseudepigraphical. Further parallels might also be drawn with early Christian apocryphal works which not only are similarly pseudonymous but also seem at least in part to have an analogous aim: the attempt to bestow legitimacy on con-temporary practices by means of apostolic fiction.

With the *Apostolic Tradition*, however, we move into litera-ture of a very different kind. Here, at least in its extant form, exhortations concerning Christian behaviour and the moral

[69] 'La documentation canonico-liturgique de l'Église ancienne', *RevSR* 54 (1980), pp. 204–19, 237–97: see especially, pp. 287ff.

qualities required of ordained ministers have almost entirely disappeared, and are replaced by directives about the correct procedure to be adopted in the appointment of ministers, the texts of prayers to be used for ordination and in the celebration of the eucharist, the ritual to be followed in the administration of baptism, and other such matters. It is the ordering of the church and its liturgy which is now the principal focus. This trend continues in the derivatives of this document, so that, for example, whereas the *Didascalia* was concerned with the proper disposition of different groups of people — ordained, lay, male, female, etc. — within the Christian assembly, the *Testamentum Domini* concerns itself instead with the proper arrangement of the church building and its furniture.

These shifts in form and content suggest that, as time passed, the focus of the church orders changed, and their 'apostolic' pedigree needed to be more firmly underscored and reinforced by more emphatic claims if it were to have any authority. This in turn raises the suspicion that not all editorial hands were necessarily modifying the received text in order to correspond with the actual historical practice of their own churches. At least to some extent, they may have been indulging in an idealizing dream — *prescribing* rather than *describing* — imagining what the organization and liturgy of their community would be like if they were allowed to have their own way and impose their idiosyncratic ideas on the rest of the congregation. Thus we may sometimes have less of a factual account than a clever piece of propaganda, which required the guise of alleged apostolic prescription to promote its cause. This has long been suspected with regard to at least parts of the later documents, but there is no reason to think that any of the church orders are free from this tendency, still less that they constitute the official handbook of a local church, as earlier scholars tended to suppose.

On the other hand, this does not mean that they should simply be dismissed as historical sources. Beneath what may be fanciful embroidery in theology and practice there is undoubtedly some foundation based on the reality either of the local tradition or of influences from other churches. But the evidence needs to be sifted with care, and reliance should not too readily be placed on the unsubstantiated testimony of a church order, without corroboration from other sources.

The change of emphasis in subject-matter also provides some clues as to why certain texts were retained and others dropped in the development of the collections of church orders which we considered earlier. It was not merely that the *Didascalia* did not lend itself easily to division into separate canons, as Botte suggested: the problem was not simply one of form but of content. What the *Didascalia* had to say was not the sort of apostolic material which later generations wanted to preserve. It was no longer relevant to their needs, and so ceases to appear in the later canonical collections. This may also explain why copies of the *Didache* do not exist in the wide variety of languages in which other church orders are found: its moral teaching was no longer important enough for anyone to consider it worthwhile to translate and copy it, and its meagre liturgical provisions were too archaic to be reconciled with the contemporary practice of the translators' world.

Equally, it explains why the *Apostolic Tradition* was translated, copied, amended, and expanded so many times: its subject-matter was exactly what later eyes were looking for — the beginnings of liturgical rubrics and canon law. Similarly, it explains why *Apostolic Constitutions* 8 should have been abstracted from the totality of the work and grafted on to the later collections, even though it partially duplicated the contents of the *Apostolic Tradition*: it too contained just the sort of material people wanted. Finally, it explains why ultimately there were no more church orders[70] and the genre simply died out: eventually apostolic fiction ceased to be used as a source of

---

[70] In addition to the examples considered within this chapter, however, we should include within the genre at least two other compositions: the Coptic *Canons of Basil*, which in its final form circulated in Egypt in the sixth century and which used the *Canons of Hippolytus* as one of its sources (text in W. Riedel, *Die Kirchenrechtsquellen des Patriarchats Alexandrien* (Leipzig 1900), pp. 231−83); and the Gallican *Statuta Ecclesiae Antiqua*, which was perhaps composed by Gennadius of Marseilles *c.* 490 and which drew on both the *Apostolic Tradition* and the *Apostolic Constitutions* (text in Charles Munier, *Les Statuta Ecclesiae Antiqua*, Paris 1960). For the continuing influence of the *Apostolic Tradition* on ordination practice in the West, see Bradshaw, *Ordination Rites of the Ancient Churches of East and West*, pp. 14−15, 45, 56, 59−60.

authority in the mainstream churches of both East and West, and collections of liturgical texts and canon law were produced which derived their authority instead from individual living bishops and genuine synodical assemblies. It was only in the lesser Oriental churches that the pseudo-apostolic directives continued to be respected and carefully preserved, and even came to constitute the foundation of much liturgical practice, while elsewhere the original Greek texts were allowed to disintegrate: they had served their purpose and ceased to be of practical use.

The *Apostolic Church Order*, however, constitutes a fly in the ointment, upsetting the neatness of this theory of development. Although it is not a liturgical document, it continues to make an appearance alongside the *Apostolic Tradition* in every single collection of church orders. Nevertheless, perhaps even this can be explained. The *Apostolic Tradition* refers in its opening words to an earlier work (or to a first part of the same work) on the subject of spiritual gifts. No trace of this has ever been found. But it is possible that someone mistakenly thought that the *Apostolic Church Order* was this missing text and placed the two together in that order to form the nucleus of all other later collections. If they were thereafter looked upon as a single work, then it is less surprising that this short treatise managed to retain its place even when its subject-matter had ceased to be of interest to copyists and translators.

Conclusion

The jigsaw puzzle is far from solved, and other pieces still need to be inserted. For example, published versions and recent critical editions are still lacking for several parts of this literature. Moreover, although what in biblical studies would be called 'source-criticism' has to some extent been done, the equivalent of serious 'form-criticism' and above all 'redaction-criticism' still wait to be tackled, so that we may further comprehend what shaped the material in its development and learn more about the world of the various editors and translators who transmitted and revised it.

Perhaps the whole church order literature is not so much a simple jigsaw puzzle but, as Friedrich Loofs suggested at the end of the nineteenth century,[71] a giant kaleidoscope capable of being arranged in a variety of patterns wherein each person can see the image that he or she wishes to find. Yet, in spite of the apparent morass which first impressions present, if we are willing to take account of the total complexity of the literature and avoid the practice of simply abstracting pieces without reference to their context—what one might call the 'hit and run' approach to historical sources—we can begin to discern an underlying pattern and a logical progression in its development, which may help us to understand it better.

[71] 'Die urchristliche Gemeindeverfassung mit spezieller Beziehung auf Loening und Harnack', *Theologische Studien und Kritiken* 63 (1890), p. 637.

5. Other Major Liturgical Sources

This chapter contains a brief introduction to some of the other major documentary resources which need to be used in any attempt at the reconstruction of liturgical practices in the early Church. It is arranged according to geographical provenance and includes both material dating from the second, third, and fourth centuries and also eucharistic prayers and other liturgical texts which in their extant form are of a somewhat later date but which may be able to cast some light on earlier practices. It can make no claim to be a comprehensive listing, for our knowledge comes from a wide variety of texts, many of which supply only one or two incidental details concerning some individual custom. Nonetheless, it does aim to provide background information to the more widely used sources, and especially those which pose critical problems or other difficulties of interpretation.

ROME

Justin Martyr, writing at Rome around 150, provides the earliest substantial description that we have of Christian worship. This occurs in his *First Apology*, which is addressed to the emperor Antoninus Pius and is obviously intended to explain Christianity to those outside the Church. There are two accounts, the first dealing with baptismal procedure, which culminates in the celebration of the eucharist, and the second outlining a regular Sunday eucharistic service.[1] These present us with two principal problems of interpretation. The first is the difficulty in deciding whether Justin is here recounting the specific form of worship practised in Rome at this time or whether he is offering a more generic description of the sort of worship which might be encountered by his readers in various parts of the world. Indeed, are we in any case justified in thinking that there was a single church in Rome at this period rather than a loose collection of Christian communities distinguished

---

[1] Chs 61–7. Justin also speaks about the eucharist in his *Dialogue with Trypho* (a Jew), probably written at Ephesus *c.* 135. Extracts from both works can be found in Jasper & Cuming, *Prayers of the Eucharist*, pp. 25–30.

from one another by significant ethnic and liturgical differences?[2]

The second problem is related to the first. Since Justin's writing is intended for non-Christians, how far has this affected the
detail that is given? For example, was 'president' a standard
piece of early Christian terminology for the (ordained?) minister, or did Justin deliberately choose it as a word that would be
more intelligible to outsiders than the technical terms regularly
used by Christians?[3] Does his vague expression 'the records of
the apostles or the writings of the prophets' really imply that the
form of the ministry of the word was very flexible, or is it so
phrased because Justin thought the precise details of this part of
the service unimportant to his readers?[4] Does the absence of a
reference to any post-baptismal ceremonies mean that there
actually were none, or only that he did not judge it relevant for
his purpose to mention them?[5]

Apart from Justin's description and the possible insight
offered by the *Apostolic Tradition* attributed to Hippolytus,[6]
there are no other substantial sources of information for ancient
Roman liturgy belonging to this early period. We do not, for
example, possess a set of fourth-century baptismal catecheses
like those belonging to some of the other major centres of early
Christianity which might have offered a step-by-step account and
explanation of the baptismal and eucharistic rites. We have to
make do, therefore, with a mere handful of brief allusions in var-

[2] See further the important study by A. Hamman, 'Valeur et signification
des reseignements liturgiques de Justin', *SP* 13 (1975), pp. 364—74; and also G.
La Piana, 'The Roman Church at the End of the Second Century', *Harvard
Theological Review* 18 (1925), pp. 214—77.

[3] See T. G. Jalland, 'Justin Martyr and the President of the Eucharist', *SP* 5
(1962), pp. 83—5.

[4] For discussion of various parts of Justin's eucharistic rite, see G. J.
Cuming, 'DI' EUCHES LOGOU (Justin Apology 1.66.2)', *JTS* 31 (1980), pp.
80—2, and the response by Anthony Gelston, *JTS* 33 (1982), pp. 172ff.;
Maurice Jourjon, 'Justin', in Willy Rordorf et al., *The Eucharist of the Early
Christians* (New York 1978), pp. 71—85; E. C. Ratcliff, 'The Eucharistic
Institution Narrative of Justin Martyr's First Apology', *JEH* 22 (1971), pp.
97—102 = A. H. Couratin & David Tripp, eds., *E. C. Ratcliff. Liturgical Studies*
(London 1976), pp. 41—8.

[5] On this question, see below, pp. 174—5.

[6] See above, pp. 89—92.

ious contemporary works and with attempts at reconstruction of earlier practices based on the evidence provided by somewhat later sources, such as the letter of **Innocent I** to Decentius of Gubbio (416)[7] and the sermons of **Leo the Great** (440–61), as well as the much later liturgical books of the Roman rite.[8]

NORTH AFRICA

There is always some difficulty in knowing how far writers are expressing their own personal opinions and how far they are reflecting the common beliefs of their culture, but the problem is greatly increased when there are virtually no alternative sources against which to check a statement. This dilemma can be clearly illustrated in the case of **Tertullian**, who was a North African lay Christian, converted to the faith *c.* 195. Although at first fiercely opposed to the Montanist movement, which among other things laid great emphasis on the continuing gift of prophecy within the Church, he eventually allied himself with it. Scattered throughout his writings, which cover both the Catholic and Montanist phases of his life, are numerous brief references to various aspects of liturgical practice.[9] But are these always descriptions of what *was* the case, or should at least some of them be treated as expressions of what the author thought *should be* the case?

For instance, Tertullian says that 'Pascha [Easter] provides the day of most solemnity for baptism. . . . After that, Pentecost is a most joyful period for arranging baptisms. . . . For all that, every day is a Lord's day: any hour, any season, is suitable for baptism.'[10] On the other hand, he claims elsewhere that lay people may baptize and even preside at the eucharist when an ordained minister is not available.[11] The majority of scholarly

[7] Critical edition by Robert Cabié, *La lettre du pape Innocent I à Decentius de Gubbio*, Louvain 1973.

[8] For an introduction to these, see John F. Baldovin, *The Urban Character of Christian Worship* (OCA 228, 1987), pp. 119–41; Gordon Jeanes, *Early Origins of the Roman Rite*, A/GLS 20, 1991; Cyrille Vogel, *Medieval Liturgy: An Introduction to the Sources* (Washington DC 1986), pp. 61ff.

[9] See E. Dekkers, *Tertullianus en de geschiedenis der liturgie*, Brussels 1947.

[10] *De Baptismo* 19.

[11] *De Exhort. Cast.* 7.3. See G. Otrano, 'Nonne et laici sacerdotes sumus? (*Exhort. Cast.* 7.3)', *Vetera Christianorum* 8 (1971), pp. 27–47; C. Vogel, 'Le

opinion has generally treated the first passage as firm factual evidence that the Easter season was already established as the primary occasion for baptism, certainly in North Africa if not in the whole Church, but has dismissed the claim to lay eucharistic presidency in the second as merely Tertullian's personal opinion with no basis at all in ecclesiastical practice. There are, however, no real grounds for distinguishing the two statements in this way, apart from the preconceptions that one brings to them, and so it is necessary to look for external confirmation before jumping to one conclusion or another.

Further information about liturgical practices in North Africa is furnished in the writings of **Cyprian,** bishop of Carthage from 248 to 258,[12] and of **Augustine,** bishop of Hippo Regius from 396 to 430,[13] as well as in various pieces of synodical legislation.[14] Unfortunately, however, because of the Arab conquest of the region at the end of the seventh century and in contrast to other parts of the ancient Christian world, no later African

---

ministre charismatique de l'eucharistie: approache rituelle', in idem, *Ministères et célébration de l'eucharistie* (Studia Anselmiana 61, Rome 1973), pp. 198–204; Pierre van Beneden, 'Haben Laien Eucharistie ohne Ordinierte gefeiert? Zu Tertullians "De exhortatione castitatis" 7.3', *ALW* 29 (1987), pp. 31–46. With regard to lay men (but not women!) baptizing in cases of emergency, see also Tertullian, *De Baptismo* 17.

[12] See A. Coppo, 'Vita cristiana e terminologia liturgica a Cartagine verso la metà del IIIo secolo', *EL* 85 (1971), pp. 70–86; V. Saxer, *Vie liturgique et quotidienne à Carthage vers le milieu du IIIe siècle. Le témoignage de S. Cyprien et de ses contemporains d'Afrique*, Vatican 1969; G. G. Willis, 'St Cyprian and the Mixed Chalice', *Downside Review* 100 (1982), pp. 110–15.

[13] See, for example, K. Gamber, 'Ordo Missae Africanae: Der nord-africanische Messritus zur Zeit des hl. Augustinus', *Römische Quartalschrift* 64 (1969), pp. 139–53; A. Gerhard, 'Benedicere/benedictio in Theologie und Liturgie nach den Schriften des hl. Augustinus', *Ecclesia Orans* 5 (1988), pp. 53–75; V. Grossi, *La liturgia battesimale in S. Agostino*, Rome 1970; R. de Latte, 'Saint Augustin et le baptême: Étude liturgico-historique du rituel baptismal des adultes chez saint Augustin', *QLP* 56 (1975), pp. 177–223; idem, 'Saint Augustin et le baptême: Étude liturgico-historique du rituel baptismal des enfants chez saint Augustin', *QLP* 57 (1976), pp. 41–55; W. Rötzer, *Des heiligen Augustinus Schriften als liturgiegeschichtliche Quelle*, Münster 1930; G. G. Willis, *St Augustine's Lectionary*, ACC 44, London 1962.

[14] See E. J. Kilmartin, 'Early African Legislation concerning Liturgical Prayer', *EL* 99 (1985), pp. 105–27.

sacramentary or other collection of prayers has survived from which earlier practice might have been inferred.

NORTH ITALY

Very early sources for this region are lacking, and the writings of the fourth-century bishop, **Ambrose** (*c.* 339−97), provide the chief evidence for liturgical practices at Milan.[15] However, since his audience were generally Christians already familiar with the rituals to which he was alluding, Ambrose is not always very explicit about the precise details, and his extensive use of metaphor also makes it difficult to know if and when references to such things as incense and anointing are to be taken literally. Moreover, the authenticity of *De Sacramentis*,[16] one of the works attributed to him which provides considerable liturgical information, has been seriously questioned since the sixteenth century. In the 1940s Otto Faller and R. H. Connolly, working independently of one another, succeeded in convincing most scholars of its Ambrosian authorship,[17] but there has been a

[15] There is a wide range of secondary literature dealing specifically with this. Among more recent works are J. Beumer, 'Die altesten Zeugnisse fur die romische Eucharistiefeier bei Ambrosius von Mailand', *ZKTh* 95 (1973), pp. 311−24; R. Johanny, *L'eucharistie centre de l'histoire du salut chez St Ambroise de Milan*, Paris 1968; W. Ledwich, 'Baptism, Sacrament of the Cross: Looking behind St Ambrose', in Bryan D. Spinks, ed., *The Sacrifice of Praise* (Rome 1981), pp. 199−211; V. Monachino, *S. Ambrogio e la cura pastorale a Milano nel secolo IV*, Milan 1973; A. Paredi, 'La liturgia del "De Sacramentis" ', in *Miscellanea Carlo Figini* (Milan 1964), pp. 59−72; H. M. Riley, *Christian Initiation. A Comparative Study of the Interpretation of the Baptismal Liturgy in the Mystagogical Writings of Cyril of Jerusalem, John Chrysostom, Theodore of Mopsuestia, and Ambrose of Milan*, Washington DC 1974; J. Schmitz, *Gottesdienst im Altchristlichen Mailand*, Bonn 1975; E. J. Yarnold, 'The Ceremonies of Initiation in the De Sacramentis and the De Mysteriis of St Ambrose', *SP* 10 (1970), pp. 453−63; idem, 'Did St Ambrose know the Mystagogic Catecheses of St Cyril of Jerusalem?', *SP* 12 (1975), pp. 184−9.

[16] Editions by Henry Chadwick, *Saint Ambrose: On the Sacraments*, London 1960; Bernard Botte, *Des Sacrements; Des Mystères*, SC 25, 1961; partial English translation in E. J. Yarnold, *The Awe-Inspiring Rites of Initiation* (Slough 1971), pp. 97−153.

[17] Otto Faller, 'Ambrosius, der Verfasser von De Sacramentis', *ZKTh* 64 (1940), pp. 1−14, 81−101; R. H. Connolly, *The De Sacramentis a Work of St Ambrose*, Oxford 1942. For a summary of the controversy, see the introduction to Botte's edition, pp. 7−25.

more recent debate between Klaus Gamber and Josef Schmitz, the former attributing the work to Nicetas of Remesiana.[18]

Some further details of north Italian liturgical practices also emerge from the writings of Ambrose's contemporaries, **Chromatius** (bishop of Aquileia, *c.* 388—407), **Gaudentius** (who became bishop of Brescia *c.* 397), and **Zeno** (bishop of Verona, 362—*c.* 375),[19] and from the works of the fifth-century **Maximus**, bishop of Turin, and **Peter Chrysologus**, bishop of Ravenna.

GAUL AND SPAIN

We are even less informed about early Christan worship in these regions than we are about the practices of northern Italy. Nearly all the sources here date from at least the fifth century and are in any case very meagre, which makes reconstruction of earlier traditions extremely hazardous and speculative.

EGYPT

The writings of **Clement of Alexandria** (*c.* 150—*c.* 215) and **Origen** (*c.* 185—*c.* 254) make a number of references to liturgical customs in their extensive writings, but they are frequently difficult to evaluate. Firstly, both writers often speak in an allegorical manner about matters pertaining to the Christian faith, and so it is sometimes hard to know whether some allusion is to an actual liturgical practice or not. A simple illustration of this difficulty is provided by Clement's comparison of the Christian catechumenate with the directive in the Old Testament Law that after three years the first-fruits of the harvest are to be dedicated to God.[20] Does he mean to imply that the catechumenate lasted for three years, or is the analogy intended

[18] Klaus Gamber, *Die Autorschaft von De Sacramentis* (Regensburg 1967) and 'Nochmals zur Frage der Autorschaft von De Sacramentis', *ZKTh* 91 (1969), pp. 587—9; Josef Schmitz, 'Zum Autor der Schrift "De Sacramentis" ', *ZKTh* 91 (1969), pp. 58—69.

[19] See the extensive bibliography in Carlo Truzzi, *Zeno, Gaudenzio e Cromazio* (Brescia 1985), pp. 15—29; and also Gordon Jeanes, 'Early Latin Parallels to the Roman Canon? Possible References to a Eucharistic Prayer in Zeno of Verona', *JTS* 37 (1986), pp. 427—31.

[20] II *Strom.* 18.

in a much less literal sense?[21] Secondly, both seem to have belonged to a somewhat elitist group of Christians, whose customs may have had relatively little in common with what the vast majority of ordinary people in Alexandria were wont to do. Moreover, in the case of Origen, we cannot be sure whether the liturgical usages to which he alludes were always those of Alexandria or were the observance of Palestine, where he spent a considerable time.[22]

The problems of describing Egyptian liturgy are further exacerbated, as at Rome, by the almost complete absence of substantial fourth-century sources. The **Canons of Hippolytus** present us with difficulties of interpretation: we do not know exactly where the document comes from, nor how far it represents what was really happening in the early fourth century.[23] And the only other major witness to the early Egyptian liturgical tradition, the so-called **Sacramentary of Sarapion**, is also problematic. The only extant text of this collection of thirty prayers attributed to a fourth-century bishop of Thmuis in lower Egypt is contained in an eleventh-century manuscript in the monastery of the Great Lavra on Mount Athos, which was first published by Aleksej Dmitrievskij in 1894, and again shortly afterwards by Georg Wobbermin.[24] The edition most familiar to English-speaking students, however, is that by F. E. Brightman in 1900, but he thought that the contents were not arranged in any proper order, and so rearranged them in what he considered the most logical form.[25] Unfortunately, Brightman's order is fre-

---

[21] Cf. the different conclusions reached by P.-T. Camelot, ed., *Les Stromates* 2 (SC 38, 1954), p. 107, n. 1; Michel Dujarier, *A History of the Catechumenate: The First Six Centuries* (New York 1979), pp. 42−3; A. Mehat, *Étude sur les 'Stromates' de Clément d'Alexandrie* (Paris 1966), p. 221.

[22] See further Werner Schütz, *Der christliche Gottesdienst bei Origenes*, Stuttgart 1984.

[23] See above, pp. 92−3.

[24] Aleksej Dmitrievskij, *Ein Euchologium aus dem 4. Jahrhundert, verfasst von Sarapion, Bischoff von Thmuis*, Kiev 1894; Georg Wobbermin, *Altchristliche liturgische Stücke aus der Kirche Aegyptens nebst einem dogmatischen Brief des Bischofs Serapion von Thmuis*, Leipzig/Berlin 1898.

[25] 'The Sacramentary of Sarapion of Thmuis', *JTS* 1 (1900), pp. 88−113, 247−77. Brightman's text and order were followed by Funk, *Didascalia et Constitutiones Apostolorum* II, pp. 158−95.

quently treated as though it were Sarapion's own. The only complete English translation of the sacramentary was made by John Wordsworth, at first from Wobbermin's edition but later revised on the basis of Brightman's text.[26]

Bernard Capelle argued that the material in the collection had all been composed by a single author, because of the repetition of certain words, and that the author was an innovator because he attributed to the Logos the role which tradition assigned to the Spirit, and even inserted a Logos-epiclesis in the eucharistic prayer.[27] This latter argument was taken up by Bernard Botte, who concluded that the text was therefore the work of a heretic and not the real Sarapion 'who evoked the letters of Athanasius on the divinity of the Holy Spirit'. He suggested that it may belong to a later date, possibly *c.* 450.[28]

Geoffrey Cuming challenged these conclusions. Against Brightman, he took up a suggestion originally made by Theodor Scherman[29] and contended that —with one simple change — the order of the manuscript was perfectly natural. The change required the assumption that in the process of copying the second half was accidently placed before the first. Against Capelle, he argued that there were clear signs of different strata in the material, indicated by features of style and vocabulary; and against Botte, he maintained that, both in the use of the Logos and in his Christology, the author was orthodox and utilized in his eucharistic prayer an earlier and simpler form of the Alexandrine Anaphora of St Mark (for which see below). He concluded that 'it thus becomes increasingly possible that the collecting and editing of these prayers was, after all, the work of Sarapion, Bishop of Thmuis, the friend of Athanasius'.[30]

[26] *Bishop Sarapion's Prayer-Book*, London 1899, 2nd edn 1909 = Hamden CT 1964.

[27] 'L'anaphore de Sérapion: essai d'exégèse', *Muséon* 59 (1946), pp. 425–43 = idem, *Travaux liturgiques* 2 (1962), pp. 344–58.

[28] 'L'Eucologie de Sérapion, est-il authentique?', *Oriens Christianus* 48 (1964), pp. 50–6.

[29] *Ägyptische Abendmahlsliturgien des ersten Jahrtausends* (Paderborn 1912 = 1967), pp. 102–3.

[30] 'Thmuis Revisited: Another Look at the Prayers of Bishop Sarapion', *Theological Studies* 41 (1980), pp. 568–75. Other recent studies include E. Mazza, 'L'anafora di Serapione: Una ipotesi di interpretazione', *EL* 95 (1981), pp. 510–28; A. Verheul, 'La prière eucharistique dans l'Euchologe de

Also important as clues for early Egyptian eucharistic prayers are a number of fragmentary texts discovered during the course of the twentieth century. The most significant of these is **Strasbourg papyrus 254**, which dates from the fourth or fifth century and by verbal parallels reveals itself to be an early version of the Anaphora of St Mark. The major controversy which has surrounded the text is whether what survives was the entire anaphora or just a part of something much longer. Its extant contents consist of praise for the work of creation through Christ, thanksgiving for/offering of 'this reasonable and bloodless service' (with a quotation of Mal. 1.11), extensive intercession, and a doxological conclusion.[31] Many recent scholars have concluded that the anaphora was more or less coterminous with the extant material, and that therefore it did not include such elements as the Sanctus or the narrative of institution.[32] Some others, however, remain more cautiously agnostic, and regard the case as unproven. The doxology might, for instance, only be the conclusion of one section of the prayer and not of the whole anaphora, as happens in *Didache* 10 and other early texts.[33]

When studied in conjunction with the other fragmentary texts, it is possible to see that the later **Anaphora of St Mark** had substantially assumed its current form, though in a less wordy ver-

---

Serapion', *QLP* 62 (1981), pp. 43–51. A more exhaustive analysis of the text is currently being undertaken by one of my doctoral students, Maxwell Johnson.

[31] Text in M. Andrieu & P. Collomp, 'Fragments sur papyrus de l'Anaphore de saint Marc', *RevSR* 8 (1928), pp. 489–515; English translation in Jasper & Cuming, *Prayers of the Eucharist*, pp. 52–4.

[32] See W. H. Bates, 'Thanksgiving and Intercession in the Liturgy of St Mark', in Spinks, *Sacrifice of Praise*, pp. 109–19; R. G. Coquin, 'L'anaphore alexandrine de Saint Marc', in *Eucharisties d'Orient et d'Occident* 2 (Paris 1970), pp. 51–82, revised version in *Muséon* 82 (1969), pp. 307–56; G. J. Cuming, 'The Anaphora of St Mark: A Study in Development', *Muséon* 95 (1982), pp. 115–29; E. J. Kilmartin, 'Sacrificium Laudis: Content and Function of Early Eucharistic Prayers', *Theological Studies* 35 (1974), p. 280; E. Mazza, 'Una anafora incompleta? Il Papiro Strasbourg Gr. 254', *EL* 99 (1985), pp. 425–36; H. A. J. Wegman, 'Une anaphore incomplete?', in R. van den Broek & M. J. Vermaseren, eds., *Studies in Gnosticism and Hellenistic Religions* (Leiden 1981), pp. 435–50.

[33] See especially Bryan D. Spinks, 'A Complete Anaphora? A Note on Strasbourg Gr. 254', *Heythrop Journal* 25 (1984), pp. 51–5.

sion, by the time of the Council of Chalcedon.[34] Its shape is distinctive, in that it begins with the elements found in the Strasbourg papyrus and so only after extensive intercession reaches
the Sanctus, epiclesis, institution narrative, anamnesis, and offering, and concludes with a second epiclesis and doxology.

Finally, there is the **Liturgy of St Basil**. Scholars generally
assume that this composition did not originate in Egypt because
the shape of its anaphora follows the pattern of Antiochene
eucharistic prayers, with the intercessions coming towards the
end rather than at an earlier point in the prayer as in the
Anaphora of St Mark. Its oldest known form, however, is a version in the Sahidic dialect of Coptic. This is extant only in an
incomplete manuscript lacking the first third of the later text and
dating from somewhere between 600 and 800, although the contents probably belong to the first half of the fourth century or
even earlier.[35] It has been thought that it may have been the
native Cappadocian anaphora brought by Basil when he visited
Egypt *c.* 357, and subsequently amplified by the saint himself
into the longer form underlying the later Armenian, Byzantine,
and Syriac versions. On the other hand, the possibility cannot be
excluded that the prayer is in fact of Egyptian origin — maybe
even actually composed in Sahidic and not Greek — and was
later exported to other parts of the East, perhaps through Basil's
own agency.[36]

SYRIA

The earliest sources which may shed some light on liturgical
practices in this region are the apocryphal scriptures, among
them the *Acts of Thomas* from the early third century.[37] Yet
these present us with a number of problems. There is, first of all,

---

[34] For full details see G. J. Cuming, *The Liturgy of St Mark*, OCA 234, 1990.

[35] Edition in J. Doresse & E. Lanne, *Un témoin archaïque de la liturgie
copte de S. Basile*, Louvain 1960; English translation in Jasper & Cuming,
Prayers of the Eucharist, pp. 67–73.

[36] See the important article by Alphonse Raes, 'Un nouveau document de
la Liturgie de S. Basile', *OCP* 26 (1960), pp. 401–10.

[37] Texts and English translations in William Wright, *Apocryphal Acts of the
Apostles*, 2 vols, London/Edinburgh 1871 = Amsterdam 1968. See also A. F. J.
Klijn, *The Acts of Thomas*, Leiden 1962.

the difficulty of establishing an original text. This material belongs to the category of 'living literature', about which we have spoken earlier,[38] and so was often reshaped by the communities through which it passed. This practice is particularly evident in the case of the *Acts of Thomas*, which exists in two recensions, a Greek and a Syriac, differing markedly from one another in a number of places. Then, too, there is the question of how the narrative form should be interpreted: are descriptions of alleged baptismal and eucharistic activities by apostolic figures, for example, to be taken as reflecting the actual customs familiar to the compilers and editors, or do they bear little resemblance to contemporary liturgical observances? Even if they are held to be based on genuine practices, whose rituals do they represent —what was common to what might be called mainstream Christianity or what was only the tradition of an esoteric group?

A major source for the liturgy of Antioch in the fourth century is **John Chrysostom** (*c.* 347−407), since his extensive writings include many references to liturgical practices.[39] On the other hand, whether the anaphora which bears his name should really be ascribed to him has been much debated,[40] as has the nature of the relationship between that anaphora and the Syriac **Anaphora of the Twelve Apostles**. Recently, however, both John Fenwick and Robert Taft have argued that the two prayers share

[38] See above, pp. 74, 101f.

[39] See A. Cesara-Gestaldo, 'Teoria e prassi nella catechesi battesimale di S. Giovanni Crisostomo' in S. Felici, ed., *Catechesi battesimale e reconciliazione nei Padri del IV secolo* (Rome 1984), pp. 57−63; T. M. Finn, *The Liturgy of Baptism in the Baptismal Instructions of St John Chrysostom*, Washington DC 1967; Reiner Kaczynski, *Das Wort Gottes in Liturgie und Alltag der Gemeinden des Johannes Chrysostomos*, Freiburg 1974; F. van de Paverd, *Zur Geschichte der Messliturgie in Antiocheia und Konstantinopel gegen Ende der vierten Jahrhunderts. Analyse der Quellen bei Johannes Chrysostomos*, OCA 187, 1970; idem, 'Anaphoral Intercessions, Epiclesis and Communion Rites in John Chrysostom', *OCP* 49 (1983), pp. 303−39; P. Rentinck, *La cura pastorale in Antiochia nel seculo IV*, Rome 1970; Riley, *Christian Initiation*; D. Sartore, 'Il mistero del battesimo nelle catechesi di S. Giovanni Chrisostomo', *Lateranum* 50 (1984), pp. 358−95.

[40] See, for example, G. J. Cuming, 'Pseudonymity and Authenticity, with Special Reference to the Liturgy of John Chrysostom', *SP* 15 (1984), pp. 532−8.

a common Greek ancestor which, in the case of the Anaphora of the Twelve Apostles, was conflated with elements from the Syriac version of the Liturgy of St James (for which see below), and in the case of the Liturgy of John Chrysostom, was conflated with elements from the Byzantine version of the Liturgy of St Basil. Taft would contend that Chrysostom himself was the redactor of the second anaphora, and Fenwick would take the argument even further to suggest that the same ancestor lies behind the eucharistic prayer in *Apostolic Constitutions* 8.[41]

Some further light is cast on Antiochene liturgical practices by **Theodore of Mopsuestia**, who was ordained as a presbyter at Antioch about 383, and served there until 392 when he became bishop of Mopsuestia, a town about a hundred miles away but still within the patriarchate of Antioch. Of his sixteen baptismal homilies, 1−10 are on the Nicene Creed, 11 is on the Lord's Prayer, 12−14 are on baptism, and 15−16 are on the eucharist, these last six being delivered during Easter week. The original Greek text has not been preserved, and all that exists is a Syriac translation made perhaps in the fifth or sixth century. There is just one extant manuscript of this, which dates from the seventeenth century. The only edition (with English translation) is by Alphonse Mingana, and it is not without fault.[42]

While the authorship of these homilies is not disputed, the date and place of composition are. Most scholars believe that they were delivered while Theodore was still a presbyter at Antioch, but some have placed them during his episcopate in Mopsuestia, 392−428.[43] This question also has some relation to

[41] John R. K. Fenwick, *'The Missing Oblation': The Contents of the Early Antiochene Anaphora*, A/GLS 11, 1989; Robert Taft, 'The Authenticity of the Chrysostom Anaphora Revisited. Determining the Authorship of Liturgical Texts by Computer', *OCP* 56 (1990), pp. 5−51.

[42] *Commentary of Theodore of Mopsuestia on the Nicene Creed*, Woodbrooke Studies 5, Cambridge 1932; *Commentary of Theodore of Mopsuestia on the Lord's Prayer and on the Sacraments of Baptism and Eucharist*, Woodbrooke Studies 6, Cambridge 1933. See also the excellent French translation by R. Tonneau & R. Devreesse, *Les Homélies Catéchétiques de Theodore de Mopsueste*, Vatican 1949; and the English translation of homilies 13−16 in Yarnold, *Awe-Inspiring Rites*, pp. 173−263.

[43] Liturgical studies of Theodore's sermons include: S. Janeras, 'En quels jours furent prononcées les homélies catéchétiques de Theodore de Mopsueste?', in *Memorial Mgr Gabriel Khouri-Sarkis* (Louvain 1969), pp. 121−3; C.

the authenticity of a passage in Theodore's description of the baptismal rite which refers to a post-baptismal anointing of the forehead associated with the gift of the Holy Spirit (15.27). Such a ceremony is not mentioned by Theodore's contemporary, John Chrysostom, nor by any other Syrian source in the first five centuries, with the exception of the *Apostolic Constitutions*, and even there it is not connected with the gift of the Spirit (3.16; 7.22; 7.44). Some scholars would therefore regard the passage as a later interpolation, while others would argue that it should not be understood as a reference to a literal anointing with oil, and still others would defend it as the genuine first appearance of an innovation which did eventually become a standard part of later Syrian baptismal rites, usually explaining the divergence from Chrysostom's rite either with the claim that there had been a recent change in Antiochene practice, or with the argument that the description reflects the rite of Mopsuestia.[44]

For East Syria, we have the writings of **Aphraates** (early fourth century),[45] the hymns of **Ephrem** (*c.* 306−73)[46] and of

---

J. A. Lash, 'L'onction post-baptismale de la 14e homélie de Theodore de Mopsueste: une interpolation syriaque?', in *XXIX Congres International des Orientalistes: Resumés* (Paris 1973), pp. 43−4; J. Lecuyer, 'Le sacerdoce chrétien et le sacrifice eucharistique selon Theodore de Mopsueste', *Recherches de science religieuse* 36 (1949), pp. 481−516; J. P. Longleat, 'Les rites du baptême dans les homélies catéchétiques de Theodore de Mopsuestia', *QLP* 66 (1985), pp. 193−202; Enrico Mazza, 'La struttura dell'anafora nelle Catechesi di Teodoro di Mopsuestia', *EL* 102 (1988), pp. 147−83; idem, 'La formula battesimale nelle omilie di Teodoro di Mopsuestia', *EL* 104 (1990), pp. 23−34; J. Quasten, 'The Liturgical Mysticism of Theodore of Mopsuestia', *Theological Studies* 15 (1954), pp. 431−9; F. J. Reine, *The Eucharistic Doctrine and the Liturgy of the Mystagogical Catecheses of Theodore of Mopsuestia*, Washington DC 1942; Riley, *Christian Initiation*; George E. Saint-Laurent, 'Pre-baptismal Rites in the Baptismal Catecheses of Theodore of Mopsuestia', *Diakonia* 16 (1981), pp. 118−26; W. C. van Unnik, 'Parrhesia in the Catechetical Homilies of Theodore of Mopsuestia', in *Mélanges offerts à Mlle Christine Mohrmann* (Utrecht 1963), pp. 12−22.

[44] See the discussion in Yarnold, *Awe-Inspiring Rites*, p. 208, n. 65; J. D. C. Fisher, *Confirmation Then and Now* (ACC 60, London 1978), pp. 115−18.

[45] See E. J. Duncan, *Baptism in the Demonstrations of Aphraates the Persian Sage*, Washington 1945; F. S. Pericoli Ridolfini, 'Battesimo e penitenza negli scritti del "Sapiente Persiano" ', in Felici, *Catechesi battesimale e reconciliazione nei Padri del IV secolo*, pp. 119−29.

[46] See Joseph P. Amar, 'Perspectives on the Eucharist in Ephrem the

Cyrillonas of Edessa (a fourth-century poet and Ephrem's nephew),[47] and the somewhat later evidence of **Narsai** (fifth century),[48] which furnish some information about liturgical customs, and also the important testimony of the **Anaphora of the Apostles Addai and Mari**. Although all the extant manuscripts of this eucharistic prayer are of very late date, the comparative geographical and ecclesiastical isolation of the region and the strong Semitic influence on early Christianity there have encouraged scholars to believe that parts of the prayer may be very ancient indeed, perhaps as early as the second or third century. Furthermore, unlike other early eucharistic prayers, it appears to have been composed in Syriac rather than Greek. The publication by William F. Macomber in 1966 of a critical edition of the text based on a tenth/eleventh-century manuscript from the church of Mar Esa'ya in Mosul[49] — at least 500 years older than any previously known manuscript of the prayer — constituted a significant development for attempts to reconstruct its earlier form, as did the publication by J. M. Sauget in 1973 of a critical text of the **Third Anaphora of St Peter** or *Sharar* of the Maronite rite.[50] Since most of the contents of Addai and Mari are also found in *Sharar*, scholars had long believed that a common source must lie behind the two texts.

Macomber himself has attempted to reconstruct the original anaphora from which these extant versions developed as it might have been *c.* 400, and which he thought belonged to the Aramaic-speaking church centred on Edessa. He believed that

---

Syrian', *Worship* 61 (1987), pp. 441—54; Edmund Beck, 'Le baptême chez St Ephrem', *L'Orient syrien* 1 (1956), pp. 111—36; Pierre Yousif, *L'eucharistie chez saint Ephraem de Nisibe*, Rome 1984.

[47] See D. Cerbelaud, *Cyrillonas. L'agneu véritable. Hymnes, cantiques, homélies*, Chevetogne 1984.

[48] See R. H. Connolly, *The Liturgical Homilies of Narsai*, Cambridge 1909.

[49] 'The oldest known text of the Anaphora of the Apostles Addai and Mari', *OCP* 31 (1966), pp. 335—71; English translation of the text, review of earlier scholarship, and bibliography of secondary literature in Bryan D. Spinks, ed., *Addai and Mari — The Anaphora of the Apostles: A Text for Students*, GLS 24, 1980.

[50] *Anaphorae Syriacae* II, Fasc. 3 (Rome 1973), pp. 275—323; English translation of this text also included in Spinks' edition of *Addai and Mari*.

the whole prayer had originally been addressed to the Son and
not the Father, as *Sharar* still is from its post-Sanctus to the final
doxology; that the Sanctus, though disputed by some earlier
scholars, was original to the text; that the institution narrative,
found in *Sharar* but absent from the Mar Esa'ya text, was part of
the earlier prayer — as the existence of an anamnesis paragraph
in the latter indicated — but had been deleted from Addai and
Mari as a result of the reforms of Iso'Yab III in the seventh
century; and that the epiclesis was probably a fourth-century
accretion to the earlier core.[51]

There is, however, no clear scholarly consensus on the question of its original form. Bryan Spinks, for example, would
regard the prayer as having a bipartite structure rather than the
tripartite shape discerned by many other scholars, and would
hold that the institution narrative and anamnesis paragraphs are
additions to the original core, but that the epiclesis has many
primitive hall-marks. He also questions whether there ever was a
single original written form, and suggests that it may be more
accurate to speak simply of common oral tradition shared by the
two prayers.[52]

JERUSALEM

Although evidence for the very early period of Christian liturgical life in Jerusalem is lacking,[53] we are fortunate in having
several substantial sources to illuminate our knowledge of practices in the fourth and fifth centuries.[54] Care needs to be taken,

[51] 'The Ancient Form of the Anaphora of the Apostles', in *East of
Byzantium: Syria and Armenia in the Formative Period* (Dumbarton Oaks
Symposium 1980, Washington DC 1982), pp. 73—88.

[52] *Addai and Mari*, pp. 12, 24—9. See also his study, 'Addai and Mari and
the Institution Narrative: The Tantalizing Evidence of Gabriel Qatraya', *EL* 98
(1984), pp. 60—7; Jean Magne, 'L'anaphore nestorienne dite d'Addée et Mari
et l'anaphore maronite dite de Pierre III. Étude comparative', *OCP* 53 (1987),
pp. 107—58; E. J. Cutrone, 'The Liturgical Setting of the Institution Narrative
in the Early Syrian Tradition', in J. Neil Alexander, ed., *Time and Community*
(Washington DC 1990), pp. 105—14; and Anthony Gelston, *The Eucharistic
Prayer of Addai and Mari*, Oxford/New York 1991.

[53] Cf., however, John Wilkinson, 'Jewish Influences on the Early Christian
Rite of Jerusalem', *Muséon* 92 (1979), pp. 347—59.

[54] For an introductory survey, see John F. Baldovin, *Liturgy in Ancient
Jerusalem*, A/GLS 9, 1989, and also his extensive study, *The Urban Character of*

however, not to generalize from this testimony to what might have been the liturgical customs of other places during the same period. Because Jerusalem was the major pilgrimage centre of the fourth-century Christian world, its pattern of worship was necessarily unique in some respects and at least in part hybrid in character, as visiting groups of Christians from other parts of the world imported into it their own local usages as well as exporting from it other practices that were novel to them. The most important sources for its liturgy are:

(a) **The Catecheses of Cyril,** who was bishop of Jerusalem from 350 until his death in 387, although exiled several times as a result of the Arian controversy. His eighteen catechetical lectures, together with an introductory address (the Procatechesis), were delivered in 348 while he was still a presbyter.[55] There is in addition a series of 'Mystagogical Catecheses', a set of five post-baptismal homilies which have traditionally been thought to have been preached by Cyril to newly baptized Christians at Jerusalem,[56] but questions have been raised about their authorship.

Since the appearance of an important article on the question by W. J. Swaans in 1942,[57] there has been increasing support for the view that the Mystagogical Catecheses were not the genuine work of Cyril, but of some later person, possibly his successor as bishop of Jerusalem, John. The grounds for this are variations in manuscript attribution (some ascribe authorship to Cyril, some

---

Christian Worship, pp. 45—104. There is an exhaustive annotated bibliography of secondary literature from 1960 to 1980 in A. Renoux, 'Hierosolymitana', *ALW* 23 (1981), pp. 1—29, 149—75.

[55] Text in J. P. Migne, *Patrologia Graeca* 33.331—1064; English translation in Leo P. McCauley & A. A. Stephenson, *The Works of St Cyril of Jerusalem*, Washington DC 1969—70.

[56] Text in F. L. Cross, *St. Cyril of Jerusalem's Lectures on the Christian Sacraments: The Procatechesis and the Five Mystagogical Catecheses*, London 1951; A. Piédagnel, *Cyrille de Jerusalem: Catéchèses mystagogiques*, SC 126, 1966; English translations in Cross, op. cit.; W. Telfer, *Cyril of Jerusalem and Nemesius of Emesa*, London 1955 (selections); McCauley & Stephenson, *Works of St Cyril of Jerusalem* II; Yarnold, *Awe-Inspiring Rites*, pp. 65—95.

[57] 'A propos des "catéchèses Mystagogiques" attribuées à S. Cyrille de Jerusalem', *Muséon* 55 (1942), pp. 1—43.

to John, some to no one), differences in literary style and theology, and the description of the Jerusalem liturgy, which suggests a more developed form than is likely to have been the case as early as 348. C. Beukers suggested in 1961 that they were by Cyril, but from a date towards the end of his episcopate, and argued that the petition 'for our emperors, soldiers and allies' (5.8) pointed to the years 383–386.[58] Edward Yarnold has also more recently championed the traditional ascription to Cyril, suggesting that they were delivered later in Cyril's episcopate (350–386). This would explain the more developed form of the liturgy, and the differences in style and theological ideas, as Cyril's thought evolved. In any case they show similarities with Cyril's other works, and are unlike the sermon on the Church attributed to John.[59] Yarnold had earlier suggested that Ambrose of Milan knew these catecheses in 391, which also implied that Cyril rather than John was their author.[60]

Quite independently of the issue of the authorship of the Mystagogical Catecheses, there has also been a considerable discussion over the structure and contents of the eucharistic prayer to which these addresses allude. In particular, the debate has focused on the question: did the prayer contain the narrative of institution? The narrative is mentioned in the fourth address, but not in the description of the eucharistic prayer which comes in the fifth address. Some have argued that the prayer did include the narrative, but the author did not refer to it because he had already dealt with it in the preceding address or because it was already being recited silently in the eucharistic prayer and so would not have been heard by those to whom he was speaking.[61] Geoffrey Cuming suggested, on the basis of an analogous

[58] ' "For our Emperors, Soldiers and Allies": An Attempt at Dating the Twenty-third Catechesis by Cyrillus of Jerusalem', *Vigiliae Christianae* 15 (1961), pp. 177–84.

[59] 'The Authorship of the Mystagogic Catecheses Attributed to Cyril of Jerusalem', *Heythrop Journal* 19 (1978), pp. 143–61.

[60] 'Did St Ambrose know the Mystagogic Catecheses of St Cyril of Jerusalem?', pp. 184–9.

[61] See, for example, Baldovin, *Liturgy in Ancient Jerusalem*, pp. 25–7; Georg Kretschmar, 'Die frühe Geschichte der Jerusalemer Liturgie', *Jahrbuch für Liturgie und Hymnologie* 2 (1956), pp. 30–3.

comment in John Chrysostom, that the author's reference to the spiritual sacrifice being 'perfected' (5.8) was really an allusion to the narrative of institution. If so, it would thus have followed the epiclesis in the prayer, in line with the pattern of eucharistic prayer which evolved in Egypt, rather than have preceded it, as was the West Syrian custom.[62] Others insist that on the contrary there are really no grounds for supposing that the prayer contained the narrative.[63]

(b) **The Pilgrimage of Egeria**. This document is a travel-diary, evidently written by a female pilgrim to the Holy Land some time in the fourth century and intended to provide an account of what she saw for the members of the religious community from which she came. The one surviving manuscript, dating from the eleventh century, was discovered in 1884 and published in 1887.[64] The manuscript is incomplete and may represent only about one-third of the original. A few quotations from the work in medieval writings help to fill in some of its missing pages. Its opening and final pages are lacking, and consequently it has no title or author's name. The work itself says that the author came from 'the other end of the earth', and compares the colour of the Red Sea with that of 'the Ocean'. Its first editor, J. F. Gamurrini, attributed it to a pilgrim from Aquitaine mentioned by Palladius: her name was Silvia, or Silvania. However, in 1903 Dom Marius Férotin recognized that a seventh-century 'Letter in praise of the Blessed Aetheria', written by a monk named Valerius, was in fact about the author of this work.[65] Most

[62] G. J. Cuming, 'Egyptian Elements in the Jerusalem Liturgy', *JTS* 25 (1974), pp. 117–24.

[63] See E. J. Cutrone, 'Cyril's Mystagogical Catecheses and the Evolution of the Jerusalem Anaphora', *OCP* 44 (1978), pp. 52–64; John R. K. Fenwick, *Fourth Century Anaphoral Construction Techniques* (GLS 45, 1986), pp. 13–15.

[64] The most recent edition is by Pierre Maraval, *Égérie. Journal de Voyage*, SC 296, 1982; and the standard English translation is by John Wilkinson, *Egeria's Travels*, London 1971, 2nd edn 1981. There is also a translation by P. Wilson-Kastner in *A Lost Tradition: Women Writers of the Early Church* (Washington DC 1981), pp. 71–134. Wilkinson includes a select bibliography of secondary literature up to 1971 (pp. 300–3; 2nd edn, pp. 334–7), and M. Starowieyski, 'Bibliografia Egeriana', *Augustinianum* 19 (1979), pp. 297–318, offers a more comprehensive one, containing 296 entries.

[65] 'Le véritable auteur de la Peregrinatio Silviae, la vierge espagnole Etheria', *Revue des questions historiques* 74 (1903), pp. 367–97.

scholars accepted this conclusion, but different versions of the name appear in different manuscripts of Valerius' letter, including Egeria, Echeria, Etheria, Heteria, and Eiheria. Subsequently other evidence has been assembled which makes it more likely that Egeria is the correct version, but it is far from certain.[66] From details given in the narrative, it has been calculated that the author was in Jerusalem from 381 to 384.

While the diary gives a wealth of useful information about the Jerusalem liturgy in the late fourth century, it has several limitations. For example, it is inevitably somewhat selective in the liturgical practices the author chooses to report, reflecting no doubt her personal interests, and in particular it supplies no details of customs widely or universally practised at the time, but only of those which would have been unfamiliar to her original readers. Moreover, because it is the work of a visitor to a foreign community, there is some uncertainty concernng how far she correctly understood what was going on. A good example of this is the apparent discrepancy between her description of an eight-week Lenten season, with seven weeks of daily catechetical instruction on both the Scriptures and the Creed, and the evidence of other Jerusalem sources for a six-week Lent, as well as the existence of only eighteen lectures of Cyril which are to be delivered in this period and which focus on the Creed alone.[67]

(c) **The Armenian and Georgian Lectionaries.** The former of these, dating from the first half of the fifth century, reproduces the readings, feasts, and a number of the rubrics of the church at Jerusalem,[68] while the latter represents a later stage of develop-

[66] See Wilkinson, *Egeria's Travels*, pp. 235–6.

[67] For further details and attempts at reconciliation of the conflicting evidence, see Maxwell Johnson, 'Reconciling Cyril and Egeria on the Catechetical Process in Fourth-Century Jerusalem', in Bradshaw, *Essays in Early Eastern Initiation*, pp. 18–30.

[68] Introduction and text in A. Renoux, *Le Codex Arménien Jérusalem 121*, 2 vols, PO 35/1 & 36/2, 1969, 1971. See also John F. Baldovin, 'A Lenten Sunday Lectionary in Fourth Century Jerusalem', in Alexander, *Time and Community*, pp. 115–22; S. Janeras, 'A propos de la catéchèse XIVe de Cyrille de Jerusalem', *Ecclesia Orans* 3 (1986), pp. 307–18; M. F. Lages, 'The Hierosolymitain Origin of the Catechetical Rites in the Armenian Liturgy', *Didaskalia* 1 (1971), pp. 233–49.

ment of the same material.[69] Peter Jeffery has also recently drawn attention to the value of the Georgian chantbook, the *Iadgari*, in reconstructing Jerusalem liturgical practice.[70]

(d) **The Liturgy of St James.** The earliest manuscripts of this eucharistic liturgy date from the ninth century, and the rite has obviously undergone a considerable degree of development from earlier times. Its core appears to be a conflation of the eucharistic traditions of Antioch and Jerusalem, perhaps having taken place around the year 400.[71] John Fenwick has developed this idea further and argued that its anaphora is the result of the amalgamation in the late fourth century of the eucharistic prayer known to the author of the Mystogogical Catecheses with an early form of the Liturgy of St Basil.[72]

---

[69] M. Tarchnischvili, ed., *Le grand lectionnaire de l'Église de Jérusalem*, 2 vols, Corpus Scriptorum Christianorum Orientalium 189 & 205, Louvain 1959 – 60. See also H. Leeb, *Die Gesange in Gemeindegottesdienst von Jerusalem*, Vienna 1970.

[70] 'The Sunday Office of Seventh-Century Jerusalem in the Georgian Chantbook (Iadgari): A Preliminary Report', *SL* 21 (1991), pp. 52 – 75.

[71] Text in A. Hänggi & I. Pahl, *Prex Eucharistica* (Fribourg 1968), pp. 244 – 61, 269 – 75; English translation in Jasper & Cuming, *Prayers of the Eucharist*, pp. 88 – 99. For other aspects of the later Liturgy of St James, see G. J. Cuming, 'The Litanies in the Liturgy of St. James', *Ecclesia Orans* 3 (1986), pp. 175 – 80; 'The Missa Catechumenorum of the Liturgy of St James', *SL* 17 (1987), pp. 62 – 71; 'Further Studies in the Liturgy of St James', *SL* 18 (1988), pp. 161 – 9.

[72] *Fourth Century Anaphoral Construction Techniques*.

6. The Evolution of Eucharistic Rites

Early attempts at discerning eucharistic origins

Since they believed that Jesus himself had instituted the eucharist, it is hardly surprising that the pioneers of liturgical scholarship were generally agreed that the variety of eucharistic rites found in the ancient Church must all be ultimately derived from a single apostolic model. Thus, when an ancient church order describing itself as *The Apostolic Constitutions* was discovered in the late seventeenth century, it seemed to many that the archetype had at last been found.[1]

As Ronald Jasper indicated in his interesting survey of the work of British scholars on the origins of the eucharistic liturgy, this view was particularly held by Anglicans, and especially the Nonjurors of the early eighteenth century.[2] But it was by no means confined to them. It was also put forward, for example, by the French liturgist, Pierre Lebrun (1661–1729),[3] and it has been said of the German scholar, Ferdinand Probst (1816–1899), that he

> devoted immense erudition through a long lifetime to attempting to establish an impossible theory — namely that the College of Apostles, before they separated from Jerusalem, had elaborated, agreed upon, and enacted a comprehensive Liturgy for the celebration of the Holy Eucharist, from which all historic rites are descended; and that this archetype ... was to be identified with the liturgy set forth in the eighth book of the fourth-century compilation known as the *Apostolic Constitutions*.[4]

That this text was of greater length than many of those which were considered to have been derived from it was not seen as

[1] For this document, see above, pp. 93–5.

[2] *The Search for an Apostolic Liturgy* (Alcuin Club Pamphlet 18, London 1963), pp. 3–5. See also W. Jardine Grisbrooke, *Anglican Liturgies in the Seventeenth and Eighteenth Centuries* (ACC 40, London 1958), passim.

[3] *Explication littérale historique et dogmatique des prières et cérémonies de la messe* (Paris 1716–26 = 1949), pp. xxxix–xl.

[4] Bayard H. Jones, 'The Quest for the Origins of Christian Liturgies', *Anglican Theological Review* 46 (1964), p. 6. Probst's theory is set forth chiefly in two works, *Liturgie der drei ersten christlichen Jahrhunderte*, Tübingen 1870, and *Liturgie des vierten Jahrhunderts und deren Reform*, Münster 1893.

presenting an insuperable objection to the theory. Until the twentieth century, as John Fenwick has pointed out,[5] ideas concerning the development of the eucharist were haunted by a short tract *On the Transmission of the Divine Liturgy* attributed to Proclus, Bishop of Constantinople from 434 to 446.[6] This alleged that the earliest apostolic liturgies had been very lengthy, but that they were deliberately abridged in later centuries so as to retain the attention of less fervent generations of Christians. Its testimony has long since been discredited,[7] and indeed it has become a well-established canon of Christian liturgical scholarship that development normally proceeds from brevity to prolixity.[8]

Even the publication in 1883 of the *Didache* with its unusual liturgical provisions,[9] and the ultimate acceptance at the end of the nineteenth century that the eucharistic rite of *Apostolic Constitutions* 8 was not in fact genuinely apostolic, did not put an end to the quest for *the* original form of the Christian anaphora. *Didache* 9 contains prayers for what it describes as a *eucharistia*: a short prayer of thanksgiving to be said over 'the cup' followed by a somewhat longer prayer to be said over the 'broken bread' (*klasma*); and *Didache* 10 a lengthy prayer of thanksgiving to be said 'after being filled', ending with the direction that the prophets were to be allowed to give thanks (*eucharistein*) as they wished. Chapter 14 also gave the brief instruction that on the Lord's day its readers were to 'break bread and give thanks' (*eucharistesate*). Clearly, if chapters 9 and 10 were describing an actual eucharist, it was of a very different kind from those otherwise known to us from Christian antiquity, and precisely because

---

[5] *Fourth Century Anaphoral Construction Techniques*, p. 4.

[6] Migne, *Patrologia Graeca* 65, 849B—852B; English translation in Warren, *The Liturgy and Ritual of the Ante-Nicene Church*, pp. 197—9.

[7] F. J. Leroy, 'Proclus, "De Traditio Divinae Missae": un faux de C. Paleocappa', *OCP* 28 (1962), pp. 288—99, argued that the tract was in any case the work of a sixteenth-century forger.

[8] This was one of 'Baumstark's laws', though Baumstark regarded *Apostolic Constitutions* 8 as an exception to the rule, as it was not a true liturgical text 'formed by spontaneous evolution and really used by a community' (*Comparative Liturgy*, p. 20), and in any case he was himself still somewhat under the shadow of (Pseudo-)Proclus: see above, p. 59, n. 7.

[9] For this document, see above, pp. 85—7.

it did not harmonize with the rest of the evidence, many scholars regarded these chapters as referring to an agape rather than to a eucharist as such, and so excluded them from their consideration of eucharistic origins.[10]

Gustav Bickell (1838–1906), building upon Probst's theory, attempted to show that the first half of the eucharistic liturgy of *Apostolic Constitutions* 8 was ultimately derived from the Jewish Sabbath morning service, and the second half from the Passover meal.[11] Although his hypothesis was at first followed by a number of other writers,[12] an alternative theory concerning the second half of the rite proposed by a leading German Lutheran scholar, Paul Drews (1858–1912), eventually won greater support. He argued that its source was not the Passover, but rather the regular Jewish evening meal which inaugurated the Sabbath and festivals, the eucharistic prayer having evolved out of the grace said on such occasions.[13] He saw *Didache* 9–10 as representing a stepping-stone in this process and reflecting a daily religious meal held in the primitive Christian community —what could be described as a 'private' celebration of the eucharist and might be presided over by any member of the community —alongside which there had already developed before the end of the first century a more official form of the celebration of the eucharist, held only on Sundays and presided over by a bishop, which was referred to in *Didache* 14.[14] Although acknowledging the *Apostolic Constitutions* to be a fourth-century redaction, Drews nevertheless defended a revised

[10] See, for example, F. Kattenbusch, 'Messe', in *Realencyclopädie für protestantische Theologie und Kirche* 12 (Leipzig 1903), pp. 671ff.

[11] *Messe und Pascha*, Mainz 1872. His work was translated into English by W. F. Skene in *The Lord's Supper and the Paschal Ritual* (Edinburgh 1891), and popularized in Britain in a series of articles in the periodical *Dawn of Day* (1895–6) entitled 'The Passover and the Holy Communion by E. M.'

[12] See, for example, F.-J. Moreau, *Les liturgies eucharistiques: notes sur leur origine et leur développement* (Brussels 1924), pp. 40–1, 58ff.; J. B. Thibaut, *La Liturgie Romaine* (Paris 1924), pp. 11–37.

[13] 'Eucharistie', in *Realencyklopädie für protestantische Theologie und Kirche* 5 (Leipzig 1898), p. 563.

[14] 'Untersuchungen zur Didache', *ZNW* 5 (1904), pp. 74–9. His interpretation was followed by M. Goguel, *L'Eucharistie des origines à Justin Martyr*, Paris 1910.

version of Probst's theory, claiming, by a comparison of its liturgy with *1 Clement* and Justin Martyr, that it had managed to preserve the substance of the early 'official' celebration of the eucharist.[15]

Drews' thesis was adopted by a number of scholars, including Anton Baumstark,[16] and further elaborated by Eduard von der Goltz, who modified it by taking up a suggestion made earlier by Theodor Zahn (1838–1933) that *Didache* 10 constituted a prayer of preparation for the reception of the eucharistic elements following the meal in *Didache* 9.[17] Von der Goltz thought that the bread and wine would have been consecrated at a previous 'official' celebration of the eucharist,[18] clearly having difficulty in imagining that the meal alone could have been a true eucharist. Edmund Bishop also hinted at a possible duality of eucharistic origins, though without specifying exactly what he meant,[19] and, as we have seen earlier,[20] Hans Lietzmann (1875–1942) developed the theory that there were from the first two quite different types of eucharistic liturgy in the Church — Pauline and Jewish-Christian, with *Didache* 9–10 having evolved from the latter.

Louis Duchesne (1843–1922), in what became a standard work for much of the twentieth century, *Origines du culte chrétien*,[21] did not go as far as that. He acknowledged that there must have been variation in the details of early eucharistic rites

[15] *Zur Entstehungsgeschichte des Kanons*, Tübingen 1902, and *Untersuchungen über die sogennante Clementinische Liturgie*, Tübingen 1906.

[16] *Vom geschichtlichen Werden der Liturgie* (Freiburg 1923), pp. 7ff. Fernand Cabrol (*Les origines liturgiques*, p. 329) thought that the primitive character of the liturgy in the *Apostolic Constitutions*, 'quoique assez probable, n'est pas absolument indiscutable'.

[17] *Forschungen zur Geschichte des neutestamentlichen Kanons und der altchristlichen Literatur* III (Erlangen 1884), pp. 293ff.

[18] *Tischgebete und Abendsmahlsgebete in der altchristlichen und der griechischen Kirche*, Lepizig 1905. This view was repeated by Theodor Schermann, *Die allgemeine Kirchenordnung, frühchristliche Liturgien und kirchliche Uberlieferung* (Paderborn 1915 = New York 1968) II, pp. 282ff.

[19] In an appendix to R. H. Connolly, *The Liturgical Homilies of Narsai*, p. 145.

[20] See above, pp. 51–2.

[21] Paris 1899ff.; English translation: *Christian Worship: Its Origins and Evolution*, London 1903ff.

and that the celebrant would have had some freedom in improvising the prayers, but he still maintained that 'at the beginning the procedure was almost identical everywhere'. It was not long, however, before 'local diversities had crept into the ritual. The uses of Rome, Antioch, and Alexandria must, in the third century, have departed widely from the primitive uniformity.'[22] He regarded the *Didache* as 'contemporary, at the latest, with St Justin' and held that the liturgy described in *Didache* 9−10 was a eucharist. But he still did not allow it to count against his theory: he dismissed it from consideration as having 'altogether the aspect of an anomaly; it might furnish some of the features which we meet with in later compositions, but it is on the whole outside the general line of development both in respect of its ritual and style'.[23]

Later in the twentieth century, Joseph Jungmann (1889−1975), in his monumental and highly influential work, *Missarum Sollemnia* (Vienna 1948), espoused a broadly similar position: 'the local diversity of the earliest liturgies . . . must be understood only in the sense that, for want of precise legislation, certain minutiae might change from place to place'.[24] Nevertheless, he thought that three different types of eucharistic prayer must have developed 'quite early': one represented by the prayer in the *Apostolic Tradition*, one derived from the synagogue, and one 'in which the thoughts of the Christian acknowledgement of God were clothed in the phrases of hellenist philosophy'.[25] However, he considered it 'hardly likely' that the meal in *Didache* 9−10 included 'the sacramental Eucharist'.[26]

William Lockton, on the other hand, in an article published in 1918 switched the search for the apostolic liturgy elsewhere and, ignoring the *Didache* completely, considered that it was from the eucharistic prayer of the 'Egyptian Church Order' (later identified as the *Apostolic Tradition*) that 'every known Eastern

---

[22] English edns, p. 54. His approach was echoed by, among others, Fortescue, *The Mass*, pp. 51−7, 76ff.; Moreau, *Les liturgies eucharistiques*, pp. 31−2.

[23] English edns, pp. 52, 53−4.

[24] English translation: *The Mass of the Roman Rite* (New York 1951) I, p. 22, n. 1. See also ibid., p. 32, n. 20.

[25] ibid., I, p. 31. For the *Apostolic Tradition*, see above, pp. 89−92.

[26] ibid., I, p. 12.

liturgy without a single exception is ultimately derived'. Since he found its language to be Johannine and Ephesine, he asked, 'is it too much to conclude that it represents the liturgy of the church at Ephesus in the later apostolic days, and was in practically its present form the work of St. John —an idea which would explain what would otherwise be very difficult, its almost universal distribution?'[27] The same point of view, although in a much less extreme form, was later advanced by Walter Frere: 'this Hippolytean Anaphora fully corroborates the norm or canon which . . . [lies] at the basis of the vast number of later Anaphoras'.[28]

Though belief in a single (or dual) apostolic parent-liturgy was widespread, it was not universally adopted by all liturgical historians. There were those who held on dogmatic grounds that Christ had prescribed no particular form of eucharistic rite for the Church to follow,[29] and there were others who opposed the single-origin theory on textual grounds: later eucharistic rites showed such diversity among themselves that it was difficult to see any real evidence to suggest that they were descended from a single archetype.[30] Scholars of this school tended to conclude that in the apostolic age and for a considerable time afterwards liturgical forms were fluid.[31] R. M. Woolley (1877–1931) thought that in the evidence from before the year 200 'there are signs of three or perhaps four different uses, based on different ideas, and yet all expressing the fact that in the Eucharist the Church is doing as her Lord bids her', one of these being the type of prayer represented by *Didache* 9–10.[32]

[27] 'The Eucharistic Prayer', *Church Quarterly Review* 86 (1918), pp. 309–13.

[28] *The Anaphora*, p. 48.

[29] An early example of this approach can be seen in Charles Wheatly, *Rational Illustration upon the Book of Common Prayer* (London 1710), ch. 6, introduction, sec. 2.

[30] See, for example, William Palmer, *Origines Liturgicae* (Oxford 1832), pp. 5–6; Philip Freeman, *The Principles of Divine Service* II (Oxford 1862), pp. 380ff.; C. A. Swainson, *The Greek Liturgies* (Cambridge 1884), p. xxxii.

[31] See, for example, J. H. Srawley, *The Early History of the Liturgy* (Cambridge 1913), pp. xiii–xiv; Armitage Robinson, 'Invocation in the Holy Eucharist', *Theology* 8 (1924), pp. 89–100.

[32] *The Liturgy of the Primitive Church* (Cambridge 1910), pp. 45–6.

What did come to be generally accepted in the twentieth century, however, was that the ultimate roots of the Christian eucharist lay in Jewish liturgical practice, and the notion that the first half of the rite was descended from the synagogue service and the second half from the Jewish grace at meals was pursued in particular by a whole series of Anglican liturgical scholars — Woolley, Lockton, W. O. E. Oesterley (1866–1950), Frank Gavin (1890–1938), Felix Cirlot (1901–1956),[33] and eventually Gregory Dix.

Gregory Dix (1901–1952)

In his classic work, *The Shape of the Liturgy*, first published in 1945, Dix was one of the severest critics of attempts to find a single original eucharistic prayer.[34] However, he did not really abandon the theory, but merely revised it: in his view, the various forms of the Christian eucharist did have a common origin, but this was to be sought in the structure or shape of the rite rather than in the wording of the prayers. 'What was fixed and immutable everywhere in the second century was the outline or Shape of the Liturgy, what was *done*. What our Lord instituted was not a "service", something said, but an action, something done — or rather the continuance of a traditional jewish action, but with a new meaning. . . .'[35] In the years since the publication of his book Dix's influence has become all-pervasive and his methodology widely followed, even if some of the details of his conclusions would now be challenged. He has thus enabled the traditional theory of a single liturgical archetype to retain its position of pre-eminence in this modified form down to the present day, and for that reason his arguments warrant careful examination.

Dix shared the standard scholarly consensus that the first half of the rite was 'in its Shape simply a continuation of the jewish

---

[33] Woolley, *The Liturgy of the Primitive Church*, pp. 48–53; Lockton, 'The Eucharistic Prayer', pp. 309–10; Oesterley, *The Jewish Background of the Christian Liturgy*, esp. pp. 172–4, 187–91; Gavin, *The Jewish Antecedents of the Christian Sacraments*, pp. 59–97; Felix L. Cirlot, *The Early Eucharist* (London 1939), esp. pp. 61ff.

[34] op. cit., pp. 209ff.

[35] ibid., pp. 214–15.

synagogue service of our Lord's time', and declared that its 'original unchanging outline ... everywhere' was:

1. Opening greeting by the officiant and reply of the church.
2. Lesson.
3. Psalmody.
4. Lesson (or Lessons, separated by Psalmody).
5. Sermon.
6. Dismissal of those who did not belong to the church.
7. Prayers.
8. Dismissal of the church.[36]

This conclusion involves two major presuppositions: (a) that the contents of the first-century synagogue Sabbath service were fixed and are known to us; (b) that the fact that these eight elements are consistently found in liturgical sources from the fourth century onwards means that they must have been in existence from early times. But all this is far from certain. We have indicated earlier how little is really known of first-century synagogue liturgy, and that the relative uniformity of later Christian liturgical customs may be the result of a fourth-century movement towards standardization rather than the faithful adherence to a primitive norm.[37]

Dix himself was prepared to admit that the opening greeting with its reply was only 'probably' an inheritance from the first days of Christianity. In fact, there is no hard evidence for its usage either in early Judaism or in Christian worship before the third century, and then only in the dialogue preceding the eucharistic prayer in the *Apostolic Tradition* and not as an initial greeting.[38] Moreover, while Dix believed that the custom of singing psalms between the readings 'must have been familiar to our Lord and His apostles, since it was universal in the

[36] ibid., pp. 36, 38. Dix regarded the kiss of peace as constituting the beginning of the second half of the eucharist (ibid., pp. 103–10), but Tertullian's description of it as 'the seal of prayer' (*De Or.* 18), if more generally valid, suggests that it should rather be seen as forming the conclusion of the first half. In any case, Dix was mistaken in thinking that it was something inherited from Judaism.

[37] See above, pp. 17–24, 63–5.

[38] See van Unnik, '*Dominus vobiscum*: The Background of a Liturgical Formula', pp. 270–305.

synagogues of their day',[39] we have already seen that more recent scholarship has cast serious doubts on this.[40] There is only one piece of firm evidence for the practice among Christians before the fourth century, from Tertullian in North Africa, and that is in relation to a Montanist service.[41] As I have remarked elsewhere,[42] this is a very uncertain foundation upon which to make any assertion about the catholic practice of the day. While it *may* have been a common custom to begin the service with a greeting and response of some sort, or to include a psalm between the readings in the second or third century, we do not *know* that this was so.

Since the 'dismissal of those who did not belong to the church' is a purely Christian development, what we are left with in terms of similarities between the worship of the synagogue and that of the early Church is simply that both had readings from their Scriptures, preaching, and prayers. These are not particularly striking parallels, especially if the ministry of the word in the synagogue liturgy followed the prayers rather than preceded them, as it did in the Christian service.[43] This is not to deny the possibility that the first half of the eucharistic rite does in fact owe its origin to the synagogue, but merely to suggest that the Christian service has undergone a considerable measure of independent development.

Nor have we any reason to suppose that this development must have involved an 'unchanging outline . . . everywhere'. Our oldest source, the *First Apology* of Justin Martyr written at Rome in the middle of the second century, merely says that 'the records of the apostles or the writings of the prophets are read for as long as time allows. Then, when the reader has finished, the president in a discourse admonishes and exhorts [us] to imitate these good things. Then we all stand up together and offer prayers. . . .'[44] Apart from a few additional details provided

---

[39] *The Shape of the Liturgy*, p. 39.
[40] See above, pp. 22–4.
[41] *De Anima* 9.
[42] 'The Liturgical Use and Abuse of Patristics', p. 136.
[43] See above, pp. 17–18.
[44] *I Apol.* 67.3–5.

by Tertullian and Cyprian in North Africa,[45] we have no other
direct evidence for this half of the rite in the ante-Nicene period,
and no justification at all for concluding that what these authors
describe as practices familiar in their region were necessarily the
universal customs of the time. Once again, this is not to deny
that some of the features found in fourth-century sources may
not also have existed in the third — or even the second —
century, but only to say that we cannot know with any certainty
which they were, nor when or where they were practised.

The shape of the second half of the rite was constituted by a
modification of the 'seven-action scheme' of the Last Supper,
when Jesus is said to have (1) taken bread; (2) given thanks over
it; (3) broken it; (4) distributed it; and later to have (5) taken a
cup; (6) given thanks over it; and (7) handed it to his disciples.
According to Dix,

> With absolute unanimity the liturgical tradition reproduces these seven
> actions as four: (1) The offertory; bread and wine are 'taken' and placed on
> the table together. (2) The prayer; the president gives thanks to God over
> bread and wine together. (3) The fraction; the bread is broken. (4) The
> communion; the bread and wine are distributed together.
>
>   In that form and in that order these four actions constituted the
> absolutely invariable nucleus of every eucharistic rite known to us
> throughout antiquity from the Euphrates to Gaul.[46]

Dix believed that the transition from the sevenfold to the
fourfold shape 'must have been very solidly established everywhere as the invariable practice before the first three gospels or
1 Cor. began to circulate with authority . . . or some tendency
would have shown itself somewhere to assimilate current prac-

---

[45] Even this evidence needs to be treated with some care. Just because, for
example, Tertullian speaks of the church at Rome, like that of North Africa, as
uniting 'the law and the prophets with the writings of evangelists and apostles,
from which she drinks in her faith' (*De Praescript.* 36), this does not *necessarily*
mean that the liturgical ministry of the word always included four readings:
Law, Prophets, Epistle, and Gospel.

[46] *The Shape of the Liturgy*, p. 48. Dix has been criticized for his introduction of the term 'offertory' in relation to the first of the four actions and for
confusing here the preparatory 'bringing up' of the bread and wine to the president with the president's taking of them into his hands in order to give thanks
over them: see further Colin O. Buchanan, *The End of the Offertory* (GLS 14,
1978), esp. pp. 3ff. & 28ff.

tice to that recorded as original'; and he connected this development with the severance of the eucharist from the context of a genuine meal.[47] While there may be some force to this argument, the truth is that we do not know whether there ever were any such attempts at assimilation. Because of the paucity of early Christian literature, we are not in a position to say exactly when this way of celebrating the eucharist did become universal. Dix dealt with *Didache* 9−10 (which might have been seen as constituting an exception to his rule) by returning to the older theory and excluding it from consideration on the grounds that what it described was an agape and not a eucharist.[48]

In spite of his insistence that it was the overall shape of the rite rather than the specific contents of any prayer which constituted the common core of the eucharist, Dix nevertheless thought that it was possible to reconstruct the general outline of the early eucharistic prayer. Like earlier Anglican scholars, he believed that it had evolved out of the standard Jewish grace after meals, the *Birkat ha-mazon*, the first two paragraphs of which 'in substantially their present form were in use in Palestine in our Lord's time'.[49] He also drew attention to part of the opening dialogue to the eucharistic prayer, as found in the *Apostolic Tradition*: 'Let us give thanks to the Lord; It is meet and right.' This, he asserted, was 'clearly derived' from the invitation preceding the Jewish grace, and the form in the *Apostolic Tradition* was that laid down by the rabbis 'when there are ten in company'. He concluded that its survival in the *Apostolic Tradition* 'would alone suffice to identify the christian eucharistic prayer with the jewish *berakah*'.[50] We have indicated earlier the uncertainty that exists as to whether the Jewish grace did have a standardized form in the first century, and also noted that what eventually came to be its regular opening dialogue is actually significantly different from the Christian version,[51] which suggests that, if indeed there was a Jewish prototype

[47] *The Shape of the Liturgy*, pp. 49−50.
[48] ibid, pp. 48, n. 2, & 90ff. He was following the position already adopted by Connolly, 'Agape and Eucharist in the Didache'.
[49] *The Shape of the Liturgy*, pp. 53−4.
[50] ibid., p. 127.
[51] See above, pp. 24−6.

behind this part of the eucharistic prayer, then either Christian usage had modified it significantly or there were variant forms of the introductory dialogue in existence in first-century Judaism.

Dix thought that the second paragraph of the *Birkat ha-mazon* in particular, which contained a series of thanksgivings, offered parallels to the thanksgiving themes in Justin Martyr and the *Apostolic Tradition*. Moreover, since 'the same themes, in approximately the same order, are found too in other traditions', he judged that

> those who believe that there was an original authoritative outline of the prayer could make out (by a comparison of traditions) an overwhelmingly strong case for regarding this series of 'Thanksgivings' as the original opening of the prayer (after the preliminary 'Naming' of God), especially if its derivation from the second paragraph of the *berakah* be admitted.

He went on to insist, however, that 'the connection —if such there be—between the jewish and christian thanksgiving is one of ideas and form only, not of phrasing. The *berakah* has been entirely re-written in terms of the New Covenant.'[52]

Nevertheless, he was aware of difficulties in suggesting this line of evolution. One was the question of the 'thanksgiving for creation', which was present in one form or another in the Christian prayers but had no parallel in the second paragraph of the Jewish prayer. While he thought that it could be argued that this was a later addition, resulting from 'disputes at Rome over the Gnostic doctrine that creation was in itself evil', he believed that 'these controversies might have led only to a change or increase of emphasis on this point in the Roman prayer, not to the insertion *de novo* of the idea itself into the scheme everywhere'.[53] Another difficulty was that there were eucharistic prayers which did not have an opening sequence of thanksgivings as such, but he argued that in these cases it had been eliminated by the later prefixing of the preface and Sanctus.[54]

Moreover, while he was convinced that early eucharistic prayers once all possessed a sequence of thanksgiving themes in their first half:

[52] *The Shape of the Liturgy*, pp. 216—17.
[53] ibid., p. 217, n. 2.
[54] ibid., pp. 217—19.

it is when we pass . . . into the second half of the prayer that the difficulties in the way of establishing the existence of any original universal model of the prayer become really formidable. . . . When one has eliminated from the second half of each of these prayers all that can safely be ascribed to later local development and to borrowings, it is not easy to detect any single scheme upon which they all arrange their parts and ideas. . . . The inference is that any original material common to them all covered only the first half and the concluding doxology.[55]

He was inclined to conclude, therefore, that these elements constituted the earliest shape of the eucharistic prayer, and that the second half was formed by subsequent expansion of the primitive nucleus during the second century.[56] This conclusion was, of course, strongly influenced by his methodological presupposition that only what was common could be regarded as primitive. As we shall see, subsequent scholarship would wrestle further with all these problems.

Sanctus and Berakah

The 1950s saw two further influential — though flawed — contributions to the debate about eucharistic origins. E. C. Ratcliff (1896–1967) expressed his conviction that the eucharistic prayer of the *Apostolic Tradition* had been extensively re-worked so as to make it conform to the norms of a later age. In his view, the original version had been closer to the pattern to which he believed Justin Martyr and Irenaeus witnessed, and consisted of more extensive thanksgiving for the work of creation and redemption, the absence of any epiclesis, and the inclusion of a final thanksgiving for the admission of the worshippers to the worship of heaven, culminating in the singing of the Sanctus.[57] He developed a similar theory in relation to a eucharistic prayer outlined in the homilies of Narsai.[58] Though Ratcliff's drastic

---

[55] ibid., p. 220.

[56] ibid., pp. 221–37.

[57] 'The Sanctus and the Pattern of the Early Anaphora', *JEH* 1 (1950), pp. 29–36, 125–34 = *Liturgical Studies*, pp. 18–40. Dix had already acknowledged that the invocation of the Spirit on the oblation was likely to have been a fourth-century interpolation: see *The Shape of the Liturgy*, p. 158, n. 1.

[58] 'A Note on the Anaphoras Described in the Liturgical Homilies of Narsai', in J. N. Birdsall & R. W. Thompson, eds., *Biblical and Patristic Studies in Memory of Robert Pierce Casey* (Freiburg/New York 1963), pp. 235–49 = *Liturgical Studies*, pp. 66–79.

reconstruction drew strong support from a few other English scholars, notably A. H. Couratin and G. A. Michell,[59] it did not ultimately succeed in convincing the majority. In particular, it seemed unlikely that the Sanctus had once formed the climax of the prayer and then later been omitted from it altogether, especially as W. C. van Unnik forcefully argued in 1951 that there was no clear evidence for any liturgical use of the Sanctus in early Christianity.[60]

Jean-Paul Audet (1903–), in a paper read at the International Congress on the Four Gospels held at Oxford in 1957,[61] attempted to examine the literary genre of the *berakah* in general, which he regarded as the true parent of the Christian *eucharistia*. He distinguished two sorts of *berakot*: what he called 'the spontaneous original benediction' (made up of two literary elements, the blessing itself and the motive for the blessing), and a supposed later development, 'the cultual benediction', which now had three elements:

> a) the 'benediction' proper, always rather short, more or less stereotyped in its forms, leaning towards the invitatory genre, an enthusiastic call to divine praise; b) a central element which I would call the anamnesis of the *mirabilia Dei*; this second element is nothing else than a more or less protracted development of the motive as it already existed in the original

[59] A. H. Couratin, 'The Sanctus and the Pattern of the Early Anaphora: A Note on the Roman Sanctus', *JEH* 2 (1951), pp. 19–23; idem, 'The Sacrifice of Praise', *Theology* 58 (1955), pp. 285–91; G. A. Michell, 'Firmilian and Eucharistic Consecration', *JTS* 5 (1954), pp. 215–20; idem, *Landmarks in Liturgy* (London 1961), pp. 84–9. Building upon the work of these scholars, W. E. Pitt, 'The Origin of the Anaphora of St Basil', *JEH* 12 (1961), pp. 1–13, argued that the original form of that anaphora had consisted of preface and Sanctus alone.

[60] '*1 Clement* 34 and the Sanctus', *Vigiliae Christianae* 5 (1951), pp. 204–48. See also the critique of Ratcliff's theory in Bryan D. Spinks, 'A Note on the Anaphora Outlined in Narsai's Homily XXXII', *JTS* 31 (1980), pp. 82–93; 'The Cleansed Leper's Thankoffering before the Lord: Edward Craddock Ratcliff and the Pattern of the Early Anaphora', in Spinks, *The Sacrifice of Praise*, pp. 161–78.

[61] 'Literary Forms and Contents of a Normal Eucharistia in the First Century', *Studia Evangelica* 1 (1959), pp. 643–62; expanded version: 'Esquisse historique du genre littéraire de la "bénédiction" juive et de l'"eucharistie" chrétienne', *Revue biblique* 65 (1958), pp. 371–99.

spontaneous 'benediction' . . . ; c) lastly, the return of the initial 'benediction' by way of *inclusio*, or doxology. . . .[62]

This short article has since been very frequently cited as authoritative,[63] in spite of the fact that its analysis of Jewish liturgical forms is quite unsatisfactory. It was criticized in 1968 by Robert Ledogar for grouping the variety of first-century praise formulae into a single classification, and in particular for translating *eucharistein* as 'to bless',[64] and in 1975 by Thomas Talley for failing to examine the *berakot* in the context of the liturgical groupings in which they are found.[65] The article's shortcomings should be even more apparent in the light of our earlier survey of first-century Jewish liturgical forms.[66]

Louis Bouyer (1913–)

In his major work, *Eucharistie*, published in 1966,[67] Bouyer focused on the 'progressive unfolding' of the eucharistic prayer throughout history. In the early chapters he examined the use of the *berakah* in Judaism more broadly than Dix had done and considered not just the meal-prayers but also other liturgical formularies, with the aim of demonstrating the Jewish roots of the whole of the eucharistic prayer, and not merely of its first half. Like Dix, he subscribed to the view that Jewish prayer-forms were already fixed in the first century,[68] and pointed out that the grace after meals possessed a threefold structure: a blessing for creation (to which he gave the designation D), a blessing for redemption (E), and a supplication for the eschatological fulfilment of the people of God (F). He compared this with a similar threefold pattern which he claimed to find in the synagogue

---

[62] ibid., pp. 646–7.

[63] See, for example, the use made of it by Aidan Kavanagh, 'Thoughts on the Roman Anaphora', *Worship* 39 (1965), pp. 516ff.

[64] *Acknowledgement: Praise-Verbs in the Early Greek Anaphora* (Rome 1968), p. 124. His own analysis, however, fails adequately to distinguish all the varieties of praise formulae.

[65] See below, n. 82.

[66] See above, pp. 15–17.

[67] English translation: *Eucharist*, Notre Dame 1968.

[68] See especially, in the English edition, pp. 52–3.

liturgy in the two *berakot* before the *Shema* (which he designated as A and B) and the following *Tefillah* (C).[69]

Bouyer argued that the oldest forms of the eucharistic prayer followed the DEF pattern, but that because the eucharistic rite came to be situated immediately after a synagogue-type service, containing the ABC pattern, later prayers show a fusion between the ABC and DEF schemas:

> quite soon more or less important modifications can be observed that synthesize the two groups so that doublets or too evident repetitions might be avoided. Once this remodeling produced a completely new mold, a new schema was arrived at, which we might characterize by the formula AD−BE−CF.[70]

He believed that 'the first formulas of the Christian eucharist . . . are but Jewish formulas applied by means of a few added words to a new content',[71] and regarded the prayers of *Didache* 9−10 as reflecting a primitive Christian eucharist.[72] The other examples which he cited as still following the DEF schema were the Anaphora of Addai and Mari (in its original version) and that of the *Apostolic Tradition*. While he regarded the first as 'an archaic formula of indisputable authenticity', he held the second to be 'the work of an archaizer' attempting to resurrect the liturgy of an earlier time before the eucharist had become joined to a synagogue-type service.[73] The Alexandrian Liturgy of St Mark, on the other hand, he believed showed evidence of a remodelling of the ABC schema combined with the older DEF pattern, because of the presence of the Sanctus and of extensive intercessions, both characteristic of the synagogue liturgy but not of the meal-prayers. He even claimed to detect a correspondence between the themes of the intercessions and those of the Jewish *Tefillah*.[74]

Bouyer's ingenious theory has the advantage of offering an explanation for a puzzling development in eucharistic prayers:

[69] ibid., pp. 88−9.
[70] ibid., pp. 89−90.
[71] ibid., p. 106.
[72] ibid., pp. 115−19.
[73] ibid., pp. 146−82. For Addai and Mari, see above, pp. 124−5.
[74] ibid., pp. 192−9. For the Liturgy of St Mark, see above, pp. 119−20.

the emergence of an element which was seemingly of Jewish origin — the Sanctus — but surprisingly late in the evolutionary process, when one might have imagined Jewish influence to have long since waned, and also in a context — in association with meal-prayers — in which it had apparently not belonged in the Jewish tradition. Yet his theory has not won much favour. It presupposes that one part of Christian worship, that derived from the synagogue, remained remarkably stable and conservative for the first few centuries of the Church's history (for which there is no firm evidence at all), while the eucharistic prayer itself evolved very freely, retaining only the broadest outline of its Jewish ancestor, until a sudden desire arose to try to fuse the two parts into a single whole. Though he may have been pointing in the right general direction in some respects, especially with regard to the later migration of the Sanctus from non-eucharistic to eucharistic use, Bouyer attempted to prove too much and with too great a precision.

Louis Ligier (1911–1989)

Bouyer was also criticized by the Jesuit scholar Louis Ligier, the next major contributor to the debate, for being more attentive to similarities than to differences, and for analysing the material more in a theological fashion than from the literary and liturgical viewpoint. Ligier believed that the main advantage of Bouyer's approach was that it did attempt to explain the development of the whole eucharistic prayer, but its principal weakness lay in the variety of extant Christian anaphoras, since this inevitably tempted one to select those documents which were most favourable to one's thesis. In particular, he questioned the use of the Liturgy of St Mark as a starting-point, since there was too much uncertainty about its primitive text to justify any firm reflection on it. He also criticized Bouyer's tendency to make a superficial abstraction of ideas and themes from Jewish *berakot* without due consideration of their literary form, place in the liturgical structure, and original context.[75] In this respect he

[75] 'Les origines de la prière eucharistique', *QLP* 53 (1972), pp. 181–202 = 'The Origins of the Eucharistic Prayer: From the Last Supper to the Eucharist', *SL* 9 (1973), pp. 161–85.

made a passing reference to Joseph Heinemann's important work on Jewish prayer-forms, apparently the first Christian liturgical scholar to do so.[76] He was also the first to recognize that the introductory dialogue of the Christian eucharistic prayer ('Let us give thanks . . .') was not exactly identical with the standard invitation preceding the Jewish grace after meals.[77]

The main advantage of his own approach, on the other hand, Ligier believed, was that the number of difficulties diminished when one narrowed the focus, for he was initially concerned not to explain the origins of the whole eucharistic prayer, but instead to concentrate on the presence of the narrative of institution within it, which he compared to the festal narrative embolisms found in some Jewish prayers.[78] He admitted, however, that two main objections could be raised to his line of argument: one was the claim that there was really no need to have to explain the presence of the narrative, as it had always been there; the other was the more serious question as to the antiquity of the Jewish embolisms which he cited. He attempted to answer the second objection by pointing out that the rabbinic authorities who were said to have discussed the use of festal embolisms in the grace after meals were all figures of the first to the fourth century C.E., and hence 'it can be maintained that the practice of embolisms goes back to the first, or at latest the second century'. He also noted that, while the usual place for an embolism was in the thanksgiving section of the grace, it could also be inserted into the supplication, which was significant in view of the two different positions in which the narrative of institution was found in eucharistic prayers.[79]

---

[76] 'The Origins of the Eucharistic Prayer', p. 170. He had already made a similar reference in 'De la cène du Seigneur à l'Eucharistie', *Assemblées du Seigneur* 1 (1968) = 'From the Last Supper to the Eucharist', in L. C. Sheppard, ed., *The New Liturgy* (London 1970), p. 135, n. 83. For Heinemann, see above, pp. 4–7.

[77] 'From the Last Supper to the Eucharist', p. 144.

[78] See his earlier articles: 'Autour du sacrifice eucharistique. Anaphores orientales et anamnèse juive de Kippur', *Nouvelle revue théologique* 82 (1960), pp. 40–55; 'Anaphores orientales et prières juives', *Proche-Orient chrétien* 13 (1963), pp. 3–20; 'De la cène de Jésus à l'anaphore de l'Eglise', *La Maison-Dieu* 87 (1966), pp. 7–49.

[79] 'The Origins of the Eucharistic Prayer', pp. 171–6.

Finally, he proceeded to combine his approach with that of Dix and Bouyer to suggest the process of evolution of the whole eucharistic prayer. Even though he had earlier acknowledged that in the first century 'the Jewish liturgy allowed the president to adapt and even to invent his own prayer',[80] he still believed that the tripartite *Birkat ha-mazon* constituted the origin of the eucharistic prayer, but that the first section devoted to creation had in Christian usage become integrated into the second and absorbed by it, as was confirmed by *Didache* 10. Then the narrative of institution together with the anamnesis paragraph ('having in remembrance . . .'), with which it formed a unity, had been inserted into the centre of the prayer, on the model of the Jewish embolisms, and this had a significant effect on the whole anaphora. Finally, the Sanctus, the commemoration of salvation-history following it in certain eastern traditions, and extensive intercession were added to complete the classical shape. All of these latter elements appeared to Ligier to show Jewish influence, but he did not think it possible to offer a clear explanation for their appearance.[81]

What is most interesting about Ligier's work is why it should be thought necessary to look for a *Jewish* precedent at all for the presence of the narrative of institution in eucharistic prayers. Why is it not sufficient to accept this as a purely *Christian* devel opment, brought about entirely by the current needs of the worshipping community? It would seem that the only reasons for seeking a Jewish background for this phenomenon are that it is being assumed either that Jewish prayer-traditions continued to exercise a strong influence on the Gentile Church of the second and third centuries or even later (which receives little confirmation from other sources), or that the insertion of the narrative happened very early in the evolutionary process, when Jewish influence was still determinative. If the latter is the true motivating force, does one detect here the long shadow of the traditional western theory of eucharistic consecration as being effected by the recitation of the words of institution? Are Ligier, and other scholars like him, subconsciously influenced by the

---

[80] 'From the Last Supper to the Eucharist', p. 117, n. 15.
[81] 'The Origins of the Eucharistic Prayer', pp. 179−85.

need to show that the use of the narrative really does go back to very early times, even if not to the absolute beginnings of Christianity?

Thomas Talley (1924–)

Talley's first major contribution to the question of the origins of the eucharistic prayer came in a paper delivered at the 1975 congress of Societas Liturgica.[82] There he criticized Audet's treatment of the Jewish *berakah* and pointed out that the threefold pattern of the Jewish grace after meals was blessing – thanksgiving – supplication, and not blessing – anamnesis – doxology as visualized by Audet. In so doing, however, he appeared to treat the third-century rabbinic rules concerning the form of the *berakah* as operative for the period of Christian origins and also accepted Louis Finkelstein's reconstruction of an *Urtext* of the *Birkat ha-mazon*.[83] He followed Finkelstein in observing parallels between its structure and that of the prayer in *Didache* 10, and in noting the inversion of the first two paragraphs from the traditional Jewish order (thanksgiving now preceding the reference to God's gift of food) and the substitution of a doxology for a concluding benediction. This led him to the conclusion that 'while the Jewish tradition is fundamental for primitive Christianity, the practices of the early Church reflect a pattern which is as meticulously different from as it is broadly grounded upon that Jewish tradition'.[84]

However, just as the switch of Christian fast-days from Monday and Thursday to Wednesday and Friday had at one time merely seemed perversity on the part of Christians and now seemed to have some affinity with the calendar of Qumran,[85] were there, Talley wondered, new similarities to be found in other directions? Acknowledging that the common tendency

---

[82] 'The Eucharistic Prayer of the Ancient Church according to Recent Research: Results and Reflections', *SL* 11 (1976), pp. 138–58. This also appeared in a slightly expanded form as 'From Berakah to Eucharistia: A Reopening Question', *Worship* 50 (1976), pp. 115–37 = Kevin Seasoltz, ed., *Living Bread, Saving Cup* (Collegeville 1987), pp. 80–101.

[83] See above, p. 4.

[84] 'The Eucharistic Prayer of the Ancient Church', pp. 138–49.

[85] See below, p. 194.

among Christian scholars to identify *eulogein* with *eucharistein* and to equate both with the Hebrew verb *barak* had obscured the recognition of the priority which had been given to thanksgiving by the early Christians, he turned to a short paper by Henri Cazelles,[86] which traced the background of the term *eucharistia* and pointed to its link with the *zebah todah*, 'the sacrifice of praise', in the Old Testament. This sacrificial connotation, Talley suggested, might provide a clue to the reason why the *Didache* had inverted the normal arrangement of the *Birkat ha-mazon*.[87]

He then went on to see in the anaphora of the *Apostolic Tradition* an emendation of the threefold blessing — thanksgiving—supplication pattern to a twofold thanksgiving—supplication pattern, and in the Anaphora of Addai and Mari the retention of the threefold structure —praise for creation, thanksgiving for redemption, supplication —'though still giving a prominence to thanksgiving'. He also found this threefold pattern 'in such classic anaphoras as those of James and Basil'. He concluded with the remark: 'no, *berakah* is not the same as *eucharistia*, and we may hope that further studies will help us to understand the meaning and consequences of that, after all, rather odd fact'.[88]

By 1982 Talley was able to say that the main outlines of the history of the eucharistic prayer 'seem much clearer now than they did a decade ago'.[89] Here he referred to the work of Heinemann, who had emphasized the variety and flexibility of Jewish prayer-content; to studies of the use of *eucharistein* in first-century Judaism, which pointed to a possible sacrificial dimension for the choice of this word by Christians; to the suggestion, made independently by both Edward Kilmartin and Geoffrey Cuming, that the Strasbourg papyrus might constitute a complete eucharistic prayer;[90] and to recent considerations of the Sanctus. Although the Sacramentary of Sarapion had

---

[86] See above, p. 50, n. 80.

[87] 'The Eucharistic Prayer of the Ancient Church', pp. 149—50.

[88] ibid., pp. 151—7.

[89] 'The Eucharistic Prayer: Tradition and Development', in Kenneth Stevenson, *Liturgy Reshaped*, pp. 48—64.

[90] See above, p. 119, n. 32.

previously been the earliest place where the Sanctus had been found in a eucharistic prayer, Hans-Jorg Auf der Maur had discovered references to it in a eucharistic setting in the Easter Homilies of Asterios Sophistes, who wrote in the vicinity of Antioch probably between 335 and 341, and those references also pointed to its use in a non-eucharistic setting, as in *Apostolic Constitutions* 7.35 and the *Te Deum*.[91]

From all this Talley developed the hypothesis that out of the tripartite pattern of the Jewish grace after meals the primitive Christian anaphora had for some reason focused on thanksgiving, even to the extent of subsuming to it the creation-theme of the first section of the Jewish prayer, and so given rise initially to a bipartite structure of thanksgiving–supplication; but that a prayer of praise of the Creator which culminated in the Sanctus had been adopted from the synagogue as an element in Christian morning prayer and was subsequently prefixed —possibly in the third century —to the anaphora itself 'especially in East Syria where Christianity remained most strongly Jewish', thus restoring the tripartite structure (praise for creation, thanksgiving for redemption, supplication) found in later eucharistic prayers. While the East Syrian pattern placed the institution narrative and anamnesis in the concluding section, further west (possibly in Antioch) it formed the conclusion of the thanksgiving, as was also the case in the *Apostolic Tradition*. With regard to Alexandria, he took up Cuming's theory (which will be discussed more fully below), that since the theme of creation was already included in the original nucleus of the eucharistic prayer there, the Sanctus was not prefixed to the beginning but appended at the end, after the supplicatory section.[92]

Talley took these ideas further in a 1984 article,[93] where he referred to a number of newer studies which were germane to his thesis. He gave considerable attention to a recent book by

[91] *Die Osterhomilien des Asterios Sophistes als Quelle für die Geschichte der Osterfeier* (Trier 1967), pp. 74–94. For the Sacramentary of Sarapion, see above, pp. 117–18.

[92] 'The Eucharistic Prayer: Tradition and Development', pp. 55–7.

[93] 'The Literary Structure of the Eucharistic Prayer', *Worship* 58 (1984), pp. 404–19.

Cesare Giraudo, which had categorized the Old Testament euchological form *todah* as having a bipartite structure of anamnesis—epiclesis, together with an embolism which served as the *locus theologicus* of the entire formula.[94] That this embolism might occur in either part of the formula was important to Giraudo, since his principal concern was with the narrative of institution, which some anaphoras put in the first half and some in the second. Giraudo's classification of the prayer pattern is much too rigid to encompass the diversity of its forms evidenced in Old Testament and Jewish sources, and one is led once again to wonder why a *Jewish* archetype was thought so important for the narrative of institution. Talley, however, while querying the division of eucharistic prayers into two fundamental types on this basis, and also the forcing of the Syrian anaphoras into a bipartite model when they really reflect a tripartite division, believed that Giraudo's work could throw valuable light on the early development of the eucharistic prayer by pointing to biblical roots for the bipartite structure.[95]

Talley also noted a reconstruction of the original version of the Anaphora of Addai and Mari by William Macomber[96] in which it was possible to see a bipartite form, beginning after the Sanctus, that might predate the opening section. This would make it similar in structure to the eucharistic prayer of the *Apostolic Tradition*, except for the position of the institution narrative, though Talley was forced to admit that 'there is no indication of a seam after Sanctus in Macomber's reconstructed text, and that text . . . may very well present to us the earliest appearance of Sanctus in a Christian anaphora', which he thought could belong to the third century.[97]

Bryan Spinks, who had already made significant contributions to the study of the Anaphora of Addai and Mari[98] and of the

---

[94] *La struttura letteraria della preghiera eucaristica*, Rome 1981. For the *todah*, see above, pp. 50—1.

[95] In a revised version of this article, 'Sources and Structure of the Eucharistic Prayer', in T. J. Talley, *Worship: Reforming Tradition* (Washington DC 1990), pp. 11—34, although still affirming the same conclusion, the author was more critical of Giraudo's work.

[96] See above, p. 125, n. 51.

[97] 'The Literary Structure of the Eucharistic Prayer', p. 415.

[98] See above, p. 124, n. 49.

Jewish origins of the Sanctus,[99] responded to Talley in an important and challenging article in 1985.[100] First, he questioned the
assumption that Jesus used the *Birkat ha-mazon* at the Last Supper, and suggested that some Jewish groups may have used other
forms of meal-grace, while Jesus himself may have radically
transformed the Jewish prayers. Second, he referred to a recent
study by Allan Bouley on the improvisation of eucharistic prayer
in the early Church,[101] and suggested that 'the models upon
which different celebrants drew as a basis for their anaphoras
may have varied widely'. Third, he questioned the 'absolute
priority' which Talley gave to *eucharistein*, and pointed to the
work of Robert Ledogar, who had suggested that this verb may
not have featured in the earliest form of the Anaphoras of St
Basil, St John Chrysostom, or St Mark;[102] Addai and Mari too
displayed variants. He also questioned Talley's claim that the
creation section of the Jewish grace was first dropped by
Christians and then reintroduced: was it abandoned everywhere
or retained in some anaphoras from their conception? Finally,
he observed how extremely limited was the evidence upon which
to construct any hypothesis concerning the origins of anaphoral
development: we have hardly any examples from the countless
prayers which must have been used in the first three centuries,
and concerning most of these — *Didache* 10, the *Apostolic Tradition*, Addai and Mari, and the Strasbourg papyrus — there were
still serious uncertainties.

Geoffrey Cuming (1917–1988)

Reference has already been made above to Cuming's claim, in a
major paper delivered at the 1979 Oxford Patristic Conference,
that the Strasbourg papyrus constituted a complete anaphora,
possibly dating from the second century.[103] In that same paper

[99] 'The Jewish Sources for the Sanctus', *Heythrop Journal* 21 (1980), pp.
168–79.

[100] 'Beware the Liturgical Horses! An English Interjection on Anaphoral
Evolution', *Worship* 59 (1985), pp. 211–19.

[101] *From Freedom to Formula: The Evolution of the Eucharistic Prayer from
Oral Improvisation to Written Texts*, Washington DC 1981.

[102] See above, n. 64.

[103] See above, p. 119, n. 32.

he sketched out the way in which he thought that the later Alexandrian Anaphora of St Mark had developed out of this primitive nucleus of thanksgiving for creation, offering, intercession, and doxology by adopting features from eucharistic prayers elsewhere. First the Sanctus was added, but appended here to the conclusion of the prayer, replacing the original doxology, and so creating the unusual pattern in which intercession preceded it. At the same time, or shortly afterwards, a first epiclesis was added after the Sanctus; then the narrative of institution and anamnesis section were appended; and finally a second epiclesis which reflected a more developed eucharistic doctrine and prayed for the change of the elements into the body and blood of Christ, the whole anaphora being rounded off with prayer for the fruits of communion.

Cuming further believed that something like the Strasbourg papyrus was also the ancestor of the Jerusalem Anaphora of St James, and that that prayer too had been built up by similar additions, but with the Sanctus and everything that followed it in this case being inserted at the end of the preface and before the intercessions. John Fenwick, one of his students, continued this exploration in his doctoral dissertation by comparing the Anaphoras of St Basil and St James (which show marked similarity to one another) and arguing that each constituted an independent reworking in the late fourth century of a common original, which was most closely represented by the Egyptian version of the Anaphora of St Basil.[104] He has since gone on to propose that the Anaphora of the Twelve Apostles, the anaphora of the Liturgy of John Chrysostom, and the anaphora of *Apostolic Constitutions* 8 are similarly all independent derivatives of a single prayer.[105]

[104] Publication forthcoming in the series OCA. Summary in Fenwick, *Fourth Century Anaphoral Construction Techniques*.

[105] *The Missing Oblation*. Other recent studies of the eucharistic prayer of *Apostolic Constitutions* 8 include: W. H. Bates, 'The Composition of the Anaphora of Apostolic Constitutions VIII', *SP* 13 (1975), pp. 343—55; Marcel Metzger, 'Les deux prières eucharistiques des Constitutions apostoliques', *RevSR* 45 (1971), pp. 52—77; idem, 'The *Didascalia* and the *Constitutiones Apostolorum*', in *The Eucharist of the Early Christians* (New York 1978), pp. 194—219; A. Verheul, 'Les prières eucharistiques dans les "Constitutiones Apostolorum"', *QLP* 61 (1980), pp. 129—43.

In a short paper at the 1983 Patristic Conference Cuming took the question of early anaphoras a stage further. Following a suggestion made by Ligier, he thought that behind the longer texts of later centuries were signs of very brief, simple, and ancient eucharistic prayers which had consisted of nothing but the expression of praise for what God had done. Even the Strasbourg papyrus might once have lacked the elements of offering and intercession found in the extant version. Some of these prayers seem to have ended with a doxology, while others — the more developed ones — appear to have led into the Sanctus as their conclusion. The later versions of the prayers would thus have evolved by the addition of further elements to the end of the original nucleus, as in the case of the Anaphora of St Mark, or by inserting them at appropriate points within it; and this conclusion was supported by the clear evidence which existed in numerous cases of a general process of piecemeal construction by the insertion of prefabricated passages into pre-existent prayers.[106]

In a subsequent paper delivered at the 1987 conference, Cuming continued to pursue his theory, but suggested that, while the *Birkat ha-mazon* was an important source for the Christian anaphora, biblical examples of prayer and other Jewish prayers also needed to be taken into account. He went on to point out that no extant anaphora exactly reproduced the tripartite structure or the content of the *Birkat ha-mazon*: some anaphoras had two thanksgivings and a supplication; others had originally a single thanksgiving later divided into two by the Sanctus (as he thought was the case with Addai and Mari); some had lengthy intercessions from the start; others probably had none, but acquired them later; others had only an epiclesis.[107] It is to be regretted that his sudden death prevented him from developing any further this promising line of enquiry.

The Sanctus again

In 1991 Bryan Spinks returned to a more thorough exploration of the Sanctus. He rejected two common theories of its point of

---

[106] 'Four Very Early Anaphoras', *Worship* 58 (1984), pp. 168—72.
[107] 'The Shape of the Anaphora', *SP* 20 (1989), pp. 333—45.

entry into Christian eucharistic prayers —the so-called 'Egyptian theory' strongly advocated by Gregory Dix and Georg Kretschmar, which maintained that its appearance can be traced to the writings of Origen in the early third century,[108] and the 'climax theory' developed by E. C. Ratcliff and discussed earlier in this chapter.[109] He pointed out that while in some early eucharistic prayers the Sanctus certainly appeared to be a later addition, in others it seemed instead to be an integral part of the original nucleus, which could perhaps best be explained by positing a variety of early models of eucharistic prayer rather than a single archetype. He thought that its use may have been derived by Christians from the synagogue liturgy, or from the Jewish tradition of *merkavah* mysticism, or perhaps directly from biblical phraseology without a Jewish intermediary. It might even be that it originated in a different way in different places, which could account for regional differences in its form.[110]

At the same time as Spinks, but independently of him, Robert Taft was also investigating the emergence of the Sanctus in early eucharistic prayers. Although in some respects reaching broadly similar conclusions, he argued that the Egyptian form of the Sanctus, which lacked the conclusion 'Blessed is he who comes in the name of the Lord', appeared more primitive than the Antiochene version, and furthermore only in Egypt was the Sanctus integral to the structure of all extant eucharistic prayers, with the possible exception of the Strasbourg papyrus. He was inclined to conclude, therefore, that it had begun to be incorporated into Egyptian anaphoras probably in the second half of the third century. But, while the *idea* of adding the Sanctus to the eucharistic prayer had later spread from there to Antioch, the *form* adopted at Antioch was instead a Christianization of the version found in the Jewish synagogue.[111]

---

[108] Dix, 'Primitive Consecration Prayers', *Theology* 37 (1938), pp. 261–83; idem, *The Shape of the Liturgy*, p. 165; Kretschmar, *Studien zur frühchristlichen Trinitätstheologie* (Tübingen 1956), pp. 180, 182.

[109] See above, pp. 143–4.

[110] *The Sanctus in the Eucharistic Prayer* (Cambridge 1991), pp. 1–121.

[111] Article forthcoming in *OCP* 58 (1992).

Conclusion

It has been the universal assumption of the last hundred years that later Christian eucharistic rites were formed by the combination of two originally distinct elements —a service of reading(s), preaching, and prayer (which may owe its origin to the Jewish synagogue), and the stylized remains of a community meal which similarly seems to have its roots in Jewish practice. This may very well be true, but it also needs to be remembered that the Jewish meal tradition itself seems to have included what might be called 'an informal ministry of the word', the custom of surrounding the repast with religious discourse and the singing of hymns.[112] Hence the first half of the later eucharistic rites may be as much an outgrowth from that tradition as a legacy from the synagogue.

On the other hand, in the search for the origins of the eucharistic prayer itself —which is where the majority of scholarly interest has centred —progress has been hindered by two major factors.

One is the widespread belief that it is necessary to trace the Christian prayer-forms back to a standard, fixed text of the Jewish grace after meals, though the real difficulties involved in this operation have to some extent been masked by the failure by most scholars to distinguish between *berakah* and *hodayah* forms of prayer and their tendency to look instead merely for a broad congruence of themes. With the exception of Bryan Spinks, even the few scholars who have acknowledged the possibility of fluidity in Jewish prayer-patterns in the first century have still seen the *Birkat ha-mazon* as the starting-point for comparison.

The second major obstacle to progress has been the general desire (to which Spinks is again a notable exception) to situate all extant examples of Christian anaphoras within a single line of development. This has generally meant either fitting *Didache* 10 somehow into this trajectory or alternatively rejecting it from consideration altogether on the grounds that what it describes is not a eucharist, defended by the circular argument that it cannot

---

[112] See Bradshaw, *Daily Prayer in the Early Church*, pp. 21—2, 44—5.

be one because it does not fit into the pattern![113] It has usually also involved treating the anaphora of the *Apostolic Tradition* as an example of the stage of evolution that all eucharistic prayers had reached by the beginning of the third century, and hence pushing any 'more primitive' types (for example, those lacking a narrative of institution and anamnesis section) back into the second century or even earlier. This seems a particularly unwarranted step in the light of the uncertainty about the status of this document, to say nothing of the possibility that the text of its eucharistic prayer may have been subject to some later emendation. Though Ratcliff may have been incorrect with regard to *how* the anaphora was reworked, that does not mean that he was necessarily wrong in supposing that it had been revised in some way.

If, however, as we have suggested in the first chapter, Jewish prayer-forms —including the grace said at meals —were far less fixed in the first century, and if primitive Christianity was as pluriform as contemporary New Testament scholarship suggests, then it should not be surprising to find a diversity of patterns of anaphoras in the evidence of early Christianity, especially once it had moved away from its Jewish roots and perhaps no longer distinguished so sharply between euchological forms which had originally been used in relation to meals and those which had only been prayed in other contexts. These appear to have included anaphoras which had a more complex tripartite structure but quite closely mirrored Jewish forms (like *Didache* 10), as well as those which had a simpler bipartite or even unitive form but showed considerable freedom in their content and style

---

[113] Among recent scholars, Willy Rordorf, 'The *Didache*', in *The Eucharist of the Early Christians* (New York 1978), pp. 1—23, subscribed to the theory originally put forward by Zahn and Von der Goltz (above, nn. 17, 18) that *Didache* 9—10 contains 'not a eucharistic liturgy in the strict sense, but prayers spoken at table before the eucharist proper', and claimed that this was 'the most common view today'. The majority of other scholars, however, seem to take the opposite view, that it is a eucharist: see, for example, the works by Bouyer, Cuming, Ligier, and Talley cited in this chapter, and by Mazza, cited in ch. 4, n. 25. Cf. also Klaus Gamber, 'Die "Eucharistia" der Didache', *EL* 101 (1987) 3—32; John W. Riggs, 'From Gracious Table to Sacramental Elements: The Tradition-History of Didache 9 and 10', *Second Century* 4 (1984), pp. 83—101, who attempts to reconstruct the evolution of the prayers.

of expression (as in the Syriac Anaphora of the Twelve Apostles). Some anaphoras which had a simple structure seem to have contained a multiplicity of themes, while others concentrated on only a single aspect. In some anaphoras thanksgiving appears have been the dominant mode, while in others praise was expressed in a quite different way. In some the theme of creation was central (as in the Strasbourg papyrus); in others it hardly appeared at all (as in the *Apostolic Tradition*).

As the relatively fluid prayer traditions began to crystallize, and more stable, written texts began to appear (perhaps in the late third or early fourth century), no doubt some styles fell completely out of use while others achieved positions of supremacy within particular geographical areas. Then apparently began a phase of standardization and cross-fertilization, as Cuming and Fenwick have suggested, with units which had emerged in one tradition (like the Sanctus, the narrative of institution, and extensive intercession) being copied into the anaphoras of other traditions —sometimes at the same point in the order, sometimes in a different place —to complete the classical shape of the eucharistic prayer with its different regional variants which characterized later Christian history.

7. Christian Initiation: A Study in Diversity

Prior to the late 1950s scholars paid considerably less attention to the history of rites of initiation than to the evolution of eucharistic rites. One of the principal reasons for this imbalance was that baptism and confirmation had in the practice of most churches generally been relegated to the status of 'pastoral offices' —rites performed more or less in private for individuals as the need arose —rather than being seen as part of the mainstream of the liturgical life of the Church. Consequently, until the later phases of the liturgical movement began to have an impact on initiation rites, there was not the same sensitivity to their theological and liturgical shortcomings nor the same pressure for their revision as was felt in the case of the eucharist, and it was these things that provided the main stimulus for historical research. What little exploration of the origins of Christian initiation there was mostly occurred among Anglicans, for whom the nature and purpose of confirmation, and to a lesser extent the question of baptismal regeneration, were hotly debated issues during the nineteenth and early twentieth centuries.[1]

We have seen that the dominant tendency in scholarly research into the origin and early history of the eucharist has been to attempt to understand the evidence largely in terms of a monolinear development from a supposed single archetypal ritual structure in the first century. We can also observe a similar tendency towards a single harmonized picture in the study of early baptismal rites. Admittedly, in this instance the nature of the data has made this approach somewhat more difficult than in the case of the eucharist, and scholars have gradually been forced to acknowledge some marked differences between the major geographical regions of Christian antiquity. Nevertheless, there has been a clear preference for emphasizing as far as possible the similarity of the various traditions to one another

[1] See, for example, Colin O. Buchanan, *Anglican Confirmation*, GLS 48, 1986; Peter J. Jagger, *Clouded Witness: Initiation in the Church of England in the Mid-Victorian Period, 1850—1875*, Allison Park PA 1982.

rather than their diversity, so as to encourage the impression that the early Church initiated new converts everywhere in basically the same manner, with only very minor differences of ceremonial being observable.

A major trait which can be observed in early twentieth-century studies was the tendency to treat evidence from one geographical region as representing the custom of the Church universal, in the absence of any clear testimony to the contrary from other sources, and to regard later western practice as the normative standard against which to measure any deviations. Thus, Duchesne, in his survey of early Christian worship, affirmed that 'the ceremonies of Christian initiation, such as they are described in authorities from the end of the second century onwards, consisted of three essential rites —Baptism, Confirmation, and First Communion'. This tripartite ritual was preceded by a catechumenate and 'ordinarily administered' at Easter 'from the earliest times'.[2] Similarly, Thomas Thompson, in a 1914 study of baptism and confirmation which was widely used as a standard text-book in the English-speaking world for the next few decades, stated that 'Easter was the general time for baptism throughout the Church, at least from the time of Tertullian.'[3]

More recent studies have often adopted a similar harmonizing approach: the chapter on baptism in Jungmann's *Early Liturgy to the Time of Gregory the Great* is a good example of the tendency,[4] and even Edward Yarnold's otherwise excellent edition of extracts from fourth-century baptismal homilies catalogues the elements of early initiatory rites in his introduction in such a way as to give the impression that a standardized shape existed.[5] On the other hand, Georg Kretschmar and Robert Cabié present notable exceptions to this rule. In a survey of early initiatory practices presented at the 1977 congress of

[2] *Christian Worship*, pp. 292—3.

[3] *The Offices of Baptism and Confirmation* (Cambridge 1914), p. 19.

[4] op. cit., pp. 74—86.

[5] *The Awe-Inspiring Rites of Initiation*. Indeed, he explicitly states that the initiation ceremonies 'conform in essentials to a common pattern' (p. 3) and speaks of John Chrysostom as 'dispensing with a rite of confirmation after baptism' (p. 33).

Societas Liturgica, Kretschmar observed that 'in the matter of the essential rites at the core of the action . . . the diversity is greater than we have hitherto been willing to admit' and so it was 'hard to go on speaking of a single original and therefore normative form of baptism'.[6] Cabié has similarly stated that when the ritual of baptism did begin to become organized in the middle of the second century, 'it took appreciably different forms in the various churches and underwent many changes in the space of four centuries', adding a footnote that 'it must be kept in mind that each document provides information only for the place and time of its origin. Even neighbouring churches might have different customs'.[7]

As we shall see as this chapter unfolds, the traditional claim that early initiation practice was fundamentally identical in every place cannot really be sustained. Not only are there differences in the ritual structures between East and West, but these external variations also reflect important divergences in their underlying theology. Furthermore, there are some significant variations within the supposed eastern and western patterns themselves which suggest that even this basic twofold division presents a false perspective. The major centres of early Christianity were not nearly so uniform in the elements of their baptismal practice as many others have tended to conclude, and a very different picture emerges if we observe not what appears to have been common but what was distinctive or unique about the baptismal process in each place.

Syria

In 1909 R. H. Connolly laid out the evidence for the apparent absence from early Syrian practice of any post-baptismal ceremonies which could be considered the equivalent of the western rite of confirmation.[8] This observation created a major difficulty for attempts to paint a harmonized picture of initiation practice, and two principal solutions were offered to this

[6] 'Recent Research on Christian Initiation', *SL* 12 (1977), pp. 93, 102.

[7] 'L'Initiation chrétienne', in A. G. Martimort, ed., *L'Eglise en prière III: Les Sacrements* (new edn, Paris 1984), p. 27 = *The Church at Prayer III: The Sacraments* (Collegeville 1988), p. 17.

[8] *The Liturgical Homilies of Narsai*, pp. xlii—xlix.

inconvenient obstacle to the standard theory that confirmation
was of apostolic origin and had been universally practised in the
early Church. One solution was to assume that it must originally
have been part of the Syrian tradition, but had simply fallen out
of use in the course of time. This approach was adopted, for
instance, by Joseph Ysebaert in 1962, who went even further and
tried to find traces of the retention of confirmation in *Didascalia*
16, where the unction of female baptismal candidates involved a
twofold action, first of the head by the bishop and then of the
whole body by a woman deacon. Other scholars have understood
both actions to be pre-baptismal and to have been divided from
one another in the case of female candidates only for reasons of
propriety. Ysebaert claimed, however, that the second action
was meant to take place after the baptism, but that it had to be
performed under cover of the water for the sake of modesty, and
this eventually led to its fusion with the first and so to the complete disappearance of a post-baptismal anointing in the Syrian
tradition.[9]

Ysebaert and Joseph Lecuyer also interpreted John
Chrysostom's reference to the bishop's imposition of the hand
on baptismal candidates during their immersion and his remark,
'it is at this moment that through the words and hands of the
priest the Holy Spirit descends on you', as meaning that the two
sacraments of baptism and confirmation were being conveyed at
the same time.[10] This interpretation, however, has not been
accepted by other scholars, especially in the light of other passages in Chrysostom's writings which suggest rather that the
Holy Spirit was seen as being present in the whole baptismal
action.[11]

The other solution to the problematic absence of any post-
baptismal ceremonies in the early Syrian tradition was to regard
the pre-baptismal anointing as really being the unction of con-

[9] *Greek Baptismal Terminology* (Nijmegen 1962), pp. 312, 360f. For a critique of his position, see E. C. Whitaker, *Documents of the Baptismal Liturgy*
(2nd edn, London 1970), pp. xix—xx. For the *Didascalia*, see above, pp. 87—8.

[10] Ysebaert, op. cit., pp. 376—9; Lecuyer, 'San Juan Crisostomo y la Con-
firmacion', *Orbis Catholica* (Barcelona 1958), pp. 365—87.

[11] See, for example, Finn, *The Liturgy of Baptism in the Baptismal Instructions of St John Chrysostom*, p. 180.

firmation. Although this involved conceding the existence of a difference in the structure of the rites, it was able to hold on to the notion of an identity of significance: even if both patterns were somewhat unalike in form, they still had the same meaning. This line was followed by a number of scholars, although with interesting variations between them.

Some, like Thompson[12] and Joseph Coppens (1896 – 1981),[13] simply noted the difference in structure without offering an explanation for it. Others, however, sought to salvage the idea that there had once been a single prototypical rite. F. E. Brightman (1856 – 1932) believed that the Syrians had 'apparently transformed what was elsewhere an exorcism into the unction of Confirmation',[14] while Gregory Dix on the other hand produced the ingenious theory that 'Confirmation was in the Apostolic age regularly administered *before* Baptism in water', that it consisted of the affusion of oil, and that it originated as the Christian equivalent of Jewish circumcision;[15] only later was it transferred to a post-baptismal position, although this move was made in the West much earlier than in the East.[16] T. W. Manson (1890 – 1969) adopted a fundamentally similar position, citing Gal. 4.6f., Rom. 8.15f, 1 Cor. 12.3, 2 Cor. 1.21f., and above all the reference in 1 John 5.7f. to 'the Spirit, the water, and the blood' as possible allusions to the sequence: unction, baptism, and communion.[17]

---

[12] *The Offices of Baptism and Confirmation*, p. 31.

[13] *L'imposition des mains et les rite connexes dans la nouveau testament et dans l'église ancienne* (Paris 1925), p. 281.

[14] 'Terms of Communion and the Ministration of the Sacraments in Early Times', in H. B. Swete, ed., *Essays on the Early History of the Church and Ministry* (London 1918), p. 350.

[15] *'Confirmation or the Laying on of Hands'?* ('Theology' Occasional Papers, No. 5, London 1936), p. 1 (emphasis in original). The notion that confirmation was the Christian counterpart of Jewish circumcision had already been put forward by earlier scholars: see Lampe, *The Seal of the Spirit*, pp. 82ff.

[16] ibid., pp. 5, 8 – 9, 15f. See also Dix, *The Theology of Confirmation in Relation to Baptism* (London 1946), p. 15.

[17] 'Entry into Membership of the Early Church', *JTS* 48 (1947), pp. 25 – 33; 'Baptism in the Church', *SJT* 2 (1949), p. 394. In 'Miscellanea Apocalyptica III', *JTS* 48 (1947), pp. 59 – 61, he also added to the list a Christian interpolation in the *Testament of Levi* 8.4 – 10 which spoke of unction, baptism, and communion, in that order. Cf., however, the critique by Lampe, *The Seal of the*

E. C. Ratcliff at first sought to play down the importance of the Syrian pattern: 'the remote and isolated church of Eastern Syria' was an exception to the 'all but universal' rule that confirmation followed baptism, and so 'we may reasonably assume that the Romano-Byzantine pattern of initiation represents the main stream of Christian tradition, as we can clearly trace it to the middle of the second century'.[18] Later, however, he acknowledged that 'the old Eastern liturgical usage of baptism differed markedly from that which obtained in the West'[19] and argued that the Syrian anointing was 'not a confirmation or completion, but an inception; the giving of the Spirit is the beginning of initiation'. On the basis of Acts 9.17–18; 10.44–8 and the passages from the Epistles cited by Manson, where the gift of the Spirit seems to precede baptism, it could be said that

> Syrian baptismal usage has its roots in the Apostolic past. In the earliest period, we may suppose, the laying-on of the bishop's hand was unaccompanied by anointing with oil. From teaching catechumens about the non-material unction of the Spirit, it is but a short step to representing that unction by an anointing with material oil. The next step is to explain the material anointing as the means of effecting spiritually that which it represents. The practice of consecrating the oil is the corollary of the explanation.[20]

While thus claiming an apostolic origin for the Syrian pattern, Ratcliff did not make it clear whether he thought that it was the sole shape that the rite then took, with the western structure a later development, or whether the two patterns had coexisted from the earliest days. However, he did draw attention to

---

Spirit, pp. 87–91. Manson's explanation was adopted by L. L. Mitchell, *Baptismal Anointing* (ACC 48, London 1966), pp. 49–50; and G. G. Willis, 'What was the Earliest Syrian Baptismal Tradition?', *Studia Evangelica* 6 (1973), pp. 651–4, argued that 1 Cor. 10.1–2, mentioned by Dix, also lent support to that same sequence as being the original Christian practice.

[18] 'The Relation of Confirmation to Baptism in the Early Roman and Byzantine Liturgies', *Theology* 49 (1946), p. 264 = *Liturgical Studies*, p. 125.

[19] 'The Old Syrian Baptismal Tradition and its Resettlement under the Influence of Jerusalem in the Fourth Century', *Studies in Church History* 2 (1965), p. 19 = *Liturgical Studies*, p. 135.

[20] ibid., p. 27 = p. 141.

another important difference from the West in the ancient Syrian tradition: Christian baptism was understood here as a *mimesis* ('imitation') of the baptism of Christ. 'What was done at Jordan is done again, *mutatis mutandis*, in the water of the font. A man comes out of that water reborn as a "son" of God. . . .' So it was that, in allusion to the concept of rebirth, some ancient commentators referred to the font as a womb, but never as a grave, and the idea of Rom. 6.3–5 (of Christians being baptized into the death and resurrection of Christ) made no mark upon early Syrian thought about baptism.[21]

On the other hand, not all scholars were determined to find an equivalent of confirmation in the Syrian tradition. The central thesis of Geoffrey Lampe's book, *The Seal of the Spirit*, written as a response to Dix, was that in New Testament times the gift of the Spirit had been mediated through baptism in water alone and that all other external signs of the coming of the Spirit were later developments, probably derived from Gnostic circles.[22] Others, notably Benedict Green[23] and E. C. Whitaker,[24] argued that the pre-baptismal unction in the Syrian documents was intended to be exorcistic, just as it was in western sources. Thus, these scholars also managed to retain the notion of a single primitive pattern of Christian initiation, but they did so by claiming that any separate ceremony denoting the giving of the Spirit was a secondary development in all regional traditions.

In the late 1970s, however, important contributions to the debate were made by Gabriele Winkler. In a paper delivered at the second Symposium of Syriac Studies in Paris in 1976 she built upon a suggestion made by Juan Mateos at the first Symposium in 1972[25] and argued forcefully that, in the light of early Armenian evidence, the original Syrian practice did not

[21] ibid., p. 28 = p. 142.

[22] He deals with the Syrian evidence briefly on pp. 186–9.

[23] 'The Significance of the Pre-Baptismal Seal in St John Chrysostom', *SP* 6 (1962), pp. 84–90.

[24] 'Unction in the Syrian Baptismal Rite', *Church Quarterly Review* 162 (1961), pp. 176–87; *Documents of the Baptismal Liturgy*, pp. xv–xxii; *Sacramental Initiation Complete in Baptism* (GLS 1, 1975), pp. 24–9.

[25] 'Théologie du baptême dans la formulaire de Sévère d'Antioche', *Symposium Syriacum 1972* (OCA 197, 1974), pp. 135–61.

involve an anointing of the head and the whole body, as other scholars had concluded,[26] but an anointing of the head alone, to which was gradually added the anointing of the body.[27]

In a further study she examined the significance of the Syrian pre-baptismal anointing and concluded that in the oldest stratum of the tradition

> Christian baptism is shaped after Christ's baptism in the Jordan. As Jesus had received the anointing through the divine presence in the appearance of a dove, and was invested as the Messiah, so in Christian baptism every candidate is anointed and, in connection with this anointing, the gift of the Spirit is conferred. Therefore the main theme of this prebaptismal anointing is the entry into the eschatological kingship of the Messiah, being in the true sense of the word assimilated to the Messiah-King through this anointing.[28]

This, she believed, explained why at first oil was poured only over the head (this was the custom at the anointing of the kings of Israel), why the coming of the Spirit was associated with it (the Spirit of the Lord came over the newly nominated king), and why the anointing and not the immersion in water was regarded as the central feature of baptism in the early Syrian sources (this was the only visible gesture for what was held to be the central event at Christ's baptism — his revelation as the Messiah-King through the descent of the Spirit).

Winkler argued that the subsequent introduction of the anointing of the whole body led to the loss of its original impact and its reinterpretation as a healing ritual. The conferring of the Spirit together with the themes of royal and sacerdotal anointing were transferred to the immersion itself in the thought of John Chrysostom, and to a newly introduced post-baptismal unction at Jerusalem in the late fourth century, while the older pre-baptismal anointing was now understood as a cathartic and

[26] See, for example, A. F. J. Klijn, 'An Ancient Syriac Baptismal Liturgy in the Syriac Acts of John', *Novum Testamentum* 6 (1963) 216—28.

[27] 'The History of the Syriac Prebaptismal Anointing in the Light of the Earliest Armenian Sources', *Symposium Syriacum 1976* (OCA 205, 1978), pp. 317—24. See also her more detailed study, *Das armenische Initiationsrituale*, OCA 217, 1982.

[28] 'The Original Meaning of the Prebaptismal Anointing and its Implications', *Worship* 52 (1978), p. 36.

apotropaic ritual. This change also led to the reinterpretation of the rite as a death/resurrection event, in accordance with Romans 6, rather than a birth event, in accordance with John 3. She therefore held that the two descriptions of baptism in the third-century *Acts of Thomas* which mention the anointing of both the head and the whole body, focus on the theme of healing, and include a prayer for the blessing of the oil (chapters 121 and 157), constitute a later stratum than the two descriptions which refer to an anointing of the head alone, associate this with the Messiah, and have no blessing prayer (chapters 27 and 132).[29]

Winkler's interpretation of the early Syrian evidence has subsequently become widely accepted. But while her division into two chronological strata may be correct, it is not the only possible explanation. Ruth Meyers, for example, has suggested that the differences between the descriptions of the anointings may be capable of reconcilation. She points out that explicit mention of the anointing of the body occurs in the *Acts of Thomas* only when female candidates are involved, who require the services of a woman to perform the action. In the other instances the body-anointing may have been presumed without necessitating detailed description, the oil perhaps simply being allowed to run down from the head over the body or the apostle Thomas himself performing the service.[30]

On the other hand, the differences in the descriptions could reflect the simultaneous coexistence of a variety of baptismal practices within the Syrian region. It should be noted that, although Winkler's analysis clearly accepts some diversity in early Christian baptismal practice, it still assumes a basically monolinear development within each individual geographical area. Thus, variations in the testimony presented by the Syrian sources are treated as representing different chronological stages in the evolution of a single pattern. There is, however, at least some evidence which would support the alternative possibility that they are manifestations of an inherently multifarious

---

[29] ibid., pp. 36—45. For the *Acts of Thomas*, see above, pp. 120—21.

[30] 'The Structure of the Syrian Baptismal Rite', in Paul F. Bradshaw, ed., *Essays in Early Eastern Initiation* (A/GLS 8, 1988), p. 41.

practice, which only later became more uniform. For example, it is not certain that unction of any sort was everywhere a part of the Syrian baptismal ritual. In one further description of a baptism in the *Acts of Thomas*, that of a woman possessed by a devil (chs. 49–50), no mention is made in the Syriac version of anything other than the use of water.

To this consideration may be added the evidence of the *Didache*, which seems to be of Syrian provenance and yet appears to make no reference to a baptismal anointing. While some scholars have simply ignored this inconvenient exception, others have put forward a variety of suggestions to explain the omission. Some have argued that the document was a manual for presbyters and deacons and so made no reference to liturgical actions which only the bishop could perform[31] —overlooking the fact that the *Didache* does not seem to presuppose a threefold ministerial order. Dix thought that it was meant for the laity, and therefore only gave instructions about the rites which they could perform in the absence of the clergy[32] —overlooking the fact that the East has always been much more hesitant than the West about accepting lay administration of baptism. Others have regarded the prayer over *myron* ('ointment') found in the Coptic version of the *Didache* and in *Apostolic Constitutions* 7 as being part of the original text, and so as indicating the existence of a baptismal anointing after all.[33] Theophile Lefort, however, has argued that the Coptic word is not a translation of *myron*, nor is the prayer baptismal in context,[34] and Stephen Gero has suggested that the original word was incense, which was burned at the meal described in *Didache* 9–10, and this was then changed to *myron* by the tradition lying behind *Apostolic Con-*

[31] A. T. Wirgman, *The Doctrine of Confirmation* (London 1897), p. 102; Charles Gore, *The Church and the Ministry* (London 1936), p. 252.

[32] ' "The Seal" in the Second Century', *Theology* 51 (1948), p. 9. Fisher, *Confirmation Then and Now*, p. 3, is uncertain whether the omission is to be explained along these lines or not, but he rejects the suggestion that the baptism rite was 'complete in itself and regarded by its author as such'.

[33] See the critical evaluation of earlier literature in Vööbus, *Liturgical Traditions in the Didache*, pp. 41–60.

[34] L. T. Lefort, *Les Pères apostoliques en copte* (Corpus Scriptorum Christianorum Orientalium 135, Louvain 1952), pp. 32–4.

stitutions 7, which arose in Egypt and was unfamiliar with the practice of burning incense.[35]

Even in the fourth-century Syrian sources, where a greater element of standardization is apparent, there are still signs of some continuing variation in baptismal rituals which seem to be remnants of an older diversity. Thus the apocryphal *History of John the Son of Zebedee* contains two somewhat different descriptions of baptism. In one case, the baptism of Tyrannus, the procurator of Ephesus, together with a multitude of people, there is a confession of faith by the crowd after the consecration of the oil and the water, and a confession of faith by Tyrannus after he is anointed. In the other case, the baptism of the priests of Artemis, again with a crowd of people, a renunciation of Artemis and a confession of faith by the multitude precede the consecration of the oil and the water, and the confession of faith by the priests follows the consecration but precedes the anointing. A. F. J. Klijn has attempted to harmonize these accounts,[36] but Winkler would again see in them two chronological stages of the development of the baptismal ritual.[37]

Furthermore, Theodore of Mopsuestia records the strange practice of the sponsor spreading a linen stole on the candidate's head after the anointing of the head and before the anointing of the body, which he says symbolizes 'the freedom to which you are called, for this is the decoration that free men wear both indoors and out'.[38] This certainly looks like the survival of an ancient local custom, as it is not mentioned in other early Syrian literature, although it is found in a different position — as a post-baptismal ceremony — in later Syrian rites.[39]

Whatever may be the case with regard to the diversity within early Syrian baptismal practice, this literature suggests that the initiatory practices of this region prior to the fourth century dif-

[35] 'The So-called Ointment Prayer in the Coptic Version of the Didache: A Re-evaluation', *Harvard Theological Review* 70 (1977), pp. 67—84.

[36] 'An Ancient Syriac Baptismal Liturgy in the Syriac Acts of John', pp. 220—1.

[37] *Das armenische Initiationsrituale*, pp. 154—6.

[38] *Baptismal Homily* 14.19. See Yarnold, *Awe-Inspiring Rites*, pp. 187—8.

[39] See S. P. Brock, 'Some Early Syriac Baptismal Commentaries', *OCP* 46 (1980), p. 45.

fered from those of Rome in more ways than just the absence of a post-baptismal anointing. There is no sign of Easter having been the preferred baptismal season, and indeed one would not expect such a connection to have been made in a tradition which did not understand initiation in terms of Romans 6. There is also little to imply the existence of a lengthy, highly formalized and strongly ritualized catechumate, such as the *Apostolic Tradition* suggests and we find in fourth-century Syrian evidence, and no mention of sponsors or of pre-baptismal exorcisms.[40]

Moreover, there are strong indications running through the later evidence that initiation was once a two-stage affair in Syria, with the profession of faith, in the form of an act of adherence to Christ or *syntaxis* (preceded by a renunciation of evil, if that is not a later development), taking place on a separate occasion prior to the baptism. Some confirmation of this division is provided by the third-century *Didascalia*, which says that 'when the heathen desire and promise to repent, saying "We believe", we receive them into the congregation so that they may hear the word, but do not receive them into communion until they receive the seal and are fully initiated'.[41] Chrysostom in the late fourth century and the Constantinopolitan rite of the fifth century seem to have known the renunciation/act of adherence as still occurring on the day before the baptism, and the testimony of Theodore of Mopsuestia and of the later Syrian baptismal *ordines* show traces of this twofold structure, even though both parts now take place on the same occasion.[42]

This pattern, of course, is quite different from that at Rome, where the profession of faith accompanied the immersion itself and took a threefold interrogatory credal form. In Syria the immersion was instead accompanied by a declaratory formula, apparently at first in the active voice, 'I baptize you in the name

[40] Cf. the unconvincing efforts of Dujarier, *A History of the Catechumenate*, pp. 64–8, to read a formal catechumenate into the earlier Syrian evidence, culminating in the assertion that 'in the third century, catechumenal practice had the same structure everywhere'.

[41] II.39, cited from Brock & Vasey, *The Liturgical Portions of the Didascalia*, p. 12.

[42] For further details, see Meyers, 'The Structure of the Syrian Baptismal Rite', pp. 31, 34–8.

of . . .', but by the fourth century in the passive, 'N. is baptized in the name of. . . .' The use of the active formula eventually spread westwards, appearing first in the *Canons of Hippolytus* in Egypt in the early fourth century, and later in Spain, Gaul, and Rome.[43] At the same time western elements were being carried eastwards, so that such things as a formal catechumenate accompanied by frequent exorcisms and other purificatory elements, initiation at the Easter season and the adoption of Pauline death-burial baptismal imagery, the use of credal interrogations in the rite, and above all a post-baptismal unction gradually began to make appearances in eastern rites, generally turning up first —not surprisingly —in Jerusalem, where pilgrimages brought East and West face to face. The result was certainly not uniformity of baptismal practice throughout Christendom, as the eastern versions were often markedly different in detail from their western counterparts, but there did emerge a broad similarity which largely masked the earlier diversity.

Ratcliff regarded the eventual introduction of a post-baptismal anointing in the East as the result of the influence of Jerusalem, and its original adoption there as the consequence of the celebration of Christian initiation at Easter in close proximity to the actual sites of the death and resurrection of Jesus, which thus led to a revival of the Pauline doctrine of baptism.[44] Botte, on the other hand, linked its emergence in the East with the practice adopted at the reconciliation of heretics.[45] Winkler disagreed with both, and thought that the change came about through:

[43] See further E. C. Whitaker, 'The Baptismal Formula in the Syrian Rite', *Church Quarterly Review* 161 (1960), pp. 346—52; idem, 'The History of the Baptismal Formula', *JEH* 16 (1965), pp. 1—12; P-M. Gy, 'La formule "Je te baptise" (Et ego te baptizo)', in *Communio Sanctorum: Mélanges offerts à Jean-Jacques von Allmen* (Geneva 1982), pp. 65—72; Paul de Clerck, 'Les origines de la formule baptismale', in Paul de Clerck & Eric Palazzo, eds., *Rituels: Mélanges offerts à Pierre-Marie Gy, O.P.* (Paris 1990), pp. 199—213.

[44] 'The Old Syrian Baptismal Tradition'.

[45] 'L'onction postbaptismale dans l'ancien patriarchat d'Antioch', in *Miscellanea Liturgica in onore di sua Em. il Card. G. Lercaro* 2 (Rome 1967), pp. 795—808 = 'Post-baptismal Anointing in the Ancient Patriarchate of Antioch', in Jacob Vellian, ed., *Studies on Syrian Baptismal Rites* (Syrian Churches Series 6, Kottayam, India 1973), pp. 63—71.

the inner change of dynamics within the ritual itself. Once baptism moved away from its original essence, being the *mimesis* of the event at the Jordan, and shifted at the same time toward a cathartic principle, it was inevitable that all rites that preceded baptism proper became subordinated to a process of thorough cleansing. The catharsis slowly became an indispensable condition for the coming of the Spirit. Consequently, only after intensive purification and the washing away of sins could the Spirit enter the heart of the baptized.[46]

It is of course possible that all these factors played a part.

Rome

The evidence for early Roman initiation practice is extremely limited. We do not possess a set of fourth-century baptismal catecheses from this city such as we have from other places, and there are only two main sources from earlier centuries, the *First Apology* of Justin Martyr and the *Apostolic Tradition* attributed to Hippolytus, both of which present problems of interpretation.

Justin's account is very brief and mentions only that converts 'are taught to pray and ask God, while fasting, for the forgiveness of their sins, and we pray and fast with them'. They are then 'led by us to a place where there is water, and they are reborn' in the name of the Father, Jesus Christ, and the Holy Spirit. Justin also describes this process as being 'washed' and 'enlightened', and says that 'after we have thus washed him that is persuaded and declares his assent, we lead him to those who are called brethren, where they are assembled', and common prayer, the exchange of a kiss, and the celebration of the eucharist follow.[47]

Many things are not said here. There is, for example, no reference to a formally structured catechumenate, though some pre-baptismal instruction is certainly implied; no indication whether baptism was restricted to a specific season of the year, or even to Sundays, though the latter seems probable; no allusion to exorcism or other pre-baptismal ceremonies; and above all no mention of a post-baptismal prayer with imposition of

---

[46] 'The Original Meaning of the Prebaptismal Anointing', p. 42, n. 63. See also S. P. Brock, 'The Transition to a Post-Baptismal Anointing in the Antiochene Rite', in Spinks, *The Sacrifice of Praise*, pp. 215–25.

[47] *I Apol.* 61, 65. Text in Whitaker, *Documents of the Baptismal Liturgy*, p. 2.

hands and/or anointing. Of course, it can be argued that since Justin is writing a brief account for pagans, we should not expect a very detailed description of every element of Christian practice, and there may well have been many other ceremonies which were included in the rite besides those explicitly mentioned. This argument certainly has some force. But the fact remains that we do not actually know which of the features of later Roman practice, or of other western centres of Christianity, were being practised at Rome in the middle of the second century and which were not. If we assume a large measure of continuity and stability, then we can argue that it is likely that what we find later at Rome and elsewhere was already known to Justin. But this assumption precisely begs the questions at issue: how alike was the practice of the early centres of Christianity, and how much change and development took place in the first three or four centuries?

Attempts have been made by a few scholars, most notably the Anglo-Catholics Dix, Ratcliff, Arthur Couratin, and L. S. Thornton,[48] to read between the lines of Justin's writings and discern there evidence to suggest that Justin did not regard water baptism as the whole of Christian initiation, but also knew of a post-baptismal rite which effected the gift of the Holy Spirit. Their arguments have, however, failed to convince many.[49]

Reference has been made earlier in this book to the difficulties inherent in interpreting the evidence supplied by the *Apostolic Tradition*: we cannot be certain whether it really originates from Rome, and even if it does, whether it represents what was the actual practice of the period and not merely the unfulfilled desires of some individual or group, or whether the text as we now have it has been subjected to a measure of later revision.[50] This means that we ought to exercise considerable

---

[48] Dix, ' "The Seal" in the Second Century', pp. 7−12; Ratcliff, 'Justin Martyr and Confirmation', *Theology* 51 (1948), pp. 133−9 = *Liturgical Studies*, pp. 110−17; A. H. Couratin, 'Justin Martyr and Confirmation− A Note', *Theology* 55 (1952), pp. 458−60; L. S. Thornton, *Confirmation: Its Place in the Baptismal Mystery* (London 1954), pp. 34−51. See also Fisher, *Confirmation Then and Now*, pp. 11−21.

[49] See, for example, Lampe, *The Seal of the Spirit*, pp. 109−11; Mitchell, *Baptismal Anointing*, pp. 13−15.

[50] See above, p. 90.

caution in treating its description of Christian initiation as reflecting third-century Roman practice. On the other hand, for what it is worth, the broad outlines of its account are consistent with the baptismal rites of the later Roman tradition.

According to the evidence of the *Apostolic Tradition*, those who desired to become Christians had to enter a period of instruction which might last up to three years. At the outset they were required to have sponsors who could attest to their capacity to 'hear the word' and also to their way of life; and at the end their lives were again examined to determine whether they were ready for baptism. There then followed a period of final preparation involving a daily exorcism and ending with two days of fasting immediately before the baptism itself, which may have been at Easter, although this is not explicitly stated.[51] The baptism began at cockcrow after a night-long vigil. Prayer was made over the water and the baptismal oils were blessed. The candidates removed their clothes, renounced Satan, had their bodies anointed with the 'oil of exorcism', and went down into the water. There they answered three credal questions and were immersed after each response. They came up out of the water, were anointed by a presbyter with the 'oil of thanksgiving', put on their clothes, and joined the congregation. The bishop himself then laid his hands on them and recited a prayer, and after this anointed their heads with the oil of thanksgiving, signed them on the forehead, and gave them a kiss.

It is the post-baptismal ceremonies of this text which have generated most debate, chiefly with regard to whether or not they envisaged a bestowal of the Holy Spirit at this point. The Latin version of the bishop's prayer reads:

> Lord God, who has made them worthy to receive the remission of sins through the laver of regeneration of the Holy Spirit, send upon them your grace. . . .

In the oriental-language versions, however, the phrase 'of the Holy Spirit' is replaced by 'make them worthy to be filled with

---

[51] On the question of Easter baptism, see further Paul F. Bradshaw, ' "Diem baptismo sollemniorem": Initiation and Easter in Christian Antiquity', in Ephrem Carr, Stefano Parenti, & Abraham-Andreas Thiermeyer, eds., *Eulogêma: Studies in Honor of Robert Taft, S.J.*, Rome 1992.

the Holy Spirit and. . . .' While both Dix and Botte in their editions of the *Apostolic Tradition* generally preferred to adopt the
readings of the Latin version as coming closest to the original, at
this point both of them opted for oriental-language versions as
reflecting the original. Dix described the Latin version as
'corrupt' here, and Botte thought that a line had accidentally fallen out of the Latin text.[52] Their conclusions have been accepted
by a number of scholars,[53] but others have argued that there is
nothing to suggest that the Latin is not the original reading and
the oriental versions a subsequent amplification made under the
influence of later doctrine which associated the gift of the Spirit
with the post-baptismal anointing rather than with the immersion.[54]

Recently Anthony Gelston suggested a third possibility and
proposed a more complicated textual history for the prayer. The
Greek original, he believed, had referred to the Holy Spirit
twice, once in relation to the immersion (as in the Latin text)
and again in connection with the petition for grace (as in the
oriental texts), and the Latin and oriental versions had each
accidentally left out one of the references but retained the
other.[55] Geoffrey Cuming responded to this by pointing out the
improbability of two different errors being made by two copyists
in the same place, and put forward a fourth hypothesis, that
there was no reference at all to the Holy Spirit in the original,
and that it was later added to the subordinate clause by the textual tradition underlying the Latin and to the main clause in the
oriental tradition.[56]

Aidan Kavanagh has taken an even more novel approach to
the passage. While accepting the Latin text as authentic, he
argued that the whole liturgical unit of prayer and the imposi-

[52] Dix, *The Treatise on the Apostolic Tradition*, p. 38; Botte, *La Tradition
apostolique*, p. 53, n. 1.

[53] See, for example, Fisher, *Confirmation Then and Now*, pp. 52−5.

[54] See, for example, Lampe, *The Seal of the Spirit*, pp. 136−42. But cf. p.
xvii of the second edition where he appears to retract his argument.

[55] 'A Note on the Text of the *Apostolic Tradition* of Hippolytus', *JTS* 39
(1988), pp. 112−17.

[56] 'The Post-baptismal Prayer in the *Apostolic Tradition*: Further Considerations', *JTS* 39 (1988), pp. 117−19.

tion of hands was originally nothing more than a *missa* —the dismissal ceremony with which ancient liturgical services generally seem to have ended —and it was only later reinterpreted as an invocation of the Holy Spirit.[57] Although his theory is not without its problems, it could perhaps be carried further still. There is some manuscript evidence to suggest that the *Canons of Hippolytus*, the oldest derivative of the *Apostolic Tradition*, may not have included the second post-baptismal anointing found in the other versions of the *Apostolic Tradition*. Might this be a clue to the original version of the *Apostolic Tradition*, which would then have included only the one post-baptismal anointing by the presbyter, the imposition of hands and prayer, the sign of the cross, and the kiss? The second anointing would thus have been added as the significance of this concluding section changed.[58]

North Africa
From the references to the rites of Christian initiation which are scattered throughout the writings of Tertullian the order of the baptismal rite seems to have been:

> Prayer over the water;
> Renunciation, with imposition of the bishop's hand;
> Triple profession of faith and triple immersion;
> Unction;
> Sign of the cross;
> Imposition of hands 'in benediction, inviting
>   and welcoming the Holy Spirit'.

Because Tertullian nowhere gives a systematic account of the whole rite, it is of course quite possible that there were other elements which he does not mention. Yet, from what he does say, it is clear that, while the general pattern was similar to that found in the *Apostolic Tradition*, there was, nevertheless, some divergence in details. The renunciation, for example, apparently

[57] *Confirmation: Origins and Reform* (New York 1988), esp. pp. 41–52. See also Paul Turner, 'The Origins of Confirmation: An Analysis of Aidan Kavanagh's Hypothesis', *Worship* 65 (1991), pp. 320–338, with response by Kavanagh.

[58] See Bradshaw, *The Canons of Hippolytus*, p. 24; J. M. Hanssens, 'L'édition critique des Canons d'Hippolyte', *OCP* 32 (1966), pp. 542–3.

took place after the candidate had gone down into the water. The most notable differences, however, are in the post-baptismal ceremonies. In North Africa there was seemingly only one anointing, which Tertullian associates with the priestly anointing of Aaron, and the imposition of hands and prayer followed both the unction and the sign of the cross. There is also no explicit mention of a kiss at the conclusion of the rite.

Other scholars have often sought to minimize the importance of these variations. J. D. C. Fisher, for example, claimed that, although the gift of the Spirit was associated by Tertullian with the imposition of hands and not the unction, 'yet unction cannot be altogether separated from the giving of the Spirit, because it conferred membership in Christ, the anointed one, so called because he was anointed with the Holy Spirit'.[59] Ysebaert argued that the imposition of the hand, the anointing, and the sign of the cross should not be regarded as three distinct rites but rather as one 'complicated liturgical act',[60] and Whitaker accepted his argument, claiming that its effect was

> to show that if there is a difference in detail between the practice described by Tertullian and that advocated by Hippolytus; if some later documents appear to connect the gift of the Spirit with the imposition of the hand, and others with the anointing; if some areas have retained only one post-baptismal anointing although others have two; then the differences arise from differences in the way in which one basic and complex act has developed and disintegrated in response to circumstances.[61]

But such a conclusion remains to be proved. It is at least equally possible that the differences arise both from the independent addition of further ritual elements to an originally simple nucleus and also from quite distinct interpretations of their significance.

Northern Italy
We lack evidence for the pattern(s) of Christian initiation practised in northern Italy prior to the fourth century, but even the later sources reveal a number of interesting variations from the

[59] *Confirmation Then and Now*, p. 31.
[60] *Greek Baptismal Terminology*, pp. 264, 289f.
[61] *Documents of the Baptismal Liturgy*, p. xv.

Roman model which appear to be of some antiquity. Ambrose of Milan takes great pains in his writings to stress the close similarity between liturgical practices in his city and those at Rome, and so we may safely assume that he would not have introduced new customs which differed from those then found at Rome, nor have willingly perpetuated existing customs which were at variance with Roman ones if he had been able easily to abolish them. This means, therefore, that practices described by Ambrose which are peculiar to northern Italy must have been long established there to resist his Romanizing tendency. These include the following:

(a) The enrolment of candidates for Easter baptism took place on the feast of the Epiphany instead of at the beginning of Lent, as was usual elsewhere.[62] The same custom also appears to have obtained in nearby Turin,[63] and Thomas Talley would see here a connection with the early Alexandrian baptismal pattern, which we shall examine shortly.[64]

(b) The pre-baptismal anointing of the body was located before the renunciation of the devil rather than after it, as in the *Apostolic Tradition* and in fourth-century eastern sources; and while these all clearly regard the rite as an exorcism, Ambrose instead treats it as a source of strength for combat with the devil, a theme also found alongside that of exorcism in Chrysostom and Theodore.

(c) The post-baptismal unction was performed by the bishop himself, in contrast to both the *Apostolic Tradition* and later Roman practice, where it was done by a presbyter.

(d) The washing of the feet of the newly baptized followed. This is the most striking difference from the practices of the other regions we have examined, and Ambrose himself reveals considerable embarrassment about this particular deviation from Roman custom.[65] There are, however, possible allusions to this custom in East Syrian sources (Aphraates, Ephrem, and

[62] Ambrose, *In Expos. Ev. Luc.* 4.76.

[63] Maximus addresses two sermons preached on the days immediately after Epiphany (13 & 65) to catechumens apparently preparing for baptism at Easter.

[64] *The Origins of the Liturgical Year* (New York 1986), p. 217.

[65] *De Sacramentis* 3.5—7.

Cyrillonas of Edessa); a prohibition of the practice in canon 48 of the Spanish Council of Elvira (300); and provision for it in later Gallican liturgical books, as well as evidence of its observance elsewhere in northern Italy at this period (although at Aquileia it was apparently a pre-baptismal rite); and so it may once have been more widespread. Indeed, Pier Franco Beatrice has advanced the theory that it may originally have been practised in place of immersion in some places and only became an adjunct to it as a later compromise.[66]

(e) The initiation ended with a 'spiritual sealing'. Some scholars have seen this as being the counterpart of the second post-baptismal anointing described in the *Apostolic Tradition* and found in later Roman usage, but while Ambrose does refer to an invocation of the Holy Spirit, he makes no explicit mention of the use of oil, which has led other scholars to conclude that the only gesture was a sign of the cross or even an imposition of hands.[67] Alternatively, it might have been a kiss.

Gaul and Spain

Although the Council of Elvira supplies some information about early Spanish baptismal practice, we lack any really detailed sources for liturgical customs in these regions prior to the fifth century, as we have indicated in an earlier chapter, and can only conjecture what older traditions might have been on the basis of the later evidence. However, Gabriele Winkler has attempted to show that the later Gallican texts suggest that there was originally only one post-baptismal ceremony in this region — an anointing — and that there are signs in the material of what are usually considered as being Syrian characteristics — Johannine rather than Pauline baptismal theology, allusions to the Jordan event in the blessing of the baptismal water, and references to the conferral of the Spirit in the pre-baptismal anointing.[68]

[66] *La lavanda dei piedi*, Rome 1983.

[67] See Fisher, *Confirmation Then and Now*, p. 57; Pamela Jackson, 'The Meaning of the "Spirituale Signaculum" in the Mystagogy of Ambrose of Milan', *Ecclesia Orans* 7 (1990), pp. 77–94; Mitchell, *Baptismal Anointing*, pp. 87–91; Riley, *Christian Initiation*, pp. 353ff.

[68] 'Confirmation or Chrismation? A Study in Comparative Liturgy', *Worship* 58 (1984), pp. 2–16.

Egypt

As I have indicated in a recent study,[69] the traditional assumption that early initiatory practice in Egypt was fundamentally western in character will not stand up to close scrutiny. Although it is true that there is some resemblance to western practice, other features seem to have more in common with what we find in Syria, while still other characteristics appear to be unique to this region. The most notable of these is the baptismal season, which appears originally to have been situated at the end of a forty-day period of fasting which began immediately after 6 January in imitation of Christ's fasting in the wilderness. Only in the fourth century was this fast and the baptismal season transferred to a pre-Easter position. Moreover, there is no strong evidence for a pre-baptismal catechumenate lasting any longer than the forty days of this fast, nor any sign of regular exorcism being a part of this preparation. Instead, the only liturgical features seem to have been an enrolment of the candidates at the beginning and a final examination of their suitability for baptism towards the end.[70]

The initiation rite itself appears to have included on the one hand a pre-baptismal anointing to which considerable importance was attached and which shows some parallels to Syrian usage, but on the other hand a credal interrogation resembling that found at Rome rather than an act of adherence of a Syrian kind. It is this latter feature which has chiefly been responsible for scholars describing the rite as 'western'. However, the interrogatory form of the baptismal confession of faith did not last but was soon replaced by a declaratory form in fivefold shape. There are some signs that this may have existed as a variant to the interrogatory form from early times and perhaps became more common after the indicative baptismal formula, 'I baptize you in the name . . .' (which was apparently introduced from Syria in the fourth century), forced the profession of faith to

[69] 'Baptismal Practice in the Alexandrian Tradition: Eastern or Western?', in Bradshaw, *Essays in Early Eastern Initiation*, pp. 5—17.

[70] For further details of the Egyptian post-Epiphany fast, see below, pp. 198—99.

become detached from the threefold immersion itself.[71] Finally, various pieces of evidence point to the conclusion that the post-baptismal unction with chrism found in the *Canons of Hippolytus*, the Sacramentary of Sarapion, and the later Coptic rite may well be a fourth-century innovation, and that, like the early Syrian tradition, ancient Egyptian initiation practice may not have known any post-baptismal ceremonies.[72]

Conclusion

What seems to emerge from this brief review is that we cannot really talk of a standard or normative pattern of early initiation practice in primitive Christianity. Nor can we simply classify the various rites as being fundamentally either eastern or western in shape. Not only does Egypt not fit into this neat division, but if Winkler's assessment of the Gallican evidence is accurate, then the traditional distinction between 'eastern' and 'western' initiation rites may only be marking off Romano-African rites from the rest, and even this group exhibit some variations among themselves, as we have seen. This is not of course to deny that there are some features which are common to many or all of the local rites known to us, and that still more may be capable of discovery. Maxwell Johnson has, for example, recently demonstrated that a three-week period of final pre-baptismal preparation can be discerned beneath the layers of many later texts from various parts of the world.[73] But there are just too many regional variations in details of structure and theology to allow us to construct a single picture in anything but the very broadest terms. To emphasize what is common and to ignore what is distinctive of individual churches —or worse still to force that evidence to fit some preconceived notion of a norma-

[71] See E. Lanne, 'La confession de foi baptismale à Alexandrie et à Rome', in A. M. Triacca & A. Pistoia, eds., *La liturgie expression de la foi* (Rome 1979), pp. 213–28.

[72] See Bradshaw, 'Baptismal Practice in the Alexandrian tradition', pp. 12–17; Georg Kretschmar, 'Beiträge zur Geschichte der Liturgie, inbesondere der Taufliturgie, in Ägypten', *Jahrbuch für Liturgik und Hymnologie* 8 (1963), pp. 1–54.

[73] 'From Three Weeks to Forty Days: Baptismal Preparation and the Origins of Lent', *SL* 20 (1990), pp. 185–200.

tive pattern — is seriously to distort our understanding of the variety of primitive Christian practice, and to lay a false foundation for the modern revision of initiation rites.

8. Liturgy and Time

This chapter explores two distinct but related areas of early Christian liturgical practice, and considers how changing interpretative frameworks adopted by scholars have opened up quite different ways of viewing the various pieces of evidence. In the first part we look at attempts to reconstruct the custom of regular prayer at certain fixed hours of the day —whether practised collectively or individually —otherwise known as the Divine Office or the Liturgy of the Hours. In the second part of the chapter we shall go on to discuss the evolution of the liturgical year.

DAILY PRAYER

The office as a fourth-century creation

For earlier generations of scholars, the divine office was generally understood as being essentially a new development of the fourth century. They were of course aware that Christians in the second and third centuries had been encouraged to pray regularly at fixed hours of the day, but they sharply distinguished such 'private prayer' from the office itself. Louis Duchesne, for example, believed that it was the adoption of these times of prayer as communal exercises by the congregations of ascetics in the fourth century which led to 'the introduction of daily prayers into ecclesiastical use proper'.[1] Pierre Batiffol (1861–1929), Suitbert Bäumer (1845–1894), and Gregory Dix all adopted similar positions.[2]

E. C. Ratcliff, in his contribution to the 1932 collection of essays entitled *Liturgy and Worship*, maintained that attempts to trace the origin of the offices to 'the observance by the Apostles and first Christians of the Jewish hours of prayer' was 'a mistake,

---

[1] *Christian Worship*, pp. 448–9.

[2] Batiffol, *Histoire du Bréviaire Romain* (Paris 1893), pp. 14–15 = *History of the Roman Breviary* (London 1898), pp. 14–15; Bäumer, *Geschichte des Breviers* (Freiburg 1895), pp. 69ff. = *Histoire du Bréviaire* (Paris 1905) I, pp. 100ff.; Dix, *The Shape of the Liturgy*, pp. 319–32.

because such observances were in no sense public acts of worship on the part of the Church; they were the private prayers of one or more individuals'.[3] Ratcliff, however, thought that the roots of the transformation from private to public prayer lay further back in Christian history than the fourth-century ascetics: he ascribed a important place to the third-century *Apostolic Tradition*, where, although prayer still remained private, 'regimen has replaced recommendation'.[4]

Continuity with Judaism

Eventually scholars were persuaded to take much more seriously the possible Jewish roots of the office, and credit for this development must chiefly go to C. W. Dugmore in *The Influence of the Synagogue upon the Divine Office*, first published in 1944. He argued that two daily services, morning and evening, had been celebrated publicly from the very beginning of the Christian Church and were a continuation of the custom of the Jewish synagogue. He was not the first to propound this theory — nearly a century earlier Philip Freeman (1818–1875) had advanced a similar claim[5] —but Dugmore's presentation was persuasive and was subsequently cited with approval by many other scholars.[6]

More recent scholarship, however, has undermined much of his case for the public celebration of these hours of prayer before the fourth century. We have already seen above that Jewish worship was much less regimented in the first century than Dugmore supposed, and that contemporary evidence for daily synagogue services is lacking.[7] The foundation for his claims concerning early Christian practice has also proved unreliable, since he failed to distinguish assemblies for the purpose of instruction and occasional services of the word from the

---

[3] 'The Choir Offices', in W. K. Lowther Clarke, ed., *Liturgy and Worship* (London 1932), p. 257.

[4] ibid., p. 259.

[5] *The Principles of Divine Service* I (Oxford 1855), pp. 59–78.

[6] See, for example, Benedict Steuart, *The Development of Christian Worship* (London 1953), pp. 195ff.

[7] See above, p. 24.

regular hours of prayer themselves, and so cited evidence for the former as proof of the public nature of the latter.

The distinction between 'cathedral' and 'monastic' offices

The study of the early history of the office took a significant step forward in the middle of the twentieth century when Anton Baumstark drew attention to the fact that there were two quite distinct forms of daily worship in the fourth century, which he labelled as 'cathedral' and 'monastic'.[8] His insight has subsequently been taken up and fruitfully explored by other scholars, most notably by Juan Mateos, Gabriele Winkler, and Robert Taft,[9] who have further refined his classification. Mateos divided the monastic type into 'desert monastic' (originating in Egypt) and 'urban monastic' (arising in Cappadocia and Syria and being a hybrid of the other two types), and Taft has suggested that within the 'urban monastic' it is possible to distinguish between offices which were fundamentally monastic in character but had absorbed some cathedral elements and those which had their origin in a cathedral pattern and had added certain monastic elements.[10]

'Cathedral' and 'monastic' were perhaps not the best choice of adjectives to distinguish the worship of the local Christian church assembled under the leadership of its bishop and other clergy, on the one hand, from the daily devotions of individual ascetics and early religious communities, on the other. But the labels have stuck and become the standard technical terms of later research. The differences between the types of worship, however, relate not merely to the people who participated in them but to their external forms and ultimately to their inner spirit and purpose.

The cathedral office, which was usually celebrated only twice each day, morning and evening, was characterized primarily by a very selective use of psalmody and hymnody, usually repeated

[8] *Liturgie comparée* (3rd edn), pp. 123ff. = *Comparative Liturgy*, pp. 111ff.

[9] For a full bibliography of the works on these scholars in this area, see Robert Taft, *The Liturgy of the Hours in East and West* (Collegeville 1986), pp. 376–80.

[10] ibid., p. 84.

every day,[11] by extensive intercessions, and by the absence of Scripture reading on most occasions. The ascetics who made their homes in the Egyptian deserts, on the other hand, attempted to fulfil more literally the apostolic injunction to 'pray without ceasing' (1 Thess. 5.17), and so occupied nearly all their waking hours with individual meditation. The emergence of the cenobitic life gave rise to more formal rules, which still expected the monk to persevere in prayer throughout the day but also came to include prescribed occasions of prayer at the beginning and the end of the day.[12] In the Pachomian communities of Upper Egypt these hours were observed in common and consisted of the alternation of biblical passages read aloud by one of the brothers with the recitation of the Lord's Prayer and silent meditation by the rest of the community.[13] By contrast, in the monasticism of Lower Egypt the daily prayers were said by the monks individually in their cells (except on Saturdays and Sundays), with the morning prayer apparently being earlier than in Upper Egypt, at cockcrow. The content of the prayer here seems to have been the alternation of psalms, recited in their biblical order, and silent prayer.[14]

[11] Pss. 148–150 seem to have constituted the primitive nucleus of the morning service apparently everywhere, with Pss. 51, 63, and the *Gloria in Excelsis* forming a second stratum in many places. The canticle *Benedicite* with its strong emphasis on creation was also commonly used on Sunday mornings. With regard to the evening, the hymn *Phos hilaron*, 'Hail, gladdening light', was widely used at the lighting of the evening lamp, and Ps. 141 is found in virtually all later eastern rites, but is not so clearly evidenced in the West, where at least in some areas Ps. 104 seems to have been used instead (see above, p. 68, n. 27).

[12] One of the main sources which has generally been used to reconstruct the nature of this pattern of daily prayer has been the account given by John Cassian in his *Institutes*, but as Robert Taft has indicated (*The Liturgy of the Hours in East and West*, pp. 58ff.), Cassian was here not simply writing as a disinterested observer: he was using the example of the Egyptian monks as an ideal to promote a reform of monasticism in his native Gaul. Hence, discrepancies between his description and evidence obtained from other sources may be signs of a desire, whether conscious or unconscious, to furnish Egyptian precedents for the Gallican practices which he favoured, and so his testimony needs to be treated with great caution.

[13] See Armand Veilleux, *La liturgie dans le cénobitisme pâchomien au IVe siècle* (Rome 1968), pp. 307ff.; Taft, *The Liturgy of the Hours in East and West*, pp. 62–5.

[14] Cassian's claim that twelve psalms were recited on each occasion cannot be accepted uncritically as the original practice. As Veilleux and Taft have

Although these two traditions — the cathedral and the desert monastic — are similar in terms of the number of times of formal daily prayer, their contents are strikingly different and indicate a radically different concept of the nature of that prayer. The cathedral office had a strong ecclesial dimension: here was the Church gathered for prayer, exercising its royal priesthood by offering a sacrifice of praise and thanksgiving on behalf of all creation and interceding for the salvation of the world. The monastic office, on the other hand, was centred around silent meditation on the word of God and supplication for spiritual growth and personal salvation. Its ultimate aim was spiritual formation: the monk meditated on Christ in order to grow into his likeness, and prayed for the grace necessary for that. It was thus essentially individualistic, and the presence or absence of other people was a matter of indifference. There was nothing inherently corporate in the worship, nothing which might not be done equally as well alone as together. It was the same prayer which was performed in the cell as in the community gathering, and neither setting was viewed as superior to the other.[15]

The urban monastic communities display some variation in the details of their prayer-patterns but they usually prayed at least five times during the day — early in the morning, at the third, sixth, and ninth hours, and in the evening — and again at some point in the night. These hours of prayer were generally observed in common, but might be kept individually if circumstances prevented a corporate assembly. In most cases the offices seem to have used psalms selectively, as in the cathedral tradition, but included prayer for spiritual growth instead of intercession for others, just as we find in the desert monastic tradition.

---

shown, the more ancient tradition was that twelve prayers be offered each day and twelve each night, in other words that one should pray every hour or constantly. The grouping of these prayers into two daily synaxes of twelve psalms each thus appears to be a later development. See Veilleux, *La liturgie dans le cénobitisme pâchomien au IVe siècle*, pp. 324ff.; Taft, *The Liturgy of the Hours in East and West*, p. 72.

[15] See Taft, *The Liturgy of the Hours in East and West*, pp. 66 – 73.

Daily worship before the fourth century

My own contribution to this subject has chiefly been to reconsider the connection of these fourth-century patterns of worship with what preceded them in the Christian tradition. Although rejecting Dugmore's conclusions concerning daily public worship, I have argued that a line of continuity can be traced from early Jewish patterns of daily prayer through primitive Christianity to the post-Constantinian practices examined by other scholars.

Because morning and evening prayer emerge as pre-eminent in the fourth century, other scholars have tended to follow Dugmore in assuming that it is these hours which must be of greatest antiquity and that there had always been a greater obligation to observe these particular times of prayer than any others. I challenged this presupposition, however, and pointed out that the early eastern sources (*Didache*, Clement of Alexandria, and Origen) refer to praying not twice a day but three times — morning, noon, and evening — and to prayer again in the night, and that the early western sources (principally Tertullian and Cyprian) speak of prayer five times during the day — morning, third hour, sixth hour (= noon), ninth hour, and evening — as well as prayer at night. When their statements are correctly interpreted, none of these sources makes any distinction between the importance of observing some of these hours rather than others. I concluded, therefore, that the oldest Christian pattern of daily prayer seems to have been threefold — morning, noon, and evening — together with prayer at night, and that there are signs that something like this may already have been current in some Jewish circles in the first century.[16]

Subsequently, one of my doctoral students, Edward Phillips, has suggested a modification to my theory which seems to fit the facts better. He has made a detailed analysis of the prescriptions concerning daily prayer in the *Apostolic Tradition*, which exhibit a number of peculiarities, among them the absence of a true evening hour of prayer. On the basis of this study, he argued that an older tradition of threefold daily prayer does underlie it, but at the third, sixth, and ninth hours, together with prayer at

---

[16] *Daily Prayer in the Early Church*, chs. 1—3.

night.[17] His thesis points to the conclusion that threefold daily prayer was indeed a widespread, if not universal, custom in the early Church, but that some communities structured it according to the natural rhythm of the day—praying morning, noon, and evening—while other communities adopted the major divisions of the day in the Roman Empire and prayed at the third, sixth, and ninth hours. These two traditions seem later to have been conflated into the fivefold pattern that we first encounter in third-century Africa.

More recently, I have argued that in the light of this earlier history we should not view the urban monastic prayer-cycle of the fourth century merely as a hybrid of cathedral and desert monastic usages. Rather, these religious communities were faithfully preserving what had been common practice among ordinary Christians in the third century. They were not innovators, but conservatives in a world which had changed.[18] The cathedral office was a departure from earlier tradition in one direction, formalizing daily worship under clerical presidency and generally reducing the hours of prayer to two, morning and evening, influenced by the Old Testament prescription of morning and evening sacrifices. The desert monastic office was a departure in the opposite direction, making ceaseless meditation the ideal and dispensing with everything which did not accord with this vision.

Such was the magnetic attraction of the spirituality of the Egyptian desert tradition, however, that the urban monastic office was rapidly drawn towards it and began to incorporate, to a greater or lesser extent, features from it into its own pattern. At the same time, as the cathedral office further evolved, newer elements from there also found their way into some urban monastic traditions, and in this way the hybrid varieties of offices to which Taft has drawn attention were produced.

For example, some communities apparently had prayer at midnight, in the morning, at the third, sixth, and ninth hours, in

[17] 'Daily Prayer in the *Apostolic Tradition* of Hippolytus', *JTS* 40 (1989), pp. 389–400.

[18] 'Cathedral vs. Monastery: The Only Alternatives for the Liturgy of the Hours?', in Alexander, *Time and Community*, pp. 123–36.

the evening and again before bed, but extended the midnight hour into a longer vigil of consecutive psalmody after the Egyptian pattern. Others began their day with an Egyptian-style office at cockcrow, culminating in Pss. 148−150 (the original core of the cathedral morning office), and prayed at the third, sixth, and ninth hours, in the evening, and again before bed, but later added a further morning office containing newer cathedral elements.[19] While some communities probably had a cathedral-style evening prayer, others appear to have had either an Egyptian-style service with consecutive psalmody or a combination of the two. To complicate matters further, some monastic traditions, among them Jerusalem, seem to have added to their own version of evening prayer another one shared with the secular church around them, and so eventually produced a composite office which contained a number of elements in duplicate.[20]

THE LITURGICAL YEAR

Sunday

The New Testament contains only three texts (Acts 20.7−12; 1 Cor. 16.2; and Rev. 1.10) which may allude to the Christian observance of Sunday, and even their meaning is a matter of some dispute.[21] Nevertheless, scholars have not generally accepted the thesis of the Seventh-Day Adventist Samuele Bacchiochi that Sunday observance only began among Christians in the second century.[22] Instead, many have tended to believe that the first Christians chose Sunday as their Sabbath day in order to differentiate themselves from other Jews, and furthermore that during the first century the Christian eucharist was usually celebrated on Saturday evening, after the Sabbath was over and as Sunday began according to the Jewish reckoning of the day.

In 1962, however, Willy Rordorf made a significant contribution to the matter, arguing that Jesus had deliberately chal-

---

[19] See Taft, *The Liturgy of the Hours in East and West*, pp. 75−91.

[20] See Bradshaw, *Daily Prayer in the Early Church*, pp. 80−1, 105−6; Jeffery, 'The Sunday Office of Seventh-Century Jerusalem', pp. 62−3.

[21] See Rordorf, *Sunday*, pp. 193−215.

[22] *From Sabbath to Sunday*, esp. pp. 90−131.

lenged not just an over-zealous interpretation of the Sabbath commandment by the Pharisees, but the very keeping of the Sabbath itself. Moreover, while the early Christians certainly retained the eschatological image of the Sabbath rest, and while Jewish-Christians may have gone on observing the actual weekly Sabbath, Gentile Christians who adhered to the Pauline view of the Law would not have done so, and would therefore have had no interest in transferring the Sabbath to Sunday. Taking up an idea first put forward by Oscar Cullmann, Rordorf suggested that instead the Christian celebration of Sunday probably arose out of the post-resurrection meal appearances of Jesus, many of which seem to have taken place on the first day of the week. He also argued that the weekly eucharistic assemblies were held at first on Sunday evening rather than Saturday evening, and only later transferred to Sunday morning.[23]

Though warmly welcomed by many, Rordorf's explanation has not met with universal approbation. Some conservative scholars have defended the traditional view of the origins of the day, insisting that the Sabbath commandment was not abrogated either by Jesus or by the early Christians.[24] Others have challenged the assumption that the eucharist emerged out of the post-resurrection meals shared by Jesus with his disciples, and argued that on the contrary the meal-stories emerged out of the eucharistic celebrations of the early Christians.[25] But support for Rordorf's general position has come from a perhaps rather surprising quarter: a collection of essays by a group of conservative scholars in 1982 agreed that Christians first began to observe Sunday not as a substitute for the Sabbath but as their day for corporate worship.[26]

[23] *Der Sonntag* = *Sunday* (1968), esp. pp. 54—153, 215—73. See also his later studies, 'Ursprung und Bedeutung der Sonntagsfeier im frühen Christentum', *Liturgisches Jahrbuch* 31 (1981), pp. 145—58; 'Sunday: The Fullness of Christian Liturgical Time', *SL* 14 (1982), pp. 90—6. For Cullmann, see above, pp. 52—3.

[24] See in particular Roger Beckwith & William Stott, *This is the Day*, London 1978 = *The Christian Sunday. A Biblical and Historical Study*, Grand Rapids 1980.

[25] See above, p. 53, n. 92.

[26] D. A. Carson, ed., *From Sabbath to Lord's Day*, Grand Rapids 1982.

Wednesday and Friday

Didache 8.1 directed Christians not to fast on Mondays and Thursdays (the regular Jewish fast-days) but on Wednesdays and Fridays, and this custom continued to be widely observed in later centuries, with regular services of the word also taking place at the ninth hour on these days. It was traditionally assumed that Christians made this change in order to differentiate their practices more clearly from those of the Jews and merely picked these days at random. In 1960 Annie Jaubert argued, however, that this assumption did not take account of how deep-rooted liturgical customs were, and pointed to the solar calendar in use among the Jewish community at Qumran, in which Wednesday and Friday had a certain prominence.[27] Scholars have subsequently concluded, therefore, that, while they were apparently not marked by fasting or by any special liturgical assemblies at Qumran so far as we are aware, the Christian choice of these particular days in place of the traditional Jewish ones was probably influenced by the familarity of some early converts with the solar calendar of Qumran.[28]

Easter

There are two major questions concerning the celebration of Easter in primitive Christianity: (a) how early in the history of the Church did it begin? (b) which came first —its observance on the Sunday closest to the date of the Jewish Passover or its observance on the actual day of the Passover (the fourteenth day of the Jewish month Nisan) found in some churches in Asia Minor (a practice consequently termed Quartodecimanism)? Many scholars have taken the view that the Christian festival of Easter goes back to the apostolic age, even though explicit testimony to its observance only appears in the second century, and that its celebration on a Sunday was normative from the first, with the Quartodeciman practice being merely a local aberration from this, part of a general Judaizing tendency observable

[27] 'Jésus et le calendrier de Qumrân', *NTS* 7 (1960), pp. 1—30. See also Rordorf, *Sunday*, pp. 183—6.

[28] See Bradshaw, *Daily Prayer in the Early Church*, pp. 40—1.

in early Christianity.[29] A few have even suggested that the annual celebration of Easter on a Sunday is older than the weekly observance of Sunday.[30]

On the other hand, some scholars have claimed that the Quartodeciman practice originated in Palestine as the early Jewish-Christian adaptation of the Passover festival.[31] Yet others have gone further still and argued that the celebration of Easter on a Sunday was a considerably later development than is often supposed, and that it was not established at Rome until around 165, though it may have been adopted at Alexandria and Jerusalem somewhat earlier.[32] Prior to this, these churches would have known no annual paschal observance at all. If this is true, it effectively reverses the usual conclusions reached by the majority of earlier scholars: Quartodecimanism is not some local aberration from an apostolic norm but is instead the oldest form of Easter celebration, with the Sunday version — although it was eventually to achieve dominance — being a secondary adaptation of the original practice. It also means that the primary focus of the oldest celebration was on 'Christ, the paschal lamb, sacrificed for us' rather than upon the resurrection.

Because it was often difficult for Christians to calculate the Jewish date, the Quartodecimans in Asia Minor appear to have settled for the compromise of celebrating Easter on the fourteenth day of the first spring month according to the version of the Julian calendar in use in their culture, which was the equivalent of 6 April. Elsewhere by the third century, especially in the West, attempts were being made to compute what would have been the exact date of the death of Jesus according to the Julian calendar. This was generally agreed to have been 25

[29] See, for example, A. A. McArthur, *The Evolution of the Christian Year* (London 1953), pp. 98—107; Jungmann, *The Early Liturgy*, pp. 25—6.

[30] See Kenneth Strand, 'Sunday Easter and Quartodecimanism in the Early Christian Church', *Andrews University Seminary Studies* 28 (1990), pp. 127—36, and especially n. 1 for other studies adopting a similar stance.

[31] See, for example, B. Lohse, *Das Passafest der Quartadecimaner*, Gütersloh 1953; Jeremias, *Eucharistic Words of Jesus*, pp. 122—3.

[32] Karl Holl, *Gesammelte Aufsätze zur Kirchengeschichte. II: Der Osten* (Tübingen 1927), pp. 204—24; Marcel Richard, 'La question pascal au IIe siècle', *L'Orient syrien* 6 (1961), pp. 212—21; Talley, *The Origins of the Liturgical Year*, pp. 13—27.

March, and August Strobel has suggested that some communities in Asia Minor, Syria, Spain, Gaul, and northern Italy celebrated Easter annually on that date.[33]

The evidence indicates that the early Christian version of the Passover was preceded by a period of fasting and vigil during the Jewish festivities of the 14 Nisan, and only began at cockcrow on 15 Nisan. When Easter began to be celebrated on a Sunday, the preceding Saturday was also kept as a fast-day, but since it followed directly after the normal weekly Friday fast, it led to the establishment in many places of a continuous pre-paschal fast of two days. By the third century in some places, notably Syria and Egypt, this was further extended back to the beginning of the week, resulting in a full six days of fasting before the feast.

Pentecost

The Christian observance of the fifty-day period following Easter as a festal season is first attested in a number of sources from a variety of regions at the end of the second century. It was regarded as a time of rejoicing, and every day was treated in the same way as Sunday, that is, with no kneeling for prayer or fasting.[34]

On the other hand, there are signs that the observance of this season may not have been quite as universal as is generally supposed. Canon 20 of the Council of Nicea refers to some who kneel on Sundays and in the days of Pentecost, ordering them to desist; and Asterios Sophistes, a Cappadocian writing probably between 335 and 341, makes no mention at all in his Easter homilies of anything other than a single week of celebration following the feast;[35] nor do Aphraates or Ephrem in East Syria.[36] Elsewhere too, the first week after Easter receives special

[33] *Ursprung und Geschichte des frühchristlichen Osterkalenders* (Berlin 1977), pp. 370−2. See also Talley, *The Origins of the Liturgical Year*, pp. 5−13; Philipp Harnoncourt, 'Kalendarische Fragen und ihre theologische Bedeutung nach der Studien von August Strobel', *ALW* 27 (1985), pp. 263−72.

[34] For details see Robert Cabié, *La Pentecôte: L'évolution de la Cinquantaine pascale au cours des cinq premiers siècles* (Paris 1965), pp. 35−45; John Gunstone, *The Feast of Pentecost* (London 1967), pp. 21ff.

[35] See Auf der Maur, *Die Osterhomilien des Asterios Sophistes*, pp. 71−3; Talley, *The Origins of the Liturgical Year*, pp. 56−7.

[36] See Cabié, *La Pentecôte*, p. 153, n. 1, & 154, n. 3.

emphasis within the fifty-day season, which may perhaps be an indication that this shorter period was at one time the only extension of the Easter festival in some places. Furthermore, Canon 43 of the Spanish Council of Elvira (300) seeks to correct what it describes as a corrupt practice and insists that all should celebrate 'the day of Pentecost'. On the basis of a variant reading in two manuscripts, Robert Cabié interprets the corrupt practice as being a recent innovation of prematurely terminating the Easter season on the fortieth day,[37] but it is not impossible that the canon is seeking to introduce the celebration of Pentecost to churches which had not previously known it.

In any case, the integrity of the fifty days does not seem to have been so deep rooted that it was able to resist erosion in the course of the fourth century. We have already mentioned the existence in many places of a special emphasis on the first week of the season. In addition to that, in Constantinople, Rome, Milan, and Spain the fiftieth day itself came to be celebrated as a commemoration of the gift of the Spirit, while in other places —including Jerusalem—both the Ascension and the gift of the Spirit were celebrated together on that day. Towards the end of the century a separate feast of the Ascension on the fortieth day emerged in a number of places, including Antioch, Nyssa, and northern Italy, and became almost universal early in the fifth century. There are also traces of the existence in some places of a 'mid-Pentecost' festival. Although some churches still continued to observe the whole fifty days as a festal season, even when punctuated in this way, others resumed the regular weekly fasts after the fortieth day, while still others (at least according to Filastrius, bishop of Brescia in northern Italy in the late fourth century) fasted even before the Ascension.[38]

Lent
Evidence for the existence of the season of Lent emerges rather suddenly in the early part of the fourth century. As Thomas Talley has commented, 'Prior to Nicea, no record exists of such a

[37] *La Pentecôte*, pp. 181—2.
[38] See Cabié, *La Pentecôte*, passim; Talley, *The Origins of the Liturgical Year*, pp. 54—70.

forty-day fast before Easter. Only a few years after the council, however, we encounter it in most of the Church as either a well-established custom or one that has become so nearly universal as to impinge on those churches that have not yet adopted it.'[39] Prior to Talley's work, scholars assumed that the association of this season of fasting with Jesus' fast in the wilderness was a secondary development, a piece of historicizing which took place only after the period of baptismal preparation before Easter (from which Lent was thought to take its origin) had been extended to six weeks for purely practical reasons. Similarly, both its focus on fasting by the whole Christian community, rather than primarily by the baptismal candidates, and its adoption as the usual period for penance for those who had committed grave sins were also thought of as having arisen later.[40]

Talley has presented a strong case, however, for a quite different understanding of the emergence of the season. Building upon a suggestion originally made by Baumstark[41] and upon research done by René-Georges Coquin,[42] Talley assembled the evidence for the existence in Egypt from early times of a forty-day fast in commemoration of Jesus' fasting in the wilderness. This did not take place immediately before Easter, but began on the day after 6 January, which the Alexandrian church observed as the celebration of the baptism of Jesus,[43] and thus was situated in the correct chronological sequence of the gospel accounts. Furthermore, it also seems to have functioned as the final period of preparation for baptism, with the rite itself being celebrated at the end of the forty days, and may have been associated with the restoration of penitent apostates.[44] The Lenten season which emerges as a universal phenomenon in the fourth century, therefore, seems to be the result of the fusion of two

---

[39] *The Origins of the Liturgical Year*, p. 168.

[40] See, for example, Dix, *The Shape of the Liturgy*, p. 354.

[41] *Comparative Liturgy*, p. 194.

[42] 'Les origines de l'Épiphanie en Égypte', in Bernard Botte et al., *Noël, Épiphanie: retour du Christ* (Paris 1967), pp. 139—70.

[43] For this, see further below, pp. 203—4.

[44] Talley, 'The Origin of Lent at Alexandria', *SP* 18 (1982), pp. 594—612 = idem, *Worship: Reforming Tradition* (Washington DC 1990), pp. 87—112; idem, *The Origins of the Liturgical Year*, pp. 189—214.

quite distinct earlier traditions —the Alexandrian post-
Epiphany fast of forty days, which had culminated in the baptism
of new converts, and the shorter (perhaps three-week[45]) period
of baptismal preparation which had existed in other churches,
being commonly situated at least in some of them immediately
before Easter. Coquin suggested that this fusion came about as
part of the settlement of the paschal question at the Council of
Nicea.[46]

When the various churches attached the forty-day fast to the
paschal season, however, they did so in varying ways, to a large
extent depending upon the shape of their own pre-existent fasting arrangements. Rome, which had previously known only a
two-day general fast before Easter, situated the forty days
immediately before this, resulting in a composite forty-two day
season beginning on the Sunday which fell six weeks before
Easter. Since there was never any fasting on Sundays, this meant
that there were thirty-six days of actual fasting here. Milan did
the same, but adhered to the custom found in the East of excluding Saturdays (apart from the day before Easter itself) as well as
Sundays from fasting and so had only thirty-one days of actual
fasting. Other churches in the East, such as Antioch, which had
already extended the pre-paschal fast to six days usually began
the forty-day fast on the Monday after the Sunday seven weeks
before Easter and ended it on the Friday nine days before
Easter, thus retaining the six-day fast in the following week as a
separate entity. Because these churches did not fast on either
Saturday or Sunday, this resulted in thirty days of fasting,
together with six more days in the final week, when Saturday was
included in the fast.

Alexandria is an exception to the eastern rule. It adopted the
pre-paschal location of the fast rather more slowly than other
places, but when it did make the move, it placed the season
immediately before Easter, thus overlapping the six-day fast
which it had previously observed, and resulting in a total of only
six weeks like Rome, but in this case with fasting on only five

[45] See above, p. 183, n. 73.
[46] 'Une Réforme liturgique du concile de Nicée (325)?', *Comptes Rendus,
Académie des Inscriptions et Belles-lettres* (Paris 1967), pp. 178–92.

days in each of the weeks, except for the last. Eventually, here and elsewhere, the duration of the season was increased in order that a full forty days of actual fasting might be kept. Egeria claims that such a development had already taken place at Jerusalem in the late fourth century, for she speaks of a total of eight weeks of Lent there, but it is hard to reconcile her testimony with other evidence.[47]

Holy Week

The emergence of what western Christians came to call Holy Week and eastern Christians Great Week —the attempt to commemorate liturgically the detailed events of the last week of Jesus' life on the particular days on which they were thought to have occurred—was thought by earlier generations of liturgical scholars to have been a fourth-century creation which began in Jerusalem, and was often attributed to 'its liturgically-minded bishop' Cyril.[48]

Once again, the true story seems rather more complex. It is highly likely that much of what later became standard Holy Week liturgy in many parts of the Church does owe its origin to the desire of pilgrims who flocked to the Holy Land in the new religious climate of the fourth century to commemorate gospel events in the very places and on the very days that they were said to have happened. But Robert Taft has shown that such 'historicizing' tendencies existed among Christians long before the fourth century, and that the degree of historicization in the fourth-century Jerusalem liturgy can be overstated: no attempt was made, for example, to locate the Holy Thursday liturgy at the supposed site of the Last Supper, nor did the procession through the city early on Good Friday seek to replicate exactly the route taken by Jesus, with detours to the house of Caiaphas or Pilate, but went directly to Golgotha.[49]

---

[47] For further details of the arrangement of the Lenten season, see Talley, *The Origins of the Liturgical Year*, pp. 168—74, and the sources there cited; for Egeria, see above, pp. 128—9.

[48] See especially Dix, *The Shape of the Liturgy*, pp. 334, 348—53.

[49] 'Historicism Revisited'; see also Baldovin, *The Urban Character of Christian Worship*, pp. 87—8.

Moreover, the research done by Talley suggests that Jerusalem may have been as much an importer of liturgical practices as an exporter at this period, with different groups of pilgrims bringing their own local customs and traditions with them and introducing them into the liturgical cycle of the city as well as carrying back with them ideas for innovations in the worship of their home churches. For example, the double celebration of the eucharist on Holy Thursday which appears to have been a feature of the Jerusalem liturgy in the late fourth century has previously been inexplicable, but Talley has put forward the hypothesis that the second celebration may have been a concession to pilgrims who came from a tradition which liturgically followed the Johannine chronology of the Passion and associated the death of the Lord with the hour of the slaying of the lambs.[50]

More significantly still, Talley has argued that the celebration of Lazarus Saturday and Palm Sunday did not belong to indigenous Jerusalem practice but were brought there from Constantinople, which in turn derived the observances from Alexandria, where they had originally formed the festal conclusion of the forty-day fast, as they continued to do at Constantinople. This suggests a relationship between Alexandria and Constantinople to which, as Talley comments, 'liturgiology has given little attention'.[51] Furthermore, it implies that Holy Week did not develop as a single integrated whole, but as the result of the fusion of two previously distinct traditions, the commemoration in Jerusalem of the final events in the life of Jesus according to the chronology of Matthew's Gospel, and the celebration elsewhere of the raising of Lazarus and of the entry of Jesus into Jerusalem (which is given a precise chronological connection to the death of Jesus only in the Fourth Gospel, being said to take place five days before the Passover).

[50] *The Origins of the Liturgical Year*, pp. 44—5.

[51] ibid., pp. 176—89, 203—14. While accepting the general outline of Talley's thesis, John Baldovin has suggested that Jerusalem may have inherited the Lazarus Saturday/Palm Sunday tradition directly from Alexandria rather than via Constantinople, and indeed that Constantinople itself may have received it from Jerusalem: 'A Lenten Sunday Lectionary in Fourth Century Jerusalem', in Alexander, *Time and Community*, pp. 115—22.

Christmas and Epiphany

While it is clear that in the fourth century 25 December had emerged as a Christian festival in the West (or at least at Rome) and 6 January as a similar festival in the East, and that through a process of interchange the two eventually spread to become virtually universal observances throughout the Church, the reason for the choice of these particular dates is not so obvious, and there have been two main scholarly theories concerning the origin of these feasts.

One theory — often termed the computation hypothesis and first advanced by Louis Duchesne[52] — attributed the festivals to the results of attempts to calculate the exact day in the year on which Jesus had actually been born. These particular dates had been arrived at, it was thought, by inference from the alleged date of the death of Jesus, since early Christians were convinced that he must have lived upon earth for an exact number of years and therefore the date on which he died would also have been the same as the date of his conception. Thus, those who regarded 25 March as the date of the crucifixion and conception would have placed the nativity nine months later, on 25 December, while those who believed the date of his death to have been 6 April would have assigned the birth to 6 January.

Later scholars generally rejected this explanation and have preferred what has been called the 'history of religions' hypothesis, first advanced in the eighteenth century, according to which 25 December was chosen at Rome because it was also the date of the winter solstice in the Julian calendar and a popular pagan feast, the *dies natalis solis invicti*, the birthday of the invincible sun, established by the emperor Aurelian in 274. After the Peace of Constantine the Christians, it was said, wanted to draw people away from these pagan festivities and point to Christ as the true Sun of Righteousness, and so instituted at Rome the feast of the Nativity on the same date. The eastern provinces of the Roman Empire, on the other hand, were said to have observed 6 January as the date of the winter solstice according to the ancient calendar of Amenemhet I of Thebes (*c.*

[52] *Christian Worship*, pp. 257—65.

1996 B.C.E.), and so the Christian feast too was established on that date there.[53]

Talley's recent work, however, has challenged the dominance attained by this second theory and revived the former hypothesis. He pointed out that Augustine in one of his sermons alluded to the fact that the Donatists in North Africa, unlike the Catholics, had not adopted the celebration of the feast of the Epiphany on 6 January, which seemed to imply that they did celebrate 25 December. This in turn suggested that Christmas must already have existed prior to the Donatist schism in 311, and hence at a date when it would have been unlikely that the Christians would have wanted any 'accommodation to less than friendly imperial religious sentiment'. On the basis of other evidence supporting the computation hypothesis (from Augustine and from an anonymous work known as *De Solstitiis* which was apparently also of North African provenance), Talley tentatively suggested the possibility that Christmas may have first appeared in that region rather than at Rome, as is usually supposed.[54]

Talley presented even stronger grounds for preferring the computation hypothesis for 6 January. He demonstrated that there never was a calendar of Amenemhet I, nor any clear evidence of a widespread pagan festival on 6 January, while Roland Bainton had shown that Clement of Alexandria as early as the end of the second century believed 6 January in the year 2 B.C.E. to have been the date of the birth of Christ. What Bainton had not known, however, was that 6 April constituted the solar equivalent of 14 Nisan in Asia Minor, and so the choice of 6 January could therefore have been dependent upon that.[55]

Talley then drew attention to the evidence of the *Canons of Athanasius*, a document probably composed in Egypt in the second half of the fourth century. Here the focus of the feast of the Epiphany is clearly the baptism of Jesus; the nativity is not mentioned; and a considerable point is made of Epiphany being the

[53] See, for example, Bernard Botte, *Les origines de la Noël et de l'Épiphanie*, Louvain 1932; idem, ed., *Noël, Épiphanie: retour du Christ*; John Gunstone, *Christmas and Epiphany*, London 1967.

[54] *The Origins of the Liturgical Year*, pp. 85–103.

[55] Roland Bainton, 'The Origins of the Epiphany', *Early and Medieval Christianity. The Collected Papers in Church History*, Series One (Boston 1962), pp. 22–38; Talley, *The Origins of the Liturgical Year*, pp. 103–21.

beginning of the year. From this Talley argued that, as a result of 6 January being regarded as the birth of Christ, it came to be treated as the beginning of the liturgical year in Egypt, just as 25 December seems to have been viewed in the Roman Chrono-graph of 354, and hence the course reading of the Gospel of Mark — the evangelist especially associated with Alexandria — was begun upon that date. Since that particular Gospel began with the baptism of Jesus, the focus of the festival there was con-sequently directed towards the baptism and not the nativity. He went on to propose that something similar may have happened in other places too. Because of the strong connection of John's Gospel with Asia Minor, its reading may have been begun there on 6 January, and so given to that feast the association with the miracle at Cana in John 2.1 – 11. In Jerusalem, according to Egeria and the Armenian lectionary, the focus of the festival was on the nativity, and there are signs that the course reading of Matthew's Gospel, in which an account of the nativity is included, may originally have been begun at this season.[56]

Conclusion

Many lessons can be drawn from the shifts in scholarship that we have observed above, but perhaps three are particularly sig-nificant. First, once again, as in the cases of baptism and eucharist, the further one digs into the primary sources the more diversity rather than uniformity is encountered in the first few centuries. Second, what has been perceived as the mainstream practice of the early Church is in many instances often a later development or adaptation of earlier traditions, and what were dismissed as seemingly local aberrations are frequently in reality ancient practices that exerted a much more powerful influence on the rest of Christian antiquity than was formerly supposed. Third, the traditional assumption that it was the calendar which gave rise to the lectionary cannot be sustained in every case. On the contrary, as Talley has argued, it may sometimes have been the tradition of reading certain biblical passages at particular times of the year that led to the institution of some feasts and seasons in the annual cycle.

[56] *The Origins of the Liturgical Year*, pp. 121 – 34.

Postscript

In 1981 the late Geoffrey Cuming concluded a valuable survey of recent scholarship concerning early eucharistic liturgies with the remark: 'The time has come to rewrite the textbooks.'[1] Now, a decade later, still further rewriting is required, as yet more advances have taken place not merely in the study of the evolution of the eucharist (in which, as we have seen, Cuming himself played an important part) but also in the investigation of many other aspects of early liturgical history. We need to take note not only of new sources which may have come to light but more importantly of the methods of interpretation which are to be employed in relation to all the sources. For, as Robert Taft has frequently stated, knowledge advances not so much by the accumulation of new data but by the invention of new systems, of a new matrix into which to set the data.

What this particular contribution to research has tried to do, therefore, is to help construct just such a new matrix for the search for the origins of Christian worship, one which takes seriously the altered face of Jewish liturgical scholarship, the basic pluriformity of New Testament Christianity and the inherent ambiguity of its witness to primitive liturgical practice, the real character of the source-documents of the early centuries and the extent of the gaps in our knowledge of the period, and above all the clues which point to the essentially variegated nature of ancient Christian worship. The resultant shape formed within this matrix may be less satisfying than the picture painted by earlier scholarship—but a much better representation of the truth.

---

[1] 'The Early Eucharistic Liturgies in Recent Research', in Spinks, *The Sacrifice of Praise*, pp. 65—9.

Index of Modern Authors

References to pages which include full bibliographical details are indicated by the use of boldface type.

Subject Index